The Muslim Community in North America

The Muslim Community in North America

Edited by
Earle H. Waugh, Baha Abu-Laban,
and Regula B. Qureshi

 The University of Alberta Press

First published by
The University of Alberta Press
450 Athabasca Hall
Edmonton, Alberta
Canada T6G 2E8

Copyright © The University of Alberta Press 1983

ISBN 0-88864-033-1 cloth
ISBN 0-88864-034-X paper

Canadian Cataloguing in Publication Data

Main entry under title:
The Muslim community in North America

Bibliography: p.
ISBN 0-88864-033-1 (bound). – ISBN
0-88864-034-X (pbk.)

1. Muslims – Canada. 2. Muslims – United
States. I. Waugh, Earle H., 1936–
II. Abu-Laban, Baha. III. Qureshi, Regula B.
E29.M87M8   305.6'971'071   C82-091219-0

Typeset by The Typeworks
Mayne Island, British Columbia

Printed by Hignell Printing Ltd.
Winnipeg, Manitoba

Contents

Preface

The majority of these studies were originally papers presented at the symposium on Islam in North America held at the University of Alberta, Edmonton, Canada from 27 to 31 May 1980, and revised by their authors for inclusion here. It was a labor of love for most of the participants because it came at a busy time at the end of the university year, and we want to indicate how crucial their active involvement was for both the success of the conference and this volume.

Special gratitude also should be expressed to the Social Science and Humanities Research Council of the Canadian Government, the Alberta Cultural Heritage Foundation, the Embassy of the Republic of Iraq, the University of Alberta Conference Committee and Alma Mater Fund, and the Department of Religious Studies. It was they who translated the gleam in our eye into reality. Special assistance for the publication of this book was generously given by Mr. Mohammed K. Abou Seoud of the Association of Arab-American University Graduates, Inc. We also appreciate the moral support by the local Muslim community in this enterprise, including the members of the Al-Rashid Mosque in Edmonton, where the jacket photographs were taken.

Finally, Mrs. Norma Gutteridge of the University of Alberta Press has been most helpful in giving direction and guidance to the editors, and her fine staff have made our task much lighter. Certainly they have made the reader's life infinitely easier, and we are delighted about that.

Contributors

Muhammad Abdul-Rauf is a professor of Islamic Studies at United Arab Emirates University in Abu-Dhabi.

Baha Abu-Laban is a sociologist and Associate Vice-President for Research at the University of Alberta, Edmonton, Alberta.

Charles J. Adams is a professor of the Institute of Islamic Studies, McGill University, Montreal, Quebec.

Isma'il R. Al-Faruqi is a professor in the Department of Religion, Temple University, Philadelphia, Pennsylvania.

Lila Fahlman is a counsellor and consultant with the Edmonton Public School Board, Edmonton, Alberta.

Yvonne Haddad is a professor of Islamic Studies at The Hartford Seminary Foundation, Hartford, Connecticut, and the editor of *The Muslim World.*

Murray Hogben, formerly at Collège Militaire Royale de Saint-Jean, Saint-Jean, Quebec, is now a reporter for the Kingston *Whig-Standard* and resides in Gananoque, Ontario.

C. Eric Lincoln is a professor of Religion and Culture, Duke University, Durham, North Carolina.

Emily Kalled Lovell is an independent researcher and editor most recently at Arizona State University and now resides in Stockton, California.

Lawrence H. Mamiya is a professor of Religion and Africana Studies at Vassar College, Poughkeepsie, New York.

Azim Nanji is Chairman of the Department of Humanities at Oklahoma State University, Stillwater, Oklahoma.

M. Siddieq Noorzoy is a professor in the Department of Economics, University of Alberta, Edmonton, Alberta.

Regula B. Qureshi teaches anthropology and music at the University of Alberta, Edmonton, Alberta.

Saleem M. M. Qureshi is Associate Dean of Arts and a professor in the Department of Political Science, University of Alberta, Edmonton, Alberta.

Mahmud Samra is Vice-President of the University of Jordan, Amman, Jordan.

Earle H. Waugh is former Chairman and an associate professor of the Department of Religious Studies, the University of Alberta, Edmonton, Alberta.

Introduction

That it is better to light one small candle than to curse the darkness, as Confucius puts it, could easily be applied to this volume. It is the first of its kind, and everyone connected with its production is keenly aware of the tentative nature of much of the research, and the vast areas yet to be explored. Most of the essays were originally presented as papers at the "Islam in North America" symposium, held at the University of Alberta in May 1980. The conference brought together scholars from a number of disciplines for the purpose of focusing upon a relatively new but growing force in North American society – Islam – and to discuss the academic potential for a multi-faceted study on the topic. A wide range of opinions and attitudes surfaced during the symposium, and are present here, and probably would have remained evident even had we exercised much more editorial control.

Some of these differences can be easily recognized, such as the tendency for humanists to deal with "Islam," while social scientists are more concerned with "Muslims." Others, such as the positions taken by students of Islamic/Muslim communities as opposed to those of representatives from the communities themselves, may be less obvious. As a consequence, even within disciplines, researchers differed upon interpretation. This became more pronounced as deep personal attitudes came into play, and complex issues (such as, whether Muslims who participated in the North American slave trade could be considered truly Muslim) were controversial. This interaction was considered one of the principal benefits of the conference, and the dialogue between various approaches and viewpoints was seen as important to preserve in this collection. Hence what you have before you reflects not only disciplinary diversity, but attitudinal and valuational divergence. By incorporating them all here, we have attempted to convey the multidimensional character of the inquiry.

These studies, for the most part, do not distinguish between Canada and the United States in terms of Muslim cultural interaction, even though it must be clear that indigenous Islam has far greater impact in the U.S.A. than in Canada. We are also aware that much more work could be done on the unique American experience of Muslim immigration. But we have settled for the descriptive term "North American" because immigrants themselves have traditionally made little distinction between the two countries in terms of social characteristics and values, and because the total cultural position of North America is one of official secularism. Doubtless further studies will flesh out several important differences in adaptation between American and Canadian Muslims, but this level of analysis would require much additional background research. We have contented ourselves with the more general perspective.

Despite these procedural difficulties, something like a crude map is visible. There are common issues and problems, shared experiences and ideals, and, above it all, the traditional values of Islam that unify deliberations. Moreover, we considered it imperative to establish this research on thorough-going academic principles, so that it could be seen in the future as a legitimate start to an important area of study. What follows, then, is an attempt to bring some of the contours of the map into relief.

How can a religious system that is much more a way of life than a theological structure adapt to North America? A number of the studies probe this problem. There is, first of all, the theoretical underpinning of the religion in the modern world, expressed in Samra's contribution, where he shows that relating Islam to the western world has not been so much a purchasing of western values at Islamic expense as the attempt to reinterpret important values perceived to be missing in Islamic societies in such a way that these values fit the Islamic experience. Such activity allows them to be appropriated without considering them to be "foreign" and thus suspect. The same theme is found in Abu-Laban from a different perspective, where he demonstrates that adaptation is not solely behavioral in meaning, but requires the remolding of theoretical and ideological conceptions so that they can be utilized in the process of coming to terms with North American society. Noorzoy approaches the problem from an entirely different direction. How can Islamic economic affairs integrate with those of the West, and what are the principal hurdles that must be overcome? He shows that decisions about what *ribā* is and how it is to be applied are crucial if Muslim doctrine on interest is to be integrated into the world economic system.

Several writers note that adaptability would be facilitated if principles already inherent in the Muslim system were expanded. Rather than trying to impose the standards of an ancient Muslim society upon contemporary believers, the case is made to put in place a theoretical device already known in early Islamic history, namely *ijtihād*. Both Abu-Laban and Adbul-Rauf suggest that this concept could be expanded and developed to accommodate Islamic views in the North American context, partly as a strategy to reconcile Islamic theological perspectives with Canadian society (Abu-Laban) and partly as a practical adaptive mechanism to allow Muslims to make social and political adjustments in an environment foreign to Muslim culture (Abdul-Rauf). Aiding their people to implement Islam in North America becomes one of the crucial tasks ahead for its leadership.

The dramatic growth of indigenous Islam in North America brings into focus another issue – just what kind of leadership is necessary for success? If, as is often pointed out, immigrant Islam had made next to no headway in creating a following among North Americans, what set of abilities must a leader possess to bring Islam to the nations of Canada and the United States? The data are not clear. First, as Lincoln points out, the indigenous movement was initially a reaction to racist attitudes in the United States, with some echoes from the religious past of some slaves. But it soon developed into a genuine religious orientation, with a distinctive theology and social system, motivated and given spiritual direction by remarkable leaders. That tradition is being carried on under the present leadership of Warith Deen Muhammad. Yet charisma is not the only ingredient, for, as Mamiya points out, Louis Farrakhan's retention of the Fruit of Islam and the original theology of Elijah Muhammad indicate religious concerns larger than just leadership. While there is a direct connection between the two conceptions, the cardinal role of leadership cannot be overemphasized, especially in indigenous Islam.

Moreover, leadership is regarded as central by Nanji and Waugh. In the latter's study, leadership is expanded to bring together both *imām* and group as vehicles for giving direction to the *umma,* in such a way as to express Islamic social values and concepts. In the former, stress is placed upon the role of the Aga Khan in guiding the *jamat khana* as the chief organizational expression of the Ismailis in North America. In addition, he sketches how the Councils function and why they play such an important part in the growth of this form of Islam. Some flavor of the key position associations have among Muslim communities is also gleaned from Lovell's overview of national organizations. In all of these studies, the multivalency of leadership is perceived as being quite in keeping with traditional Islam's ambivalence about investing any authority with sacerdotal power.

One could argue that it is precisely because indigenous North American Islam is not hampered by this ambivalence that it is most successful. But, the lack of a common authority means a lack of single-mindedness, of decisiveness, and creates debilitating tensions. Waugh deals with some of the problems that arise because of these tensions, and the Qureshis show that difficulties attend the "family model" as it is extended into the impersonal sphere of Canadian social structure. Both articles imply that significant research could be carried out in this area in the future.

The stark case could hardly have been put better than in Al-Faruqi's article:

The "immigrant" mentality stands on two necessary assumptions: a country and culture perceived as bankrupt, despised, hated, forsaken, left behind; and a country and culture seen as alien, awesome, superior, admired, and desired but not yet appropriated or mastered.

The resulting eddies have scarcely been noticed, let alone studied. Still, some measure of their impact can be taken by looking at education, that front line of many social movements in North America. While we have no systematic data for the whole of North America, Charles Adams gives a fresh and candid insight into establishing Islamic studies in institutes of higher education in Canada. What we find there is a microcosm of the widespread and almost universal indifference on the part of Canadians in general. Various levels of government respond only to active concerns on the part of the population, and hence show no interest in a cultural study that has so little local impact; university structure must be harnessed in careful and deliberate ways or Islamic institutes wither and die; the population at large is not sensitized to Islam, so programs suffer for lack of students or proper funding; regional loyalties militate against the development of truly national centres with federal funding and moral support; largess from abroad may seem helpful in the short term, but ultimately it cannot be relied upon to sustain long-term development, and responsibility must come back to North American society.

But indifference is not the only irritant. There has been and continues to be significant distortion of the meaning of Islam in publications that should know better. Admittedly some of this is pure laziness, and reflects an attitude on the part of publishers and writers alike to accept antiquated ideas rather than draw from contemporary research. But some of it arises from deep-seated prejudices that have been perpetrated in the West and reinforced with political and social mythologies. Children face these in their books, or among their teachers. Moreover, Fahlman's article shows that antagonism to drugs and alcohol can bring about a kind of cultural shock that alienates Muslim children. More research will have to be done to see if they are not relegated to a sub-culture because their values differ from those held by the majority of their peers, or if other non-Muslims of similar values are equally designated as outsiders. But it is obvious that misunderstandings and reactions from the past continue to frame host culture attitudes in negative ways, and Muslims experience these very directly.

Some of these result in conflicts between the Muslim system and North American culture. Hogben traces a few of these, indicating that Muslims in Canada must adapt with regard to prayer times, Ramaḍān, and other religious festivals, as well as in more technical areas like law and values. A number of studies deal with some aspects of this conflict, but another dimension is added by Haddad, where she shows that the revolution in Iran brought to the surface important Muslim aspirations among the community in Montreal that can only be interpreted as a recovery of a Muslim sense of pride and self-respect. Some would see this as part of Muslim attitudinal baggage from their homelands, but there must be more to it than that. It reflects the attempt to regain something lost and perceived as never having been replaced in this country. Thus, in spite of the religious tolerance of secularism, these Muslims are seemingly unable to find fulfilment for all their feelings in this environment. One is left to contemplate the impact that various forms of reform in the Muslim world might have upon a nascent community, and how Muslim triumphalism might eventually be expressed in North America. It also leads to some consideration of home culture linkages.

Immigrant Islam did not come to North America to secure religious liberty, hence the motivations that propelled the Pilgrim Fathers have no place in our analyses. The very diversity of the home cultures, along with the distinctiveness of indigenous Islam, poses some critical academic issues. To these must be added the complexity of immigration policy, which has encouraged or discouraged immigration depending upon a number of factors (the unemployment figures, for one). The result has had an effect on Muslims. Almost all the adaptation studies here have detailed some characteristic derived from this situation. Continuous immigration constantly renews the homeland ties, reaffirms a cultural distinctiveness, and chides "securlarized" Muslims; it helps resist integration and acculturation and thereby idealizes the "home" culture. There are positive and negative linkages with that culture, and these place further stress on the individual trying to adapt to a new environment.

But the home culture also provides the conceptual framework by which adaptation processes are begun. The Qureshis particularly demonstrate that the mechanisms for establishing the Pakistani Canadians were not *ad hoc*, but were derived from the social system in place at home, and are continued in the new world. Abu-Laban details some of the difficulties which ensued when these mechanisms begin to break down, usually in the second generation. One issue is particularly trying: children reject the social control systems adopted by their parents when they first arrived in North America, and the result is dislocation and antagonism, even the desperation of failure. Further research is needed to determine what happens when the immigrant comprehends that he cannot return "home," nor feel at home here. The dislocation may be particularly trying for the elderly.

We may also see studies such as Haddad's as a means of determining a true international consciousness on the part of Muslims. Up to this time, the Jews have been the group who have most invested their religious value here. What we are perceiving may be an aspect of the long-held view of Muslims that how one orients oneself to another place is more significant for religious value than *this* place. What is not clear is whether Muslims will respond to the religious values of North America by redefining Islam (although Warith Deen Muhammad seems to be trying to do this) rather than filtering Islam through the realities they perceive in another time and place. The experience of defining Islam, whatever its motivation, is seen by Abdul-Rauf to be a positive thing, promoting awareness, and developing character in future North American Muslims, and one that will probably remain a principal activity for some time to come.

I

Islam & the Modern World

Muslim Leadership
and the Shaping of the Umma:
Classical Tradition and Religious Tension
in the North American Setting

Earle H. Waugh

The past, says Northrop Frye, is functional in our lives only when we neither forget it nor try to return to it. Then he clarifies:[1]

> Everybody's sympathies with the past are highly qualified: everybody has to make very selective efforts to make a personal contact with the chosen part of one's cultural heritage, and more means for expressing one's deeper personal interests have constantly to be provided.

The resulting model is that of a continuous movement from contemporary life to the fount of the past in order to build a rich and meaningful existence. This is certainly applicable to those of us fascinated by the impact of the ancient ways upon culture today, but it has special significance for our interest in Islam. For one of the essential ingredients of that faith is the normativeness of the past, that is, of the time of the Prophet and the Word of God as revealed in the Qur'ān, in establishing the community today. From the credo of tawḥīd of the earliest *suras,* the belief that the *umma* is a single community whatever its temporal, cultural, or social trappings, has played a fundamental role.

But the community itself has had great difficulty in determining just what constituted the unity of the first century of the *hijra*

... some of the sources are doubtful, and we lack precision in the interpretation of key theological concepts. Some of these problems have spilled over into today. Consider the difficulties faced in the modern state of Pakistan, where conservative 'ulamā' lobbied to have the Ahmadiyya declared non-Muslim. Who, then, is a Muslim? A special court of inquiry was set up to determine who could fittingly be given that appellation, and the leading scholars, steeped in religious sciences, were called to testify. The result is best described by the report:[2]

> Keeping in view the several definitions given by the 'ulamā', need we make any comment except that no two learned divines are agreed on this fundamental? If we attempt our own definition as each learned divine has done and that definition differs from that given by all others, we unanimously go out of the fold of Islam. And if we adopt the definition given by one of the 'ulamā', we remain Muslims according to the view of that 'ālim (scholar) but kāfirs (infidels) according to the definition of everyone else.

To this essentially theological problem must be added one of more recent vintage: issues that are quite secular can be clothed in religious language. Thus, Ahmad Taleb writes about the Prophet as a radical reformer because he is looking for a common language to inspire a wide range of social classes to espouse a radical ideology.[3] Gran's point that "the language of religion is the only way the affluent bourgeoisie-cultured rulers can try to communicate across class lines"[4] then becomes relevant on a much wider scale. Using religious language for such purposes may be culturally acceptable, but Islam moves from being a universal tradition to a mere vehicle for fashionable causes every time it is done.

An additional problem is that the classical tradition is mediated to contemporary Muslims through complex institutional forms that are likely to provoke new interpretations in American culture. This can be quickly demonstrated by the experience of freedom. A glance over the recollections of the earliest immigrants soon makes us realize the importance of freedom for them. They cherished America's freedom. What did they mean by it? It had both religious and political overtones, since the authority of the Islamic regimes they left behind rested upon a network of associations drawn from both religious and political elites. The ʿulamāʾ, *qāḍīs,* and religious functionaries were part of the apparatus of caliphal or sultanal power, forming what might be called the clerical bureaucracy of their governments. They were joined by regional princes, village overlords, family heads and tribal *shaykhs* who represented the governmental structure to the masses and who incorporated the ordinary Muslim into the Islamic society. Consequently, the immigrant to North America had lived in an environment where his entire being was structured by forms identified as traditionally Islamic (whether they were or not).[5] The North American situation could hardly have been more of a contrast; his identity, so long as his neighbor had any opinion at all, was shrouded in mystery. At times he was "Syrian," at times "Turk." His name would not be of much help, since he may well have changed it, either under the influence of an impatient immigration official, or because it was easier to do business with a western name.[6] In Simmel's term he was *der Fremde* ("the stranger"),[7] moving at the edge of a society that valued individual initiative. He found, usually, extraordinary rewards for his work, all without the network of family and kinship that he required back home. The experience was heady and freedom came to play a cardinal role in the kinds of institutions he organized and fostered.[8]

Thus it would be an error to consider immigrant Islam as merely the transferral of a creed to a North American environment. We must also consider how the Islamic immigrant perceives his past and how he understands it to inform his new situation; then, how he must deal with the new situation with yet more understanding drawn from his past experience.

It would be too much to expect that these complex movements could occur without friction or conflict. The following discussion is guided by Max Weber's concept of "tension" as an operative tool in analysis. Briefly, Weber observes that a process of rationalization begins when a religious world view faces a conflict with the "real" context – what ought to be as against what is. The same applies at the institutional level. Thus the conflict between the "prophetic" and "priestly" traditions is slowly reduced through a series of compromises, until a new form of institution is in place that resolves the tensions in a manner acceptable to those participating.[9]

This posits a system in which people progressively rationalize as they perceive tensions, encounter, and subdue them. It is usually assumed that the "givens" of a tradition remain constant throughout, but as we have seen, in the case of Islam in North America, it is not so much that a fixed system of beliefs must be rationalized as that the meaning of the beliefs is itself unclear. The tensions are more diverse when the terms themselves will not stand still, and something like *ecclesia reformata semper reformanda* (the reformed congregation is ever reforming) obtains. As a result, our analysis will suggest that the classical tradition must simultaneously face defining itself while being the material of construction. The resulting tensions identify the quality of religious experience unique to believers here.

While Islam has had no priestly tradition in the Christian understanding of that term, it has had religious functionaries, and has experienced a wide range of religious leadership. This has continued in North America where local family heads have endeavored to hand on the classical tradition by constantly pushing for Muslim religious rites and mosques, indulging in charismatics (like Malcolm X) who attracted a dedicated following, and forming groups such as the Muslim Students' Association, which lobbies for a distinctive Muslim response to society. These leaders have shaped and continue to shape the umma in North America and give it a distinctive character, especially in the reaction to tensions both within and without.

The Example of Muḥammad as Leader

Few non-Muslims in North America appreciate the significance of the Prophet-image for Muslims. But this is necessary if immigrant loyalty to the tradition is to be comprehended. Just before his death, the Prophet spoke to his followers and, depending upon the sources, said either, God has given two safeguards to the world: His Book and the *sunna* (example) of His Prophet, or, God has given two safeguards to the world: His Book and the family of His Prophet. In effect, all the essentials for Muslim existence can be found in these statements. Drawing upon experiences recalled from his life, the community slowly developed a system that rejected institutional

segregation of any element of society, be it political, social, or religious. The model of the primitive Medinan community, headed by
one individual, is the basis of the Islamic vision of a moral order
incumbent upon all mankind:[10]

> Emerging from a bleak background – Arabia Deserta –
> orphaned in childhood; unfettered and untutored, he [Muḥam-
> med] arose and towered to become an organizer who moulded
> the warring tribes of his race into a nation which justified him
> and itself in the verdict of history; a social mentor and law-giver
> by whose code today one-fifth of the human race is governed; a
> prophet who led human souls from idolatry and paganism into
> the simplest and clearest conception of the Creator and His wor-
> ship; rational and humane, he struck at all fetters and brought
> forth the first true Reformation by Faith and reason, he opposed
> slavery and abolished caste, class, color, and race distinction; he
> encouraged learning and mercy, taught charity and good will.

As the attempt was made to extend that model into an international empire, the various ingredients in Muḥammad's final bequest
to the community came into play. Qurʾān and *ḥadīth* (traditions) became the basis for that development. The relative position of each
should have made the Qurʾān primary, but in reality, ḥadīth became
a privileged source, since it fleshed out the sometimes elliptical
verses of the Qurʾān and gave a more concrete interpretation of the
revelation. Ḥadīth of all kinds were suddenly discovered, and some
were truly amazing. For example, Mahmud al-Kashghari, born in
the early part of the 11th century C.E.* in the city of Kashghar in
Central Asia, related two ḥadīths: "The Prophet said: 'Learn the
Turkish language, for their rule will long endure'," and, "God said: 'I
have a host which I have called "Turk" and settled in the East. If any
people shall arouse my wrath, I shall give them into the power of
this host'."[11]

Despite this exuberance in discovering ḥadīth, we can see the
motivation for the principle: ideas or acts require prophetic sanction
before they can be accepted by the Islamic establishment. Thus,

---

*Common Era

right from the umma's inception, religious language, or more rightly, prophetic language, has been a medium that can legitimize non-religious intentions. It should also be noted that this facility led to much inner debate and considerable tension, as the history of caliphate and imāmate show. But that should not blind us to the evident truth, that the community's life has been characterized by a constant interaction with the paradigmatic nature of the Prophet, establishing him as a firm symbol in the life and work of the believer. In Weber's phraseology, the prophetic tradition is constantly being rationalized.

Yet the model ever recedes, easier models attract and hold sway, and frustration develops over the failure to realize the Prophet model in the present. In North America, these problems are even more pressing, as the following testimony shows:[12]

Muhammad is, as mentioned in the Qur'ān, to be and was for all time the beautiful pattern of conduct ... the hassan al-hasaba ... the best model. The 'ulamā' of the Muslim school, usually the Bahrain, is the inheritor of the prophet, so the same rule of the prophet is supposed to be done by the Imām. He tries every time to come closer (to him). We respect, for example, the hadīth that says "I am sent in an era and an age where if you heed ten percent of what has been revealed to me, you would be destroyed, but it will come a time if you follow ten percent of what has been revealed to me you will be safe." That is one of the least-known sayings of the Prophet to his people. We know that people here and the Imām here cannot do what they do in a very conservative village in upper Egypt or Saudi Arabia, but the model is still living and we cannot forget that. It is a fundamental thing for children to know his behaviour and conduct; and not only him but all prophets, including Jesus Christ. But how much of that is ten percent for following or neglecting, or how near we are to approaching this period is very difficult to say. We struggle to see his behaviour as he was acting in relation to neighbours, and how he dealt with his wife, as a husband, as a father, as a ruler, as a judge. There are confrontations with other things, other discouragements, but still the model is there and Muhammad should be looked at all the time as a pattern of conduct.

The Claim of Loyalties in Building the Umma

Muḥammad's leadership was also to be interpreted another way – as the impact of a special family upon the community. This perspective was to pose crucial questions for the early umma and was destined to become a minority view permanently enshrined in the Shī'a, but it was an idea born out of the belief that neither the Qur'ān nor the ḥadīth could adequately be understood without the special interpretive abilities residing in the family of the Prophet. Yet it is not the development of Shī'a theology that interests us here, but the loyalties to family and kin that were harnessed for a religious cause, thus intensifying them. Many Muslims, while rejecting the political claims of the Shī'a, were sensitive to these values, and prized the old Arab tribal loyalties as forms of interaction that should be perpetuated.[13] In the 10th and 11th centuries these loyalties were given formal expression, and it is worth surveying them for their continuing effect on family perceptions in the 20th century:[14]

> I claim from you that oath of allegiance [bay'a] which you have affirmed time after time. Whoever has sworn allegiance to me has sworn allegiance to God, so that whosoever violates that oath, violates the covenant with God ['ahd Allah]. I also claim gratitude for benefits and favours you enjoy, benefits and gifts from me that I hope you will acknowledge and consider binding.

Such was the statement of Caliph al-Muqtadir to his troops, who already were in a conspiracy to overthrow him. The *bay'a* was an oath taken before God that signalled the allegiance of Muslims to the caliph. But it was only one of a range of compacts that governed the Muslim; it took as its foundation the covenant between God and man first expressed in Adam, and since then it has been repeated in each and every covenanted relationship with others. Muslims of this era took very seriously Qur'ān 2:25–27: "Those who violate the covenant with God ('ahd Allah), after its confirmation (mithāq), and who cut the ties which God has ordered to be joined, and do evil in the earth, those will truly lose." Not living up to an oath was to bring God's curse.

Commitments are thus more than declarations of support. Rather, they require the entire resources of an individual being put into action to bring about a desired goal, formally binding him to a course because he has so sworn before God. This sense of obligation was to become further established in the Middle East through the institution of *istinā*ʿ:[15]

> Istināʿ is a surprisingly formal and serious relationship; a man expected from his protégé [muṣṭanaʿ or ṣaniʿ or ṣaniʿa] not an easy gratitude and affection, but a lifelong commitment of sizeable dimensions. To say "He is my *ṣaniʿa*" meant, "He is the person I have reared, educated, and trained well," and the obligation to such a patron was like the obligation to a parent, except that it was neither inherited nor transferable by legacy. It was, moreover, an obligation that could be made between men more nearly equal in age than father and son.

This institution was begun by the ʿAbbāsids and played a central role in the Near East into the 19th century. But this sense of obligation is more pervasive and far-reaching than its political form alluded to here. Ibn Khaldun (14th century) puts his finger on the networks of commitments in his description: "When people of group feeling (ʿasabiya) take as followers, people of another descent; or when they take slaves and clients (mawālī) into servitude and enter into close contact with them, as we have said, the clients and followers (muṣṭanaʿ) share in the group feeling of their masters and take it on as if it were their own group feeling."[16] This sense of obligation still exists in the Near East, as I recently discovered while researching in Egypt. A member of the Muslim aristocracy had been expelled during the Nasser era and only recently returned. He had only to go back to the servants and friends of his family to have them readily accept him and provide assistance, sometimes at significant cost to themselves. Recalling the scene later, he said to me with obvious emotion: "Imagine that, after all those years and the public abuse my family had received and my penurious state, these people said, 'We served your grandfather and your mother. We are indebted to your family . . . we will serve you whatever people say'."

This sense of obligation is significant, especially in connection with the cultural mores of Middle Eastern Muslim immigrants. The lines of responsibility have always rested in religion for Muslims—in fact, the language of obligation took the language of Islam, and in this way even everyday obligations assumed a religious import. This value was linked to family, kin, association, and group, so it should not surprise us that Muslims of North America also have this kind of strong interconnectedness. It may be traced in the sense of community at Cedar Rapids, Iowa, and Lac La Biche, Alberta, to mention only two.[17]

Those born into this network react against a society that has little place for these ties. The sense of loss is reflected in the words of Dr. Ilyas Ba Yunas: "Living as an Islamic family within the non-Islamic society is strainful. It demands conscious efforts and sacrifices. Those who are concerned should start by creating a community of the like-minded among themselves."[18] The strong sense of commitment is an influence in the role the family is given among Muslims in North America, as they try to recreate that warm connectedness they see at the heart of Islam,[19] and it poses severe emotional strains when family solidarity breaks down.[20] Hence something like a priesthood of the family has become a distinctive ingredient of North American Islamic experience, with the sense of obligation enshrined in family loyalties.[21] The model of the Prophet and his family adds special nuances to this new focus of commitment.

Group Leadership and Community Direction

In some respects, the umma was successful only to the extent that all other group loyalties were eradicated. Indeed, the decadence of the old tribal kinship system was a common theme in the debates between Muḥammad and his detractors. As the community expanded into empire and beyond, it adopted a way of life that transcended the narrow parochiality of language, geographical region, or kinship group. Islam values permeated all social forms. Thus, in Van Nieuwenhuijze's analysis:[22]

To be a Muslim is not something that results in, or qualifies for, membership in the umma: the two are fully synonymous. The irrelevance of city, village and tribe is basically a matter of their being necessarily and completely superseded by the umma; they simply are not meaningful any more, from the very moment when the umma appears. The question is what this basic irrelevance means in actual practice. At its worst, it amounts to mutual aloofness between patterns of social organization; at the best, it promotes optimal permeation of the so-called alternative or subsidiary patterns by the normative content of the umma. The family, the town quarter, will then tend to feature as small *ad hoc* replicas of the umma, for purposes of face-to-face contact. Hence the fundamentally unwarranted but practically most important process of islamization of any kind of social unit pre-existent to Islam — mediating the conversion to Islam of those concerned.

The ramifications for immigrant Muslims are significant. For, on the one hand, the umma is not easily identified apart from the smaller social units. In North America, after prayers, "the Pakistanis return to their curries and the Arabs to their kebabs," as one immigrant put it, is an acknowledgement that the smaller, ethnically oriented group has more validity as communal Islam than the universal concept of umma. This is why there are ethnic mosques and organizations and why there are fragmented groups vying for control of mosque organizations. If the religious leadership, and particularly the imām, becomes allied with one, usually conservative, faction, then the larger sense of Muslim community suffers.[23] This is, perhaps, why acculturated Muslims are "turned off" by mosque organizations.[24] But as the Muslim leadership relies upon and fosters small-group identity, it side-steps the larger issue of creating Muslim awareness. Muslims born in North America, with no connection to the ideological grounds of their faith, tend to consider the leadership out of touch with the contemporary scene, and feel even more alienation.[25]

But there are positive dimensions of this situation, and one of them is the vigorous growth of mosques and associations. Without a hierarchical structure to impose an organization from above, the umma has had to take the form of loose associations, with a focus on developing common cultural and religious convictions. Such organizations as the Federation of Islamic Associations, the Muslim Students' Association, and the Council of Muslim Communities in Canada, are all attempts to give structural identity to the umma in North America. Like other voluntary organizations, they face the vagaries of waxing and waning membership, and, more importantly, the problem of rotating leadership. But they reflect a move by Muslims to express symbolically the larger reality.

The Muslim community in North America, because of its small-group orientation, has a problem peculiar to it, that is, facing the task of bringing Black Muslims into the fold of "orthodox" Islam. Conflict arises over doctrinal questions as well as leadership qualities. For example, when Muhammad Abdul-Rauf, former Director of the Islamic Center in Washington, D.C., wrote a conciliatory article in *al-Islam* about Elijah Muhammad, it brought the following denunciation from a Sunni in Ohio:[26]

> We read an article quoting you as saying: "We have come to express our admiration for your work and the great achievements of the beloved leader, The Honorable Elijah Muhammad. I would like to assure you all that the whole Muslim world which includes 700 million people is behind you."

> Your support of elijah poole's "X-movement", and advocacy of his deeds as being profound, has left a great deal of anger in the hearts and minds of those who believe in Allah (Exalted be He) and in Muhammad ibn Abdullah (pbuh) as His Last Prophet.

> The whole Qur'ān is a testimony against kufrs like elijah poole, in that it states, "Who is it that does more wrong than one who invents a lie against Allah?"

> Poole claims to have received revelations from Allah, and that Allah appeared to him in the form of a man named Wallace Fard Muhammad (Astaghfirullah Adheem). This very same nigger, wallace fard muhammad, served time in San Quentin Prison on narcotics charges.

> elijah poole has deliberately slandered our beloved Prophet Muhammad ibn Abdullah (pbuh), whom Allah chose as His Last Prophet. elijah poole has stated many times that he is Allah's messenger, *refuting* the revelation from Allah that Muhammad (pbuh) is the Seal of the Prophets (pbut).

> —Where do you receive your authority to proclaim that the whole Muslim world is behind elijah poole? What you have said is that 700 million Muslims have denied the whole of what Islam is about, beginning with the first pillar, the first article and the first point!!!

> It is not easy to express the feelings of Sunni Muslims with regard

to this matter, but we hope the following will give you an idea of the disservice to Islam that your support of elijah poole has been to Sunni Muslims.

There has been too much compromise now – from presidents inaugurating masjids to advocating masturbation (in your "Muslim Prayer Book") . . . and now the greatest of all sins, associating partners with Allah, which elijah poole alias james poole bey alias elijah muhammad has done. Is Allah an ex-convict dope pusher (astaghfirullah Adheem)?

By you being from an eastern country and not experiencing this man's program – which most of us Sunni Muslims in this country have – it may be hard for you to understand what he is about. So we are offering you our past experience with this charlatan.

We implore you to immediately retract your statement of support and publicly make it understood that you were speaking for yourself, or were in error, and were not in any way speaking for 700 million Muslims.

The intensity of this rebuke should not blind us to the issues it raises: Who can speak with authority and give direction to the umma? How are traditional leadership standards in Islam to apply to an indigenous group? How can theological principles be interpreted to apply in situations totally foreign to their origins? One solution is to regard the local organization as a sort of "parish."

The "Millet" System in North America

Immigrants from the Middle East, especially from Lebanon, whose ancestors had lived under the Ottoman empire, had had experience of a society where just such a "parish" system once flourished. Sopher defines the *millet* (sometimes transliterated as *millât*) as "a 'religious community,' a legal entity . . . with virtual autonomy in religious and social matters. Each millet had a religious leader who was responsible to the state for the payment of taxes and the observance of public order . . . the millet occupied a well-defined space, often bounded by walls and gates."[27] This system allowed minorities to build their own sense of identity, while assuring their participation in the larger corporate whole, and it guaranteed freedom of religious expression.

While no such system per se existed in North America, the argument here is that some elements of the pattern do exist here, sufficient to provide a setting for the development of a modified millet system among some North American Muslim communities.

One element of the millet system was geographical cohesion. With its vast distances and urban lifestyle, America militates against such commonality. Yet immigrant communities have retained cohesion in a few large cities, like Detroit, where one whole area is Arab-Muslim,[28] or Edmonton, where immigrant Muslims tend to live on the north side.[29] Even in the Alberta town of Lac La Biche, famous for its high percentage of Muslims, the believers are overwhelmingly located in the lake area of the town.[30]

But the social organization most reminiscent of the millet system is the mosque community. Sadler has argued that the parish situation is the very opposite of "virtuoso" religion (another of Max Weber's terms). Sadler described the former as the religion of the masses and virtuoso religion as that of the charismatics, best observed in Islam among the Sufis.[31] My point is that a Muslim parish tradition has developed in North America, and that the roots of its growth were not something radically new, but rather were Islamic, sometimes remarkably so. Hence, rather than Sadler's term, "parish," we will use the phrase, *mosque community.*

At the heart of the mosque community is the religious functionary, the imām. Apart from his official prayers at the mosque, his main importance is in the part he plays in the ceremonies that accompany the great events of human life. When someone dies, he is called upon to lead the special prayers in the home of the bereaved, both at the time of death and on anniversaries. He may also lead special prayers at the mosque or graveside. Since he is likely to be the only one who knows the Qur'ān, he will be called upon to recite in honor of the deceased. He may also participate in the funeral procession, providing a focus for community grief by reciting poems of the Last Judgement and, in some cases, providing a funeral oration. He may also attend the grave after interment and instruct the spirit of the deceased in the correct phrases to use when the angels question him in the afterlife. If the funeral is a joint Muslim-

Christian affair, he may be asked to give a sermon, or otherwise participate in the funeral rites. Moreover, he may take on ameliorative roles such as counselling the bereaved, organizing community participation in the funeral rites, or initiating Muslim activities in the family. He may well also be called upon to explain the meaning of death to the children, and generally reinforce the living.

Likewise at weddings, he may have a hand in the pre-marital arrangements, assuring that proper attention to dowry and financial details has been paid. He may well instruct the couple on how to recite their vows, or even lead them in those vows. He will also participate in the special prayers in the mosque that precede the wedding. If difficulties develop between the couple, he will act as an independent arbitrator, especially if the couple is without the assistance of close family members.

Celebrations connected with the passing of exams, successful journeys, or prospective business possibilities may also involve his services. On these occasions he may lead the gathering in songs of praise to Muḥammad, a festive activity distantly related to the elaborate *moulids* of the Middle East.

As the most learned person in religious affairs in the mosque community, he is often called upon to give an opinion on matters of doctrine and practice.[32] It is also his responsibility to represent Islam to the larger community by taking part in public activities and giving a reasoned and understandable interpretation of Islam to a society that largely does not understand it. On Friday, he may act as the *khaṭib*, bringing the sermon in traditional, stylized form (sometimes in Arabic, but regularly in English). Occasionally he will express issues of pressing importance to the community in the traditional manner. He is likely to be a member of the mosque committee, usually ex officio, but nevertheless with opinions on mosque direction. In most places he will be responsible for teaching Arabic, and especially the memorization and recitation of the Qurʾān. He may also be regarded as the head of the "Sunday School," the Muslim equivalent of educational outreach. He is responsible for teaching children the proper rituals of the mosque.

This latter role is so important that a plea was recently made for a new type of imâm: "Full-time Islamic scholar-workers should direct such [mosque] centres. They should be looked [upon] more as educators-counsellors than imāms in the traditional sense. They must work in close cooperation with the community and be accountable to the representatives of the community."[33]

Finally, in North America, the imām is expected to express the values that are the verities of Islam – he should personify reverence and piety, honor and good judgement, respect and fellowship, and the pageantry and simplicity that mark the Islamic community. While only a salaried functionary within the mosque, his role in defining Islam is central.[34]

In all of these activities, the imām is intent upon transferring the social-cultural traditions of Islam to the North American milieu. However, the means that are available to him and the pull of success require him to adopt a professional stance similar to that of his co-religionists, the rabbi and minister, a development most evident among Black Muslims. As the umma has become more institutionalized, the requirement that its leaders be educated according to requisite North American values has led to institutes by the Council of Imāms, and calls for a more educated imāmate.[35] If corporate integration between indigenous and immigrant Islam continues, the process is likely to be accelerated, since the Black Muslims place much greater stress on the charisma of the leader. On the other hand, it may well lead to loss of some autonomy as colleges or seminaries provide a common link with all mosque communities.

Mosque communities face the difficulty of defining differentiation from their neighbors, and one means has been activism based on political affairs. During the Iranian revolution, Khomeini factions lobbied for control of the Washington, D.C., centre, and utilized its prominent position to hang banners praising the new regime. A number of Muslims from Canada and the United States visited Iran at the invitation of the Khomeini regime, and many of them returned with inspiration and a new desire for activism. The so-called Muslim revival in the Middle East has also had an impact here, especially on the well-educated immigrants.

Activism throws into relief the close interaction of politics and community in Islam, and raises important issues vis-à-vis Islam's development in the modern world. As Nasir Islam has noted, "Until recently, Islam has been a successful integrating or mobilizing factor only when it has been shown to be in danger or when foreign policy issues or relations with Muslim-Arab States or India are concerned."[36] Studies have also shown that discrimination has played a role in the development of Black Islam. Lincoln notes, "Because Christianity is the white man's religion, the repudiation of Christianity is an overt act of aggression against the white man. To be identified with such a movement that openly rejects the fundamental values of a powerful majority is to increase vastly one's self-esteem and one's stature among one's peers." [37] Yet continued growth and differentiation cannot continue to be based upon prejudice, for that will do little to promote an accepting environment through which major progress can be made in the conversion of North Americans. Hence the more the millet system, and its most evident expression, the mosque community, serves as an effective instrument of differentiation, the less it becomes attractive to assimilated Muslims.[38]

The Movement of Islam into Non-traditional Forms

With the diversification of religion in North America during the last few decades, it should come as no surprise that other types of Islamic groups have sprung up. Various Sufi organizations such as Pir Ilyat Khan have had more success in attracting secular youth than have traditional groups, especially among college students and disaffected Americans.[39] Unlike traditional Islam, they rely almost wholly upon the spiritual insight and acumen of the leader, and they focus on small intimate cells of participants. These groups appear to have benefitted from the interest in the East of recent years, and may now be suffering some retreat with the waning of that interest.[40] But the doctrinal commitment to oneness, and the exciting practice of finding union with God, have helped many people to overcome the initial strangeness of Islam, and may have helped promote its intellectual treasures in the West.[41]

All North Americans have been affected by values collectively known as secularism. As Bibby points out in a recent survey in Canada, "The vast majority of contemporary Canadians, including many church members, have consciously or unconsciously adopted a secular outlook on life."[42] One characteristic of this secularism has been the compartmentalization of life, at least at the conscious, most public level. This allows contradictory values and attitudes to be held at the same time. In a publication directed to Americans, the great Egyptian poet Salah Abdul Sabour suggests that some kind of accommodation is necessary:[43]

> Islam, like all religions, is not hostile to technology. Technology is a technique, a method for extracting the potential of life, but it is not an intellectual or philosophical style of life. Western Christianity has been able to give God what is God's and Caesar what is Caesar's. I think Muslims could do the same. Probably, Christianity has been more amenable to asceticism and abstract thinking than Islam. Christianity today is confined to the area that is beyond science. Any talk about the contradition between Islam as a faith and technology as a method is like comparing a rose to a nail. As progressive Muslims we have a special obligation to re-examine our souls and recreate a balance among emotion, reason and manual labour.

This segregation will require leadership of a type hardly known among the religious functionaries of contemporary Islam. It is no surprise then, that Sabour looks to the poet as the inspiration: "[He] is singing of freedom on individual and collective levels. Right now his role is that of the prophet and guardian of the future, and no longer that of the literary historian chronicling the past and its negativism."[44] His striking use of religious language suggests that this new leadership will respond to the deepest values of Islamic tradition, the prophetic dynamism of Muḥammad. It seems that the Muslim leaders in North America can neither be apologetic in the vein of many old world imāms, nor traditionalist in restating loyalty to patterns developed and nurtured in settings far from this culture. As a Pakistani student noted upon attending the Islamic Center in Cedar Rapids: "It certainly isn't Islam as we knew it at home. The religion has adapted to American culture. But that is good. Islam is a religion that can adapt, despite its many ancient traditions."[45]

Islam is not exhausted by its institutional forms. Some Muslim leaders are trying to bring Islamic values to bear upon American society. Thus, when M. Siddiq responded to Joseph Kraft's article doubting Islam's ability to adapt to modern life, he singled out sexual values as the centre of his concern:[46]

> To the narrow and limited mind of the writer the only way to modernize is to follow the footsteps of the West. The author be-

wails that Islamic leadership does not permit adultery and prom-
iscuousness as some Christian leaders have done (by allowing
female public exposure, dating, easy mixing, pre-marital "games,"
extra-marital relations and open marriages, homosexuality and
unisex marriage).

Siddiq obviously feels that the cost of moving away from a traditional value system has been too great for the West. But the point to
be stressed here is that moral issues are highly sensitive for Muslims
encountering North American values, and they react strongly to
them. As Ayoub says, "The most important problem is with our
young people. They are constantly confronted with western customs which are forbidden by the Koran – such as boys and girls playing sports together – yet these customs are very attractive to them.
... Yet we have chosen this country, and we must learn to love it
and participate fully in it."[47]

The development of an ethical sensitivity may be one option
open for those Muslims who do not participate in Muslim institutions. As one Edmonton Muslim pointed out, he is a North American
in cultural commitment, but Muslim in the application of ethical values. The same individual sees no locus for his perception of Islam
within the traditional mosque community. Rather, he finds mosque
leadership unsophisticated with regard to North American value
systems, and, more seriously, opportunistic, that is, ready to use the
Qur'ān to justify a favorite position when everyone knows full well
the verse was given in an entirely different setting. His ethical sensitivity is little represented by a mosque leadership that is beset by the
politics of personalities, some of which degenerate into almost tribal
conflict reminiscent somewhat of Middle East village sectarianism.

At the same time, he is often critical of the lack of moral stability
in contemporary society, and is distraught by the lack of ethics
among his fellow business associates. He feels isolated because he
thinks Islamic values would help Canadian culture, but he sees no
way of making them known and appreciated.[48] The tenor of his remarks, and the ethical sensitivity behind them, suggest a similar
pattern to that found in secularized Jews.[49]

Finally, we can note that Islamic values are regarded by some
Muslims as having great potential for North Americans, apart from

their institutional expression. Speaking from the context of immigrant Arabs, but underlining the aspirations of not a few Muslims, is the statement of Hitti:[50]

> This may be termed the era of making a spiritual, an intellectual, a scientific and artistic kind of contribution. . . . We are now in a position to participate in the higher things of life, the more abundant life that America can provide. It is not enough to say that we have made money; we should use our money for a higher end, a nobler purpose. Here, at last, is our chance to prove to the Americans that we are not only merchants and businessmen, but heirs of an ancient culture and a venerable tradition which we like to have them share with us. We want to prove that we are here not only to take but to give and that we have behind us a noble language, a rich literature, a glorious history and a store of religiousness and spirituality that can enrich the new heritage into which we have entered in our new homeland.

These are worthy ideals, but the sad truth is that the transmission of these values to North America will be impeded by a reluctance of the host culture to tolerate religious triumphalism, particularly of a type not derived from its own religious roots. Much research has to be done to determine just what impact this cultural Islam has had and is likely to have on this continent.

Conclusion

Weber's concept of tension deriving from the clash between the ideal and the real, and between one form of religious structure (prophecy) and another (priesthood) has allowed us to see how part of the Muslim experience in North America has occurred. But it is clear that tensions have also developed between the mosque community and the larger umma owing to ambiguities within Islam itself about the meaning of umma. Moreover, some of the conflicts that have arisen in founding the community in North America must derive from inadequacies inherent in the institutional forms traditionally adopted by Islam, and which are accerbated by the secular milieu in which it must labor.

Yet, as the umma continues to take form, the leadership given to it reflects the movement from the ideals of the founding moments of Islam to the diversified situation it faces in contemporary North

America, in a continuous affirmation, revaluation, and adaptation process. Thus, to modify Frye, the past is neither forgotten, nor lived in, but present, albeit sometimes completely transformed.

Notes

1. Northrop Frye, "Presidential Address 1976" (Paper delivered at the 91 Annual Convention of the Modern Language Association, New York, 27 December 1976).

2. *Munir Report* (Lahore, 1954), p. 218. Quoted by Marlin W. Inniger, "The Ahmadiyya Movement: Islamic Renewal?" in *Dynamic Religious Movements: Case Studies of Rapidly Growing Religious Movements Around the World*, ed. David J. Hesselgrave (Grand Rapids, Michigan: Baker Book House, 1978), p. 169.

3. Ahmad Taleb, *Lettres de Prison, 1957-61*, trans. Kenneth Cragg (Algiers: Editions nationales Algériennes, 1966), pp. 109ff.

4. Peter Gran, "Political Economy as a Paradigm for the Study of Islamic History," *International Journal of Middle East Studies* 2 (1980): 517.

5. By the 11th and 12th centuries, political élites and religious élites had become distinct; but the relations between them continued to control Muslim society. *See* Ira M. Lapidus, "Hierarchies and Networks: A Comparison of Chinese and Islamic Societies," in *Conflict and Control in Late Imperial China*, eds. Frank Wakeman and C. Grant (Berkeley: University of California Press, 1975), pp. 26-42, esp. p. 34.

6. *See* "Old-timer Remembers Young Days as a Peddlar," *Edmonton Journal*, 25 August 1980, Section B3 for Ali Ahmed Abouchad's account of changing his name to Alexander Hamilton.

7. Georg Simmel, *The Sociology of Georg Simmel*, ed. Kurt Wolff (Glencoe, Illinois: Free Press, 1964).

8. It is still enlightening to discuss emigration to the West with young Egyptians, as I did the winter of 1981-82 in Cairo, and to hear the value of "personal freedom" underlined as the most important one in North American society.

9. *See* Max Weber, *The Sociology of Religion*, trans. E. Fischoff (Boston: Beacon Press, 1964), and "The Social Psychology of World Religions" and "Religious Rejections of the World and Their Directions," in *From Max Weber: Essays in Sociology*, eds. H. Gerth and C.W. Mills (New York: Oxford University Press, 1958).

10. G.I. Keirallah, *Islam and the Arabian Prophets* (New York: Islamic Publishing Company, 1938), Introduction.

11. *See* Robert Devereux, "All-Kashghari and Early Turkish Islam," *Muslim World* 48/49(1958–59): 134–35.

12. *See* E.H. Waugh, "Imam in the New World: Models and Modifications," in *Transitions and Transformations in the History of Religions*, eds. Frank E. Reynolds and Theodore M. Ludwig (Leiden: E.J. Brill, 1980), p. 148.

13. *See* W. Robertson Smith, *Kinship and Marriage in Early Arabia* (Cambridge: Cambridge University Press, 1885), chap. 1 and 2.

14. Found in Miskawaih, *Tājarib al-Uman*, vol.1, p. 191, and quoted in Roy P. Mottahedeh, *Loyalty and Leadership in an Early Islamic Society* (Princeton, N.J.: Princeton University Press, 1980), pp. 40–41. I am indebted to this excellent study for what follows.

15. Ibid., p. 83.

16. Ibn Khaldun, *The Muqaddimah: An Introduction to History,* trans. Franz Rosenthal (New York: Pantheon Books, 1958), vol.1, p. 276.

17. For a good description of the beginnings of the former community, *see Aramco World Magazine* (November-December 1976): 33–34. On Lac La Biche, *see* the studies by H. Barclay, especially "The Perpetuation of Muslim Tradition in the Canadian North," *Muslim World* 59 (1969): 64–73; and "A Lebanese Community in Lac La Biche, Alberta," in Jean Leonard Elliott, ed., *Minority Canadians: Immigrant Groups* (Scarborough: Prentice-Hall of Canada, 1971), pp. 66–83.

18. *Islam Canada* 1 (June 1972): 17.

19. On Muslim marriage and its meaning, *see* M. Abdul-Rauf, *Marriage in Islam* (New York: Exposition Press, 1972), esp. ch. 1.

20. One young Muslim in his mid-twenties, and raised largely in Canada, purchased a car without his father's consent; the result was a traumatic battle, which ended in the youth's leaving home amid great alienation. Other Muslims have confirmed that such decision-making is tantamount to rupturing family structure.

21. To get some sense of religious solidarity in marriage, *see* M. Abdul-Rauf, op. cit., p. 30f.

22. C.A.O. Van Nieuwenhuijze, *Sociology of the Middle East* (Leiden: E.J. Brill, 1971), pp. 463ff.

23. Waugh, "Imām in the New World," p. 144.

24. Only between one and five percent of immigrant Muslims attend mosque, according to "Islamic Practice in America," *The Link* 21, no. 4 (September-October 1979): 10.

25. This point is drawn from Van Nieuwenhuijze, *Sociology*, p. 484. The loss of authority that attends this is not lost on most imāms and leaders, at least not those I have interviewed. In fact, it may be a more general phenomenon. Imāms from Kuwait and Lebanon candidly acknowledged this loss (pers. comm., B. Abu-Laban, 1981).

26. *Al-Jihat* (Columbus, Ohio, Masjid Al-Mu'min Awwal Annex, Ohio Penitentiary) 1, no. 1 (1972): 3.

27. David E. Sopher, *Geography of Religions* (Englewood Cliffs, N.J.: Prentice-Hall, 1967), p. 95. The term is used as the name of an association, Millat Community Association, in Thornhill, Ontario.

28. On the community in Detroit, in comparison with Toledo, *see* Aldo A. Elkholy, *The Arab Moslems in the United States: Religion and Assimilation* (New Haven: College and University Press, 1966), esp. pp. 139ff.

29. Edmonton information is based upon an unpublished paper by L. Fahlman (1980). Mrs. Fahlman ran for election in that ward in a recent election and came in second.

30. From Muhammad Deeb, longtime resident of the town (Summer 1981).

31. Albert W. Sadler, "Islam: The Parish Situation and the Virtuoso Community," *Muslim World* 21, no. 3 (July 1961): 197–210. The following description is drawn from him and from personal observation.

32. For example, the question of Friday vs. Sunday prayers, *see* Waugh, "Imām in the New World," p. 142.

33. "Editorial," *Islam Canada* 11, no. 7 (July 1975).

34. B. Abu-Laban, *An Olive Branch on the Family Tree* (Toronto: McClelland & Stewart, 1980), p. 144.

35. "Editorial," *Islam Canada* 11, no. 7 (July 1975).

36. Nasir Islam, "Islam and National Identity: The Case of Pakistan and Bangla Desh," *International Journal of Middle East Studies* 13 (1981): 69.

37. C. Eric Lincoln, *The Black Muslims in America* (Boston: Beacon Press, 1961), p. 29.

38. A perceptive observation by a Muslim academic in the United States, and borne out by the number of Muslims who attend mosque services.

39. *See*, for example, the Habibiyya Sufi Group, with branches in London (England) and Berkeley (California).

40. Immediate experience was a highlight of religion in the sixties, taking preference over doctrine, according to Robert N. Bellah, "New Religious Consciousness, and the Crisis in Modernity," in *The New Religious Consciousness*, C.Y. Glock and Robert Bellah, eds. (Berkeley: University of California Press, 1976), p. 346.

41. *See* the number of publications by Diwan Press, Norwich, England.

42. Reginald Bibby, *Alberta Conference Research Project (1977) Report,* Alberta Conference, United Church of Canada, 9 November 1977, "Conclusions."

43. Interview in *Arab Views* 16, no. 5/6 (May-June 1970): 7.

44. Ibid., p. 6.

45. Quoted in *Aramco World Magazine* (November-December 1976): 36.

46. Quoted in "Islamic Practice," *The Link,* p. 11. On the other hand, the problems of mixed marriage have been little researched. *See* "Un couple islamo-chrétien," *Revue Monchain* 14, no. 2, cahier 71 (April-June 1981): 15–20.

47. *See* K. Bagnell, "The Faith of Our Fathers," *The Review* 64, no. 6 (1980): 5.

48. A.L.K. Interview (1981) anonymity requested. Second generation businessman, mid-forties, university-educated, Lebanese origin, seldom attends mosque.

49. *See* James A. Deepen and Alan L. Mintz, eds., *The New Jews* (New York: Vantage Press, 1971).

50. Quoted in J.R. Haiek, ed., *The American Arabic-Speaking Community 1975 Almanac* (Los Angeles, California: The News Circle, 1975), p. 11.

Islamic Modernism:
Self-criticism and Revivalism in Syrian Muslim Thinkers

Mahmud Samra

Most studies in Muslim reform begin with the models either of adapting Western cultural formations to Islamic society, or of rediscovering in "traditional" Islam, values held to be "truly" Muslim. Both imply an orientation of rejection, the former of Islam's own heritage, and the latter of the contemporary reality in which Muslims live. The author, a leading student of Islamic modernization, shows that another pattern exits—to respond creatively to the problems that confront Muslims in Muslim contexts. This model has the advantage of placing the West outside, so that it is neither the source of all problems nor the panacea for all difficulties. [Eds.]

This is an attempt to analyze the ideas of Syrian Muslim thinkers in reaction to the impact of Western ideas. "Syria" here means the region extending from the southern boundaries of Turkish-speaking Anatolia in the north to Sinai and Northern Hijaz in the south. It includes what came to be known, after the First World War, as the countries of Syria, Lebanon, Palestine, and Trans-Jordania. Our period begins with the massacre of 1860, a significant date in the history of the country, and ends with the First World War when fundamental changes took place.

Nineteenth-century criticism by missionaries and Westerners of certain Islamic principles, claiming that Islam was the cause of Muslim decadence, was answered in Syria by the re-interpretation of these principles in such a way as to bring them into conformity with the spirit of the age. Some Syrian modernists went so far as to claim that Islam embodied the new social standards of Europe at their best. Having denied that Islam was the cause of Muslim decadence, as the West claimed, Syrian Muslim writers looked for other causes of the malady and found that there were two: corruption of religious belief, and despotism. No revival, they believed, could ever be built on sure grounds unless Islam was purified to withstand later innovations, additions, and restrictions; and unless the people were educated. In arriving at these conclusions they were influenced by the Protestant Reformation, the French Revolution, and the British educational system.

An analysis of the Syrian Muslim writers' ideas on self-criticism and revivalism shows that their contribution to modernism in Islam was not less than that of the Egyptian Muslim modernists. If it is a popular conception that Muslim modernism centred around Muhammad 'Abduh and his school, it is because Muhammad 'Abduh held a high theological position and his ideas, therefore, had the weight of office behind them. Moreover, Egypt at the time was under British rule, and the Muslim modernists there were prominent men who, by virtue of their office, came into contact with western politicians and men of letters who wrote about them. Thus much came to be known about these Egyptian thinkers in the West.

The case of the Syrian Muslim modernists was different. Most of them came from noble and wealthy families, and many were obliged, under Turkish despotism, to leave their country from time to time to take refuge in Egypt. Unlike their Egyptian contemporaries, they were not in the limelight.

From the outset I would like to draw a clear distinction between the attitude of Muslims towards western thought that pertained about the middle of the 19th century, and their attitude later on. In the earlier period, the Muslim thinkers used to look upon western civilization as a product of two factors – justice and liberty – the lack of which had caused the decline of the Muslim world. Though they urged their co-religionists to break away from their attitude of blind admiration for their past, they did not feel inferior to western man.

They took the view that the advance of the West and the decline of the Muslims had nothing to do with either Christianity or Islam. The writings of the Egyptian Rifāʿah al-Ṭahṭāwī, the Tunisian Khair al-Dīn Pasha,[1] and the Syrian Aḥmad Fāris al-Shidyāq,[2] represent this attitude, which gained support even among the Christian Arabs.[3] But later in the century, when they started to feel the vehemence of western civilization as evidenced by the power of its science, and its attacks on certain Islamic beliefs, the pressure caused them to take another attitude. The new attitude can be described, in general terms, as a mixture of fear and fascination on the one hand, and a feeling of inferiority on the other. The modernists thought that, by some strained and intricate process of reasoning, they could make the ideas of past centuries conform with the practices of the 19th and 20th centuries.

The modernists, to accomplish the defence properly and make the task easier for themselves, tried first to break the old ties and get rid of all that had been heaped up through the ages and attributed to Islam. They looked to the West for this, and were inspired by the Protestant Reformation in the Christian church. Protestantism was favored by al-Afghānī[4] and Muhammad ʿAbduh,[5] because it ignored everything attributed to Christianity other than the Bible, and gave everybody the right to read it and understand it. Following this, Muhammad ʿAbduh started a campaign against the traditional belief that the *ijtihād* was closed, and stated that "It is the right of everybody to read and understand the Qurʾān according to his faculties; the learned and the ignorant alike."[6] He thought that the Muslims of his own time were more fitted to understand the Qurʾān than their predecessors because they were acquainted with modern ideas and new inventions.[7] In Syria, Muhammad ʿAbduh's views were favored by Muhammad Jamāl al-Dīn al-Qāsimī in his commentary on the Qurʾān.[8] The first volume is devoted to how to understand the Qurʾān, quoting Muhammad ʿAbduh at length.[9]

ʿAbd al-Ḥamīd al-Zahrāwī took a further step and a bolder one in declaring that Islam was the Qurʾān only, and rejected the Traditions altogether because they were so muddled up it was impossible to distinguish the true from the forged.[10] All that was recorded in the *fiqh* was not binding on Muslims, he said, and did not form a part of Islam, and so should be discarded, because those who wrote it had in mind their own time, not ours.[11] This was shocking even to modernists, who adopted a more flexible view: they chose from the Traditions whatever suited their purpose, and rejected what did not, arguing that the discarded elements were either forged or misinterpreted.

This is the broad line on which the modernists started their revaluation of certain Islamic ideas, such as: the status of women (polygamy, divorce, the veil); Islam's attitude towards the non-Muslims (the *jihād,* slavery, the *dhimmīs;*) and Islam vis-à-vis modern science, heaven and hell, etc.[12] But what really concerned them most was: what is the true cause of Muslim decadence? As could be expected, they stated from the very beginning that Islam was not the cause, and started looking elsewhere. According to these modern thinkers, Westerners accused Islam of being the cause of the decadence of Muslims because they were judging it by its people, and such a judgement was unfair. It was Muhammad 'Abduh who gave them the following axiom: "Islam is veiled by the Muslims."[13]

The Muslim modernists agreed that one of the main causes of Muslim decadence was that they had not followed the teachings of their religion and had added things which were alien to it. Thus they had to provide answers to the questions such as: What were those alien elements? What was the true Islam? How could revival be achieved? etc. Attempts had been made long before this time to purify Islam from corruptions, and the *Wahhābī* movement had been significant for its call "Back to the Qur'ān," condemning both the worship paid to holy men , and the neglect of the writings of Muslim theologians. They also adhered to the literal meaning of the Qur'ān. In a word, Wahhabism denied all subsequent additions, regardless of their character. This leads us to draw a clear distinction between Wahhabism and this modernist movement. Though the two groups agreed that religion should be purified, they differed over intrinsic issues. Wahhabism had arisen from tension inside Islam itself; the modernist movement was a reaction to contact with the West. A major difference between them was that the first movement was backward in spirit, sticking to the literal meaning of Islam as manifested mainly in the Qur'ān, while the call for purification in the second movement was intended to give the modernists the freedom to reconcile Islam with western ideas.

All the Syrian modernists agreed that the causes of the malady were two: the corruption of religious belief[14] and the tyranny of Muslim rulers. Both had combined to cause the decline.

Despotism: A Major Cause of Decline

THE INFLUENCE OF THE FRENCH REVOLUTION

Despotism, to the Syrian Muslim modernists, was a major cause of decline. In this they had in mind the poor and miserable conditions of their country under the despotic rule of the Ottoman sultans, especially ʿAbd al-Ḥamīd II. Their ideas, in condemnation of despotism, were those of the French philosophers of the 18th century who had paved the way for the French Revolution. This had razed all forms of despotism as represented by absolute monarchy. The names of Montesquieu and Rousseau were most favored in the area at the time. The Syrian writers admitted openly that these thinkers taught them to hate tyranny and had opened their eyes to the disasters it caused.[15] From the second half of the 19th century onwards Syria produced a long line of thinkers who were much influenced by these ideas. In Turkey a similar change was taking place, and from Midhet Pasha to the constitution of 1908, and until the great change under Mustafa Kamal, there was a long list of Turks who were similarly influenced by the ideas of the French Revolution.[16]

The Syrian writers learned from the French that revolution against despotism was necessary if peaceful methods could not prevail. This trend of thought is very clear in the writings of the Christian and the Muslim modernists, who were united in condemning the tyranny of the Turkish sultan. They only differed about the suitable time for it. Some held the view that the first step towards revival would be to overthrow despotism, because no progress could be achieved under a despotic ruler. The reasons these writers gave to sanction revolution were similar to those given by the French thinkers. They declared that sovereignty was the legal right of the people, and the ruling class had to be responsible to them. If they ruled against the interests of the people, they should be overthrown by force if peaceful methods did not succeed.[17] Al-Afghānī went so far as to claim that to overthrow tyranny with peaceful methods was impossible, and that history had never recorded that any king, prince, or usurper had admitted willingly to rule only in name while the nation ruled in fact. To him, first among things that would never be granted were freedom and independence.[18] This became, later on, the axiom of the Arabs in their revolt against the mandatory powers after the First World War. King Faisal I is reported to have said: "Independence is obtained by force, and never granted." This attitude was mostly represented, before the First World War, by Christian writers; the writings of Amīn al-Raihānī[19] and Adīb Ishāq [20] are good examples.

Others argued that nothing could be built on firm ground, even if despotism were overthrown, until the people were educated in their beliefs and prepared to defend them. This attitude was advocated by Muhammad ʿAbduh and the majority of the Muslim modernists because they were primarily concerned to preserve Muslim unity and hoped the Ottoman tyranny could be reformed by peaceful methods. The failure of the Turkish Revolution of 1908 was explained away by them on the grounds that the people were not ready for such ideas and so could not defend even what they had. Al-Ghalāyīnī says: "the true liberty is what the people can get through their own struggle, not by the help of an external power,"[21] such as the army. The failure of the Turkish Revolution of 1908, though it gave the people the constitution prepared by Midhet Pasha, which was, in fact, the constitution of the French Revolution with slight modification, made the Syrian writers discuss what was needed for a revolution to be successful. They came to believe that the people had to be prepared for change before it could take place, and that the thinkers were those who should prepare them for it, as the French people had been prepared for the Revolution by the French philosophers of the 18th century.[22]

ISLAM AND DESPOTISM

In condemning tyranny, the Muslim thinkers had a distinct attitude, which colored their campaign. The Ottoman sultan represented the Muslim caliph. The Muslims had, therefore, to assert that despotism was alien and against the very spirit of Islam. Some Westerners thought that Islam, with its autocratic nature, seemed to encourage despotism, and so was responsible for the bad conditions prevailing in the country at the time; but still other Westerners believed that it was not Islam and its doctrines which had brought about the sad state of things but the tyranny of the Muslim rulers, who had wilfully perverted and corrupted Islamic doctrines.[23] As for the Muslims, they all stressed and did their best to prove that Islam was an enemy to tyranny.[24] Qur'ānic verses and events in Muslim history were quoted at length and discussed to prove that claim,[25] but commentators differed as to the date when despotism first started to overwhelm Muslim countries. Some gave the reign of al-Mutawakil, the 'Abbāsid caliph, as the first time in which despotism colored the rule of the Muslim caliph, because he took full power to himself, placed the Arab commanders at a distance, and even killed some, and favored the Turkish commanders to whom he entrusted the army. Thus, it was said, later on, he came to rule over the Muslim world tyrannically.[26] The Shī'ī writers went back as far as the rising of the Umayyad dynasty, which changed the Muslim caliphate into kingship.[27] Others did not hesitate to declare that the whole history of the Muslims, apart from the reign of the first four caliphs and the reign of 'Umar II, was a series of tyrannical reigns in which Asian despotism and Pharoanic tyranny were mixed.[28] This uncontrolled despotism had given the Muslim rulers full power to act as they liked, and gave Harūn al-Rashīd the power to execute the Barmakīds. It could be fairly said that the history of Muslims was a series of Barmakī executions.[29] The despotism of Muslim rulers seemed to some so shocking and unrestrained that they preferred the freedom they enjoyed under the just rule of a non-Muslim government such as the English one in Egypt to their persecution under the Turks.[30]

AL-KAWĀKIBĪ AND ALFIERI

Though the Syrian Christians were the first to condemn and attack despotism, it was a Muslim who wrote the most detailed study of it.[31] Although al-Kawākibī, like his Christian and Muslim contemporaries, looked to the French philosophers, especially Montesquieu, as masters to teach him, his ideas were mainly drawn from the Italian tragic dramatist, Vittorio Alfieri (1749–1803). He came to know Alfieri's ideas, most probably, through the Turkish translation of his book, *On Tyranny*, by ʿAbd ʾAllah Jaudat. Some even claimed that al-Kawākibī's book was a mere translation of *On Tyranny*, with slight modifications.[32] This side of al-Kawākibī has never been noticed by those who have tried to study him. In a French study on al-Kawākibī, the writer does not seem to have noticed the influence of the Italian dramatist on him, of whom no mention is made.[33] He also assumes that al-Kawākibī knew French,[34] but we are told by his son, the late Dr. Saʿd al-Kawākibī, that his father knew only his mother tongue and Turkish.[35]

The book is a collection of articles written on tyranny, which were later published in book form with comments and notes. Though it appeared before his other book, *Umm al-Qurā*, it was certainly conceived later in the mind of the author because it is an elaboration of one of the ideas given in *Umm al-Qurā* to explain the causes of decline. The author states from the very beginning how he came to write it:

> In the year 1318*, I arrived in Egypt, which was enjoying freedom under the rule of its Khedive ʿAbbās. Under such favorable conditions, I published in a certain journal articles on the nature of tyranny and its downfall. Some of the ideas are quoted and others are the result of study. No reference here is made to a certain despot, or government, but my aim is to open the eyes of the ignorant to the cause of all evil, so that the people of the East may know that they themselves are the cause of their decline.... I was asked, then, by some dear friends, to collect the articles in book form, and so I have done, after making some additions.[36]

When the book was published, it was much praised and hailed by the writers, and some even went so far as to say that "no philosopher, either in the East or the West, has ever written such a book."[37] Some may object that it is not enough to copy the ideas of others in order to be hailed in this way, but, in fact, the circumstances in which this book appeared gave rise to the warm reception it received. Al-Kawākibī was brave enough to attack tyranny at a time when ʿAbd al-Ḥamīd II was ruling the Ottoman empire. He

---

*1900 in the Common Era

was also well qualified for such a task since he had suffered torment and oppression under the Hamidian regime in his native town, Aleppo. His house was very often attacked by Ottoman soldiers and he was imprisoned in 1303 H.* on a charge of plotting against the life of the *wali* there, though he was later tried and acquitted. The authorities plotted against his life, accusing him of high treason, and he was barely saved from execution. His personal papers and library were destroyed, among which were his manuscripts of two books ready for publication: "Ṣaḥāʾif Quraish" and "al-ʿAẓamah li Allāh."[38] Al-Kawākibī can also be credited with being the first Arab writer to devote a whole book to such an important theme; all the others were satisfied with articles. We can also add that though he copied, sometimes word for word, the ideas of Alfieri, he tried to apply them to the tyranny existing in his country at that time. The number of original ideas put forward is limited, but the importance of his contribution lies in the fact that the ideas themselves were expressed clearly and vigorously at the very time when they were needed.

On reading the book one can tell why al-Kawākibī favored the ideas of Alfieri more than those of Montesquieu and the French 18th century philosophers, though the first was hardly known in the area, while the others were admired and copied. Alfieri, we are told, was a hater of tyrants and a fervent lover of liberty, but he was undisciplined and unsystematic and, though he was much influenced by Montesquieu and the French philosophers, he could not absorb their rational way of reasoning. Perhaps his lack of education was responsible for that.[39] The same thing comes through very clearly to us on reading the writings of al-Kawākibī: *Umm al-Qurā* is a set of disconnected ideas, and *Ṭabāʾiʿ al-Istibdād* consists of attractive ideas put in moving flowery language, but there is no systematic reasoning or deep discussion. He appears to be more of an orator.[40]

On Tyranny was written in 1777 when the Italian author was 28 years old. The two main subjects addressed were the relation between despotism and religion, and its influence on literature. These are also the two main topics in al-Kawākibī's book.

According to Alfieri, religion is one of the main pillars on which

---

*1885 in the Common Era

tyranny stands, because of the great influence it exercises over men. The Catholic church is the twin sister of despotism, because it teaches obedience to leaders, and therefore it is impossible for a people to be at once Catholic and free. He goes on to say that in Catholicism there are certain doctrines that are favorable to despotism, such as the belief that a man can be the representative of God and infallible, a belief that leads to a form of slavery. Belief in confession also makes Catholicism favor despotism, because its people, in the hope of redemption, give their possessions to the church, and so, becoming impoverished, become too discouraged to make any attempt to gain freedom. The result of all this is that tyrants and priests become rich and so do not desire any change in the established order. They become bound by common ties. The attack here was not directed against religion as such, but on its corrupted form; he stressed that religious leaders, prophets, and saints were bitter enemies of oppression. The Protestant movement was hailed by him, and interpreted as a revolt against the abuses of Christianity as represented by Catholicism. Thus, he regarded the first principles of Christianity as not incompatible with liberty or the greatness of the people.[41]

Alfieri's violent attack on the authority of the Pope and the priests, and upon innovations in religion, appealed to the Syrian reformists, who considered the religious heads in Islam similarly responsible for decline because they had allied themselves with despots and corrupted religion for the self-interests of both. According to al-Kawākibī, when despotism ruled in Muslim countries, honest theologians refused to work for the authorities, and therefore people not qualified for the office of qāḍīs and shaykhs were admitted into them and favored by the rulers. Al-Kawākibī gave astonishing ideas on this point when he claimed that despotism and religion went together.[42] It needed much courage from a Muslim at the time to say:[43]

Political despotism has originated from religious despotism, and if not, they are at least, twins, united together to humiliate man, because one rules his body and the other rules over his heart. ... The revealed books call him to worship an unseen power, which threatens him at any moment with severe punishment in life and after death. Such a threat troubles his life, weakens his mental faculty, and makes him surrender to stupid and fanciful imaginations. Salvation is promised by the religious heads and the price is man's deep reverence and humility to them.

The despots, according to him, used to go so far as to claim that they themselves had godly elements in order to rule over man's body and soul. Whenever there was religious despotism, there was political despotism and the destruction of one led to the downfall of the other. The best way for a reformation to come about was to start purifying the religious belief, and a renewed political life would follow. This could be clearly seen in the way the Protestant movement led to the reformation of political life among the Saxons; a far deeper reformation of political life than ever took place in Catholic countries[44] such as France. Al-Kawākibī differed from Alfieri in rejecting his claim that Islam, with its belief in one omnipotent God, was in favor of despotism,[45] and gave an enthusiastic defence, quoting Qurʾānic verses.[46]

On the influence of despotism on literature, both held the view that the promotion of true literature and the existence of despotism were incompatible. Tyrants had always tried to exploit literature in order to strengthen their power, but the true literary man would never condone vice. Therefore, there could be nothing in common between a despot and a writer, because their ends were entirely different. Al-Kawākibī takes this idea and elaborates it, applying it to conditions in his country. He rejects the idea prevailing in Syria at the time, that true knowledge is the acquiring of facts, or rote learning such as of the books on fiqh. Al-Kawākibī knows that the tyrant does not fear that kind of knowledge because it does not lead to the inculcation of noble feelings or ideas. The tyrant does, however, fear philosophy and great literature, which teach the love of a moral life. Al-Kawākibī then, joins Alfieri in giving the true writer the highest position in world history. No ruler, however distinguished, can approach a writer in greatness: Alexander the Great and all the other celebrated rulers have sunk into semi-obscurity, but Dante and the great poets and writers are eternal, and their influence continues down the centuries. A man of letters feels it is his duty to teach a servile people how to defend its rights, and hence arises the necessity for writers to attack tyrannical power.[47]

In addition, al-Kawākibī adopted some of Alfieri's major conceptions, which could produce serious results if one came to believe in them. Alfieri's violent attack on despotism did not mean that he was in favor of the rule of the mob. On the contrary, he hated the results of the French Revolution, because the common man came to rule. In his writings, Alfieri expresses his deep dislike and loathing of the mob, the merchants, and the shopkeepers. He was an aristocrat who moved among the upper classes of society. He had met a number of royal persons in his travels, but disliked all of them and refused to be presented to some.[48] His conception of the people is certainly not that of Rousseau or of an advanced democrat; in fact he was far from being a democrat and used to call the people the "lazy and needy dregs."[49] As for the government he advocated, he did not give a clear idea of it, but we understand that he wanted the intellectuals to rule, as he openly expressed his contempt for the aristocrats of his time. He was much in favor of the ancient republics of Greece and Rome, but his warm praise of the English monarchy makes him seem in favor of constitutional monarchy. One of the characteristics of English political life that most impressed him was the disagreement of parties as reflected in parliament by the conflict between the government and the opposition.[50] England alone was exempted from his attack on the hereditary tyrannies existing all over Europe, and he was so fond of it that "he wrote in his declining years an epitaph to adorn a possible burial place" in appreciation of it.[51] In al-Kawākibī, we find the same dislike of the mob, the merchants, the uneducated; and the same warm enthusiasm for the political life of England, and of ancient Greece and Rome.[52] He agrees with Alfieri that the learned should rule, but gives the idea an Islamic interpretation. To him the *shūrā* in Islam should be revived, which meant to him a democratic government based on the aristocratic authority of the nobles.[53] The word *ashrāf* (nobles) in the Arabic text can be misleading, since we do not know exactly what he means by it.

Al-Kawākibī differs intrinsically from Alfieri when he comes to discuss how to get rid of despotism. To Alfieri, force and the "theory of the dagger" are the most effective means of putting an end to oppression.[54] Al-Kawākibī, on the other hand, followed his fellow Muslim modernists in believing that the overthrow of despotism did not mean that the revolution would necessarily be successful. In his

view, before getting rid of tyranny, the people should be first educated and brought up to hold beliefs that they would be ready to
defend. Deciding what should replace despotism, and making the
people believe in it, had to precede the actual overthrow of despotism.[55] It was a fixed belief among the Syrian reformers, both Muslims and Christians, that without educating the people, no progress
was possible, but with that goal achieved, every sound and solid reform might be accomplished. It can be fairly stated that among these
reformers there was a spreading mania for education, which
amounted to what could be described as hysterical worship. This
enthusiasm for education arose from the fixed belief that the progress made by the West was the result of education and was not owed
to any other cause. But that is another story.

Epilogue

Lord Cromer lived for many years in Egypt, ruling there as Britain's
representative. For him, Islam could never be reformed, and if it
were, then "reformed Islam is Islam no longer; it is something
else."[56] Thus, according to him, Islam as represented by these modernists would not be the true Islam. On the other hand, Hugronje[57]
and Gibb[58] hold that the Muslims have the right to reinterpret their
beliefs as they like, and as the Christians did. But, in commenting on
the methods used by the Muslim modernists, Gibb describes this
modernist movement as having "intellectual confusions" and "paralyzing romanticism."[59] One can hardly accept a sweeping statement
like this, however much the two phrases exactly describe the general trend. We cannot overlook the fact that there were thinkers
who produced constructive ideas, which might have been colored
with romanticism but not a paralyzing one. Gibb also claims that
what leads the Arab to this paralyzing romanticism is his intensive
imagination and aversion to rationalism;[60] while Grunebaum, on
the other hand, believes the opposite, and states that the Arab's
mind is "unimaginative" and is distinguished by "sober realism."[61]
One thinks, again, that it is not possible to agree with either, but
must rather look upon the question from a different angle. No nation
can be described as either imaginative or unimaginative, because
these qualities are not characteristics of nations. They are, rather,

indicative of certain stages of development. If the Muslim Arabs started reinterpreting their beliefs in a romantic way, it was because they were still immature, and not because romanticism is a trait of their character.

Perhaps the main failings of the modernist Muslim Arabs, without exception, are: their defective understanding of the western thought on which they tried to base their religious principles; and their fascination with the science and standards of a certain human development at a certain time to the extent of believing that they were final. Europe took centuries to adjust to the impact of Greek thought and scientific discoveries, while Islam had tried to do the same in something less than a century. These ideas also did not develop naturally, but came in the shock of conquest and domination by superior powers. It is no wonder, then, that this movement failed to bring to light any outstanding intellectual achievement in the way of reconciling Islam with modern thought, but it did produce sincere and creative thinkers. The intellect was called upon to prove that Islam did embody these values, believing a priori that it did, rather than to find out whether Islam did really embody them. In any intellectual movement, the material under consideration must be examined by pure reason. The defect of having a priori beliefs still colors the writings of even the foremost Muslim Arab thinkers of today.

Notes

1. Khair al-Dīn Pasha al-Tūnisī, *Aqwam al-Masālik fī Maʿrifat Aḥwāl al-Mamālik* (Tunis: 1284 H.), p. 20.

2. *Al-Sāq ʿala al-Sāq Fī Mā Huua al-Fāriyāq*, 1st ed. (Paris: 1885); *Kashf al-Mukhabbā ʿan Funūn Aurubbā*, 1st ed. (London: 1859).

3. Thabit, Ayyūb, *ʿIbrah wa Dhikrā* (in) *Kalimah Ḥaul al-Dustūr* (Beirut: 1909).

4. *Al-Radd ʿalā al-Dahriyyīn*, M.ʿAbduh, trans., ʿUthmān Amīn, intro. (Cairo: 1955), pp. 83–84.

5. *Al-Islām wa al-Naṣrāniyyah* (Cairo: 1323 H. [1905]), pp. 42–4.

6. *Muqaddimah fī al-Tafsīr* (Cairo: 1319 H. [1901]), pp. 8-9.

7. *Risālat al-Tauḥīd,* 16th ed. (Cairo: 1373 [1953]), p. 159.

8. *Maḥāsin al-Ta'wil* (Cairo: 1957).

9. Ibid, I, pp. 322-31.

10. *Al-Fiqh wa 'al-Taṣawwuf* (Cairo: 1901), pp. 2-4. The same attitude was taken by Sir Sayyid Ahmad Khan in the 19th century; *see* on him, W. C. Smith, *Modern Islam in India,* (London: 1946), pp. 6-23.

11. Al-Zahrāwī, pp. 3-8. This attitude was adopted later on and strongly defended by the Egyptian physician Muḥammad Taufīq Ṣudqī in *Dīn Allah fī Kutub Anbiyā'ih* (Cairo: 1912), pp. 211-20.

12. This is an important and interesting topic for research and deserves a separate study.

13. *See al-Nibrās,* 1909, I, pp. 372-4; al-Ghalāyīnī, *Arīj al-Zahr,* Beirut: 1911, pp. 207-10; Muḥammad Rashīd Riḍā, *Shubuhāt al-Naṣārā, wa Ḥujaj al-Islām,* 2d ed. (Cairo: 1367, H. [1947]).

14. For details *see* M. Samra, *Arabic and Islamic Garland* (London: 1977), pp. 200-212.

15. *See* especially: *al-Nibrās,* 1909, I, pp. 58-65; Aḥmad kurd 'Alī, *Al-Ummah,* Damascus, February 9, 1909.

16. *See* Ra'īf Khūrī, *al-Fikr al-ʿArabī al-Ḥadīth* (Beirut: 1943), pp. 97-103.

17. *See* especially Amīn al-Raiḥānī, *al-Raiḥāniyyāt,* Vol. III.

18. *See* al-Afghāni's article in *Al-Manar* 3(1900), pp. 577-82; R. Khūrī, *al-Filar al-ʿArabī al-Ḥadīth;* p. 117.

19. *Al-Raiḥāniyyāt,* (Beirut: 1923), IV, pp. 144-58.

20. Adib Isḥāq, *Al-Durar* (Beirut: 1909), especially pp. 42-50, 155 ff.

21. *Arīj al-Zahr,* p. 155.

22. *See* R. Khūrī, *al-Fikr al-ʿArabī al-Hadīth,* pp. 120-23.

23. Arminius Vambery, *Western Culture in Eastern Lands* (London: 1906), p. 307.

24. *See* R. al-ʿAẓm, *Al-Jāmiʿah,* pp. 77-8; al-Kawākibī, *Ṭabā'iʿ al-Istibdād,* pp. 17-21.

25. *See* especially, al-ʿAlamī, ʿAbd Allah, *al-Ḥurriyah wa al-Musāwāh wa al-Mabʿūthān min Taʿālīm al-Qur'ān* (Beirut: 1326 H. [1908]), passim.

26. R. Al-ʿAẓm, *Al-Bayān,* (Cairo: 1887) pp. 45-67.

27. *Al-ʿIrfān* 3 (1911): 130-31.

28. Al-Khālidī and Muḥammad Rūḥī, *Asbāb al-Inqilāb al-ʿUthmānī wa Turkya al-Fatāh* (Cairo: 1326 H. [1908], pp. 15-7.

29. Ibid., pp. 22-23.

30. Al-Kawākibī, *Umm al-Qurā (Cairo*, 1320 H. [1902]), p. 16.

31. Ibid., *Ṭabāʾiʿ al-Istibdād wa Maṣāriʿ al-Istiʿbād*, Cairo, ?

32. Aḥmad Shuʿaib, *Al-Daulah wa al-Jamāʿah*, Arabic translation from Turkish by Muḥibb al-Dīn al-Khaṭīb (Cairo: 1912), pp. 5–6.

33. Norbert Tapiero, *Les Idées réformistes d'al-Kawākibī* (Paris: 1956).

34. Ibid., p. 13.

35. *Al-Ḥadīth*, Aleppo, September-October, 1959.

36. Al-Kawākibī, *Ṭabāʾiʿ al-Istibdād*, p. 2.

37. *Al-Manār*, 1902, V, p. 240.

38. *See* for details, *Al-Ḥadīth* (September-October 1952) : 548–52.

39. *See* G. Megaro, *Vittorio Alfieri: Forerunner of Italian Nationalism* (N.Y.: 1930), pp. 13–40.

40. *See* especially Al-Kawākibī, *Ṭabāʾiʿ al-Istibdad*, pp. 93–106.

41. G. Megaro, *Vittorio Alfieri*, pp. 77–85.

42. Al-Kawākibī, *Ṭabāʾi ʿal-Istibdad*, pp. 11–25.

43. Ibid., pp. 11–12.

44. Ibid., pp. 14–15.

45. G. Megaro, *Vittorio Alfieri*, p. 77.

46. Al-Kawākibī, *Ṭabāʾi ʿal-Istibdad*, pp. 12, 12–27.

47. Ibid., pp. 26–31, 75; G. Megaro, *Vittorio Alfieri*, pp. 63–76.

48. G. Megaro, *Vittorio Alfieri*, p. 72.

49. Ibid., p. 49.

50. Ibid., p. 54.

51. Ibid., p. 51.

52. Al-Kawākibī, *Ṭabāʾiʿ al-Istibdad*, pp. 15, 28, 35–36, 50.

53. Ibid., p. 19.

54. G. Megaro, *Vittorio Alfieri*, p. 47.

55. Al-Kawākibī, *Ṭabāʾiʿ al-Istibdad*, pp. 113–26, M. Samra, "Al-Kawakibi and Alfieri," *Faculty of Arts Journal*, University of Jordan: 33–48.

56. Lord Cromer, *Modern Egypt* (London: 1908), II, pp. 228–29.

57. S. Hugronje, *Mohammedanism* (N.Y.: 1916) pp. 139–40.

58. H.A.R. Gibb, *Modern Trends in Islam*, 3rd impr. (Chicago: 1954), pp. xi–xii.

59. Ibid., p. 105.

60. Ibid., pp. 109–10.

61. G. von Grunebaum, *Islam* (London: 1955), p. 67.

Islamic Laws on Ribā (Interest) and Their Full Economic Implications[1]

M. Siddieq Noorzoy

Introduction

The Islamic fundamentalist doctrine on *ribā* states that the rate of interest is zero, a doctrine based upon the Qur'ānic injunctions against it.[2] The word "ribā" means "increase" as interpreted by Imām Razi,[3] which corresponds to the word "interest" as defined by *Webster's New World Dictionary*. In both cases the increase refers to the amount beyond what is owed. Thus, the strictest interpretation that can be given to the word ribā is that it means interest – an amount, or rate, due above the principal of a loan. The word ribā, however, is commonly translated as "usury,"[4] which is defined by *Webster's Dictionary* as "an excessive or unlawfully high rate or amount of interest." Thus, the fundamental aspect of the controversy about the doctrine of interest in Islam is whether the rate of interest is zero, in which case ribā is interpreted to mean interest per se, or whether a positive rate of interest is permissible, in which case ribā is interpreted to mean usury.

The purpose of this paper is a limited inquiry about some aspects of the controversy on ribā as they affect contemporary economic transactions in a Muslim society.

Since the writing of this paper arose in the context of the workings of Islam in North America, at first sight it was tempting to confine our discussion of the applications of the laws on ribā to the problems and issues of adaptation of Muslims in North America. However, even though some issues such as on mortgage instalment payments, as discussed below, have arisen recently in the context of the workings of Islam in North America, the issues surrounding ribā including mortgage instalment payments on construction loans for mosques, community centres, or purchases of housing, are universal in applicability in minority Muslim communities anywhere in the world. Therefore, the question to address is what are the full range of implications of adherence to interest-free transactions by a subset of a society when these transactions are also carried out between the subset of the society and the rest of the society that operates with a positive rate of interest.

Some of the issues raised in this context clearly also have relevance to a larger model that encompasses economic transactions between a fundamentalist Muslim state that adopts the full workings of interest-free economic system and the non-Muslim world, which functions with a positive rate of interest. The analogy would also apply between Muslim states at large and the rest of the world if the former invoke Islamic laws on ribā along the same lines.

There is no full-fledged working model of a mixed economy based on the initial assumption of a zero rate of interest. This problem may be solved at the theoretical level and the resulting model must lead to functional policy tools on output and employment, on prices, and the balance of payments, before a fundamentalist Islamic state can adopt such a model with its full workings. Clearly a partial substitution of interest-free transactions for some sectors and their neglect in other areas would not only tend to misallocate resources, but also would not be in conformity with the spirit of Islamic laws as interpreted by fundamentalists. No attempt is made in this paper to construct such a model. However, the broad outlines of such a model are stated below without the detailed requirements of its workings.

The Nature of the Controversy on Ribā

The controversy on ribā is not due merely to the meaning attached to it by some translators of the Qurʾān; for it that were the case then the insertion of the word "interest" for "usury" in the translation would resolve the matter. The fact that there was room for different interpretations of the Qur'ānic injuctions against ribā can be traced to the time of Hadhrat-i-Omar in the first century of the Islamic period, who was quoted as saying: "The last to be revealed was the verse of usury and the Prophet expired without explaining it to us. Therefore, give up usury or anything resembling it."[5] This statement implies not only that Omar wished there were a greater explanation regarding all aspects of ribā, but also that to be safe he opted for an interpretation according to which one must avoid anything that might resemble ribā in dealings with others. It is of immediate interest to note that in this translation the word "usury" is used rather than "interest." The question then arises: Did Omar mean usury or interest by ribā? If he meant that ribā is usury, then Islamic behavior would require two kinds of patterns, one a following of the given interpretations case by case as established by fiqh ("systematic interpretation of Qur'ānic injunctions"), and the other, in case of doubt, in which a person must follow his best judgement until assessment is given by iftā' ("the scholarly exercise of such judgement"). If, on the other hand, Omar meant interest in his statement, then only barter transactions may involve some problems of interpretation. For monetary transactions, any interest above zero would qualify as ribā. In the case of barter transactions there are also two types of behavior patterns under the latter interpretation of ribā: first, avoiding examples involving barter that had been declared as constituting ribā by the Prophet Muḥammad (discussed below), and second, conducting monetary transactions through the market and thus avoiding problems of interpretation.

Probably the most common objection to the zero rate of interest on a business loan from which otherwise dividend income is lawful has been the implicit argument that such a loan involves an opportunity cost to the lender determined by the foregone profits that the lender would have earned had he invested the funds in a business investment. The discussion of ribā that recognizes this argument is given in the work of Imām Razi. Razi countered this argument by stating that there are no guarantees that higher profits will always accrue from such self-investment.[6] Clearly what is implicit in this argument is the assumption that the degree of risk involved in alternative uses of funds is the same in all cases. This, of course, need not be the case except under conditions of perfect market certainty, which is an additional assumption that must be attributed to Imām Razi's argument if the argument is to hold.

This interpretation comes close to the argument that a modern capitalist would make in favor of charging a positive rate of interest on a business loan under uncertainty with varying degrees of risk, without, however, winning acceptance for interest charges from Imām Razi. The most clear-cut case in favor of a positive rate of interest within the structure of modern credit and banking systems is given by Yusuf Ali, an eminent translator of the Qur'ān, who, among others as noted above, translates ribā as usury and states that: "My definition [of usury] would include profiteering of all kinds, but exclude economic credit, the creature of modern banking and finance."[7]

This position, however, is rejected by several modern writers on the subject of ribā. These writers generally interpret ribā to mean interest rather than usury, and thus are arguing for a zero rate of interest on all transactions.[8] Moreover, in a recent issue of *Daawa*,[9] iftā' was given by Muhammad Abdullah al-Khatib in response to questions asked by Shaber Ahmad al-Said, a representative of the Muslim community in Houston, Texas, regarding ribā. The clear implication of this iftā' is that ribā is interest per se.

Kinds of ribā and their implications

There are two kinds of ribā according to Imām Razi:[10] *ribā nasia* or ribā on credit; and *ribā faḍl*, which relates to barter transactions. The injunctions stated by the Prophet Muḥammad on ribā faḍl also have broad implications for ribā nasia. These injunctions are reported by Abu Said al-Khudari as: "Sell not gold for gold except in equal quantity, nor sell anything for the same thing in lesser quantity . . . nor sell anything present for that which is absent."[11]

This statement implies that barter exchanges of the same products were unlawful unless the exchange took place at parity and in the spot market. Further, in the context of contemporary terminology, if the quality of the products within the same code classification differed and the exchange at parity would end up unfair to the owner of the higher quality goods, then both the higher and lower quality products must be sold at their respective market prices and the demand for each grade of the same product must be satisfied through monetary purchases from the market. At the same time, barter transactions between products of different code classifications were lawful as long as such transactions took place in the spot market and future deliveries were based on spot market prices.[12]

In general, given the above kinds of issues involved in the interpretation of ribā faḍl it would be desirable to fully monetize transactions and remove barter trading altogether. Barter trading is inefficient by its nature and its removal through monetization of transactions would eliminate any doubts about the implications of ribā faḍl. In fact, full monetization of transactions, which is lacking in many developing Muslim countries in the Middle East and other areas, should be part of a national monetary reform since it accelerates development through greater efficiency of transactions, introduces more accurate measurement of national income, and facilitates in the monetization of savings for investment purposes and public financing. This aspect of the interpretation of the statement by the Prophet about ribā faḍl is, in essence, independent of whether ribā is translated to mean usury or interest, since in either case barter transactions involve imprecise assessments of values. Thus, it would be much easier to effect monetary transactions than to obtain īftā' on all cases that might involve ribā faḍl.

The interpretation of the Islamic laws governing market transactions which follow the pronouncements on ribā faḍl requiring that trading involving loans and other types of transactions be carried in spot market prices whether deliveries are intended for the spot or future periods, would present no difficulty as long as these transactions occur under conditions of constant prices and in the same currency. The same argument would hold in international trade when the exchange rate is fixed and constant prices prevail. However, the interpretation of these laws becomes more difficult when one or more of the above conditions change. These difficulties are independent of whether ribā is interpreted to mean usury or interest. The effects of some of these issues, which are part of the contemporary scene, such as the presence of inflation and aspects of the foreign exchange market, are discussed below.

Reasons for Prohibitions on Ribā

Loans may be taken out for two purposes: first, for consumption and, second, for investment in a business venture. Ribā is unlawful on both of these types of loans.[13] The basis of the injunction against ribā on consumption loans is that those who borrow are assumed to be in need of such loans for purposes of maintaining some minimum standard of living. To make a loan to another without ribā, then, is an act of charity. Thus, those with higher incomes and, therefore, higher savings (surplus funds) are asked to make loans to those with lower incomes who are in need without exacting ribā from them. Achieving equity among different levels of income and wealth is a fundamental aspect of the Islamic value system. Islamic taxation in the form of *zakāt* is directed toward this end. The prohibition of ribā on consumption loans is clearly also aimed at the redistribution of purchasing power from the rich to the poor.[14]

In the case of loans for business investment it is generally argued that the basic reason for the prohibition of interest is that it generates income without "labor" (work) on the part of the lender.[15] It seems that this prohibition is directed at those who would, in essence, be clipping coupons from fixed interest earning assets. But this reasoning also has the implication that money has no productivity per se. The argument is aimed at encouraging capitalists to invest directly, through proprietorships or active partnerships, or indirectly through silent partnerships (*mudaraba*) and purchases of shares in corporations, rather than hold idle cash balances. Thus, capital formation should proceed through the expenditures by any of these types of business on new buildings, machines, equipment, or inventories from their available capital funds. Along these lines physical capital is clearly considered to be a factor of production in the conventional sense. However, Islamic laws on interest substitute the earning of profits, which is a measure of the productivity of an enterprise as a whole, for interest, which is the net productivity of physical capital in the conventional theory of capital. Entrepreneurs, when calculating their profits, must apply a measure of cost attributed to the use of physical capital in production. There are no interpretations of the Islamic laws on interest that rule out earnings on the rental of physical capital such as rent from new buildings, or, for example, an entrepreneur's setting up a machine and tool rental enterprise, the rent for which is determined by the market demand and supply of equipment. The rental cost can be included in the total cost in determining profits by a business concern. The problem arises when the net productivity of heterogeneous physical capital and of different vintage has to be evaluated for investment or for capitalization purposes. In the neoclassical theory of capital the market rate of interest is the net productivity of capital (after depreciation). A positive net productivity of capital and, therefore, a positive rate of interest are required for saving to take place and, thus, for capital formation to continue. For a zero rate of interest to prevail, the net productivity of physical capital must reach a floor of zero and no net saving must take place. But these results occur under conditions in which there is no change in technology or factor supplies.[16] Despite the central role for the rate of interest in the theory of capital and in the process of capital formation, the empirical role of the rate of interest in determining saving behavior is at best uncertain.[17] Thus, as a guiding mechanism for the allocation of scarce capital goods to alternative uses in the economy, the rate of interest (or discount rate) could assume a positive value without violating the Islamic injunctions on ribā. This will continue to hold as long as no attempts are made by policy makers to influence saving behavior through changes in the rate of interest, and the owners of capital do not receive interest income.

Constructing models of business organizations that show earnings of variable dividend income declared from profits instead of earning fixed interest income from bonds and debentures is not problematic.[18] However, before such models can be put into operation to meet the requirements of Islamic laws on ribā, the methodology of calculating total costs under standard assumptions (where the business concern employs physical capital and attempts to minimize costs by obtaining an optimal mix of the different factors of production including capital) must be worked out. This has not been done in the literature on ribā. The Islamic model of a business concern using physical capital considers capital a factor of production and, therefore, in the calculation of optimal factor combinations and in the calculation of total costs, the purchase price of capital good or its rental can be used. This means that the standard assumptions of economic theory are accessible to business concerns in Islamic societies, except for allowing the raising of funds through interest-bearing loans in order to meet capital costs. Capital costs can be met from the sales of shares (which in turn can earn dividends as a lawful incentive) and business savings – internally generated funds from undistributed profits and the depreciation allowance.

Comparative Doctrines and Practices on Ribā

In the non-Muslim world, the history of the arguments against usury, or for that matter interest per se, is long – beginning with the Aristotelian declaration that money is "barren," and, therefore, the accumulation of wealth through interest is unjustifiable. The pagan Arabs were concerned about using "clean wealth" (wealth without usury) for work on the *Ka'ba*.[19] During the Roman period there were laws that regulated the relations between creditors and debtors, and during the Middle Ages there were usury laws passed by various European nations that in some cases survived operationally to the middle of the 19th century.[20] In fact, Adam Smith in his *Wealth of Nations* (1776) approved of the usury laws in Britain, which limited the rate of interest to five percent.[21]

In the Christian world, the solution to the controversy over usury was in part given by the Reformation of the 16th century, which separated the affairs of the church from those of the state. One effect of this was that income from interest became lawful, whereas at the same time the concept of usury was retained with the result that limitations had to be placed on the maximum rate of interest on loan transactions. Even though some laws regarding usury might still be found, their operational effectiveness clearly has faded with time – especially when it is considered that during the early part of 1980 the prime rate of interest in the United States reached 20 percent, and that the carrying charges on consumer loans are commonly 18 percent or above, both in the United States and in Canada. These are results of the operations of money and capital markets, both domestic and international, as determined by the prevailing forces of supply and demand and by the controls exerted on these markets by the central banks directly or through commercial banks and other financial intermediaries.

In brief, in this long process in the evolution of the regulations on loan transactions in the Christian world, what has transpired has been a substitution of the economic concept of market pricing of loans for the traditional view on usury.

In Islam only a limited degree of secularization has been attempted by some Muslim states. In general, the Islamic state derives the basis of its laws and their interpretations from the Qurʾān, ḥadīth, the orthodox Muslim law schools (Maliki, Shafi, Hanbali, and Hanifi) and iftāʾ. Within the framework of sharīʿa, Islamic jurisprudence permits differing interpretations of Islamic laws. Accordingly, the degree of state regulations governing economic transactions has varied among different Muslim states, based either on differing interpretations given to the laws, or in some cases on the neglect of the laws altogether. The laws on ribā are a case in point.

The interpretations of the issues on ribā have varied among the different schools of Islamic thought. There is evidence, for example, in the case of cash waqf (an interest-bearing trust fund), that its use was acceptable according to some interpretations of Ḥanifi fiqh, whereas it was unacceptable to the other schools. While this controversy continued in 16th-century Ottoman Turkey, the actual practice of founding cash waqfs apparently was established in the 15th century, and by the 17th century it was generally accepted in the Ottoman legal and economic systems.[22]

Moreover, there is also evidence that a rate of interest of ten percent was in common use in Egypt during the 19th century.[23] In this case, it seems that the determination of the rate of interest resulted from the workings of the domestic and international money and capital markets rather than being influenced by arguments on ribā.

Fresh research is clearly needed on the question of the practical applications of the laws on ribā to determine the status of these laws during the earlier Islamic periods.

At the present, banking practices in general and practices on loan transactions regarding interest vary among the Muslim countries. From a recent survey of banking in some Middle Eastern countries and of Middle Eastern international financial institutions, a mixed picture emerges on the role of interest in banking and commercial transactions.[24] While charging interest seems to be common in the domestic money and capital markets in these countries, 15 international banking and other types of financial institutions operate in the Middle East, organized with varying aims of assisting the less developed Muslim countries that do not have a uniform interest policy. Among these are eight institutions that offer loans free of interest but include a minimal service charge for transaction costs, whereas the other seven institutions charge interest rates that range between two and seven percent. However, it seems that the "softness" of these loans is a function of the degree of economic development in a Muslim country, such as in the case of the Kuwait Fund for Arab Economic Development, rather than the interpretation of ribā as usury, whereas others, such as the Islamic Development Bank, which makes loans free of interest, are adhering to interpretation of ribā as interest.

Consideration of Some Broad Theoretical Issues

If ribā were to be interpreted to mean usury, making a "reasonable" rate of increase (interest) permissible, then the burden of determining what is reasonable would fall basically on the structure of the market: whether the market functions under competition in which prices and values are impersonally determined by the market forces of supply and demand, or whether monopoly power exists and thus unreasonable prices and rates in return would prevail. Since monopoly is condemned in Islam owing to its undesirable effects,[25] and its regulation is deemed desirable,[26] under this interpretation of ribā, the task of restructuring a capitalist economy to fit the Islamic economic model is not difficult. It would basically mean the adaptation of the standard model of workable competition for different markets and the dissolution and dismemberment of monopolies as well as the institution of antimonopoly codes of conduct such as are required for enterprises like public utilities.

In this system the central bank would function as a state instrument for generating and implementing models of workable competition in the money and capital markets, while the primary role of the central bank as the controller of the money supply and the credit system would be maintained as it is in mixed economies such as those of Canada and the United States.

We proceed, however, with the argument that ribā means interest, the rate for which is zero as determined by Islamic law. This argument clearly has broad implications for the workings of the money market, the capital market, commodity markets, the foreign exchange markets, and, in general, for all transactions involving forward markets. A zero rate of interest will not only change the behavioral assumptions and structural conditions of these markets, but it will also have profound effects on income determination and on the applications of monetary and fiscal policies. In effect, to fully understand the implications of a zero rate of interest as an initial condition in a mixed economic system in which both the private and public sectors play a part in decision-making processes that involve the use of resources for the production of output, we must have a full-scale theoretical model of the economy. Based on such a model, appropriate policy decisions would then be made for helping the system achieve its goals. No such full-scale model has been presented so far, although some partial attempts for particular markets have been made.[27] Consideration of such a model is beyond the scope of this paper. But it must be recognized that within the framework of an Islamic system this kind of a model must contain private ownership of resources and the profit motive as *modi operandi* for the free enterprise system to function through privately organized markets.

Islam permits public enterprise. But the Islamic economic system per se is not fundamentally a socialist system. Inherent in Islam are the basic principles of property rights and freedom of enterprise. At the same time the state is encouraged to adopt the principle of maximization of its social welfare function, defined by absolute equality of the participants. An operational model of an Islamic economic system would resemble that of a mixed economy, with the basic exception that a zero rate of interest is built into its structure. The degree of this mixture of public and private enterprises can clearly vary in different Muslim countries, since the extent of public enterprise is not defined in all its aspects within the set of laws governing economic activities that would comprise an Islamic economic system.

Effects of the Laws on Ribā on Economic Transactions of Muslims in Non-Muslim States

In a non-Muslim state, a model of an Islamic community interpretating ribā as interest would have the following basic structure:

First, it has been a long-standing tradition that according to the laws of ribā it is lawful to earn salaries and wages from different forms of employment, rent as income from land, rent from buildings and other types of physical capital (which may vary from spades to high-speed computers), profits as residual income to entrepreneurs reflecting the productivity of their enterprise, and, in general, income from sales or lease of natural resources on the land or underneath it.

Moreover, in terms of investment activities, it is clear that the direct establishment of commerce and service industries including banking, enterprises that produce goods, such as manufacturing and agriculture, or indirect participation in these enterprises through purchases of shares in any existing forms of business organizations, are also lawful. In the above categories of activities the only prohibitions are on the purchase and sale of fixed income-bearing assets such as bonds, debentures, commercial papers, and interest-earning time deposits.

While the above conditions are implied in the laws concerning ribā nasia there are certain implications of ribā faḍl that also affect the conduct of economic transactions in such a community. For example, since no two parcels of real estate are exactly alike, direct exchange of real estate may involve ribā. Barter transactions of ribā faḍl, which also affect the conduct of economic transactions of services such as those between doctors and lawyers, may also involve ribā. The same would hold for exchange of stock, such as the splitting of shares practised by various corporations and the conversion of preferred stock into common stock. Clearly these kinds of issue require closer scrutiny on a case-by-case basis. But as indicated above, only monetization of these transactions will remove the difficulty.

One area of economic transactions has not received due attention in the literature: the question of whether capital gains are lawful, that is, the appreciation of the value of an asset which otherwise would earn either no income or variable income subject to market conditions for the period that the asset is held. Clearly, all types of assets such as financial portfolios consisting of stocks, real estate, or even commodities such as gold and wheat fall in this area. The basic premise for obtaining capital gains is that an asset is held for a period in anticipation of an appreciation of its value. This involves some degree of speculation. There seem to be injunctions against speculation in Islam.[28] However, it is not clear whether the injunctions apply against all speculative activities, even those that have a stabilizing effect on market prices, or whether they refer to destabilizing speculation, which would tend to create shortages in the spot market, and thus higher prices when speculators buy at the spot in rising markets in expectation of even higher prices. Stabilizing speculation, of course, has the effect of increasing supply and thus will reduce prices during rising markets when speculators sell to take advantage of higher prices. In falling markets speculators will buy, thus increasing demand which tends to stabilize falling prices.

It is my interpretation that the injunction against speculation in Islam is aimed at the destabilizing kind that generally leads to shortages in the short run rather than at the desirable effects that stabilizing speculation creates. This argument must hold for the orderly development of a stock market, which is central to the existence of a capital market in an Islamic economic system. In this system private firms or public institutions cannot raise long-term capital by selling long-term interest-bearing obligations. They may, however, sell stocks in order to raise capital. Since purchasers of stocks will want to maximize their income from stock portfolios, they will expect dividend incomes as well as appreciation of the value of their portfolios. Further, private firms and public enterprises will compete for the limited supply of funds provided by purchasers of stocks. Thus, they will pay out dividends as well as increase the profitability of their enterprises in order to meet the expectations of stock purchasers. It is clear that under these conditions, various degrees of speculative activity will be present in the stock market as stock prices change. Expectations formed about stock prices will be the basis of these speculative activities. Thus, to rule out speculative activities that are involved in stock market transactions is to rule out active participation in the stock market per se. This kind of ruling would effectively eliminate the workings of the capital market and along with the means of channeling funds for capital formation.

Second, for a Muslim community in a non-Muslim state, commercial banks and other financial intermediaries can perform all of the conventional services except acting as depositories for interest-earning savings or as sources of loans for consumption or investment purposes. Savings may be deposited in these institutions for safekeeping just as demand deposits are made for transaction purposes. Maintaining savings (time) deposits with financial institutions serves no purpose other than offering some degree of safety; these institutions by law must pay a minimum rate of interest on deposits, which the Muslim community, interpreting ribā as the nominal rate of interest, will reject. Clearly the opportunity cost of maintaining such deposits in view of earning any positive income from dividends or profits is not zero. To abide by the laws on ribā, the Muslim community and its members should therefore hold portfolios that will augment their incomes and capital gains instead of holding idle balances, for example, savings deposits.

Third, interpreting ribā as the nominal rate of interest also requires special consideration of consumption patterns by the Muslim community and its members. Consumption will depend on current or past income (assets) of families or individuals, and interest-free loans that other members of the community are willing to make. The conventional credit system will be of limited use to the community. Since most business concerns provide interest-free loans through the conventional credit system in the form of credit cards, for a limited period the consumer can clearly use such interest-free loans up to their limits without violating the laws on ribā. A problem arises with instalment-payment schemes which stretch over a longer period and therefore, by convention, will contain interest charges. This practice covers purchases of most durable consumer goods including housing.

In a recent iftā᾽ the conventional mortgage instalment scheme has been declared unlawful.[29] This means that the demand for housing and other expensive consumer durable goods must be satisfied with cash purchases. This pattern of satisfying demand is, of course, more critical in the case of housing, which requires substantial funds. The community may, however, form co-operatives or other commercial partnerships, thus pooling its resources to purchase or build dwelling units. But, clearly, such transactions will fall outside the conventional money markets. Alternatively, the community and its members can resort to renting dwelling units. This, of course, will deprive the consumer of obtaining any capital gains that might otherwise result from holding real estate. The same set of difficulties arise in building mosques and community centres, when insufficient gifted funds are available and the Muslim community resorts to borrowing from the conventional money markets. Recently, several communities in North America, having been unable to raise the required funds, have simply borrowed from the money markets at the prevailing rates of interest in order to purchase real estate for conversion into a mosque and Islamic centre (e.g. in the case of San Jose, California) or to construct these facilities (e.g. in the case of Edmonton, Alberta). Clearly, the reasoning has been that it is better to ignore the application of the laws on ribā in such instances rather than do without these important facilities.

The Effects of Change in Prices

An issue that requires special attention is the interpretation of the laws on ribā under inflationary and deflationary conditions. It is significant that the Prophet was aware of the effect of inflation.[30] There is, however, no ḥadīth on ribā that considers the effects of inflation and deflation on loan transactions. Inflation reduces the real purchasing power of money, whereas deflation increases its purchasing power: thus, a loan of $100 at a zero nominal rate of interest between t and t + 1 periods of time at an average rate of inflation of ten percent will be worth only $90, whereas with an average fall in the general level of prices, the same loan, ceteris paribus, will have a real purchasing power of $110 at t + 1.

The conventional interpretation of the laws on ribā indicate that no "increase" is permitted on the principal of a loan when ribā is translated to mean interest. But should this "increase" be measured in real or nominal terms, and, therefore, should a real or nominal rate of interest be applied on loans? The interpretation of the increase is contained in both nominal and real terms under the laws covering ribā. Under ribā nasia the increase refers to a nominal measure over the principal of a loan. But under ribā faḍl the increase is measured in real terms, since the law refers to barter transactions which are not monetary and any change in value is measured in real terms.

The application of these two interpretations of the laws on ribā becomes a function of the conditions under which they are considered. Clearly the issue of interpretation arises irrespective of whether ribā is translated to mean interest or usury. Under inflationary conditions a creditor receiving payment of a loan made at the zero nominal rate of interest will receive less than the real principal of the loan. Further, under deflationary conditions a lender receiving the same nominal amount of a loan will obtain an increase over the real principal of the loan. If prices vary randomly in either direction so that their effect on the purchasing power of money is nil during a given loan period, a nominal or real measure of the increase may be applied in interpreting the laws on ribā. But recent experience indicates that inflation will not be eliminated completely in the world at large. Under these conditions it seems equitable for the lender to obtain the same level of purchasing power at which a loan was initiated. It seems, then, that the application of the law on ribā faḍl is more appropriate under inflationary and deflationary conditions. This in turn means that when ribā is interpreted to mean interest the real rate of interest will be zero, which will permit nominal increases or decreases over the principal of the loan equivalent, respectively to the rate of variation in the price level under inflationary and deflationary conditions.

Conduct of Economic Transactions Between Countries

Whether international economic transactions are carried out between two Muslim countries or a Muslim and a non-Muslim country, the effects of the laws on ribā will clearly be the same on these transactions as long as one of the parties invokes them. Economic transactions between residents of two countries, including their governments, fall within the framework of the balance of payments as a periodic record of these transactions. Both international trade in commodities and international capital movements fall into this framework. Further, foreign exchange markets as an integral part of international economic transactions, which exist simultaneously in all trading countries, are also affected by the laws on ribā. The conduct of international economic transactions that are affected by the laws on ribā may be categorized in three broad areas:

1. International trade in commodities
2. International capital movements
3. Operations of the foreign exchange markets.

1. For international trade in commodities, the laws on ribā nasia and ribā faḍl imply the same set of market conditions as they do for domestic trade. The basic difference is that in this case monetization of trade takes place through the foreign exchange market instead of the domestic money market. A country invoking the laws on ribā will carry out its international trade transactions in the spot market. Therefore, spot market prices will determine the value of its exports and imports. Receipts for exports and payments for imports may be made in the spot market, or they may be part of future contracts involving lump sum or instalment payments. In addition, a country may extend interest-free loans to finance its exports. But generally a similar way of accommodating capital inflow to finance its imports free of interest charges will be unavailable, unless the Muslim country confines its imports to other Muslim countries applying the same laws on ribā. Whereas the application of the laws on ribā will not adversely affect a country's pattern of export trade, the same will not necessarily hold for the pattern of its import trade. This in turn may affect the country's balance of trade, depending on a new set of relative prices that may emerge as a result of dealing only through the spot markets and trading with a reduced number of countries. Yet at the same time any interest-free financing of exports should expand exports and improve the balance of trade. Since Muslim countries in general have a relative scarcity of capital and capital goods form only part of their imports, a shift of their import trade from the relatively capital-rich non-Muslim industrial countries to

Muslim countries will not be feasible. The alternative of purchasing capital goods in the spot market at a scale that would meet development requirement in Muslim countries will be available only to those countries that have large exportable resources. As indicated, only a limited amount of interest-free loans from international financial institutions in the Middle East are available to the lesser-developed Muslim countries to finance required imports. Consequently, these countries, when invoking laws on ribā, will have to adopt a strategy for development that will enable them to meet their import requirements from their export earnings.

2. The laws on ribā will clearly affect both short-term and long-term international capital movements. Accommodating short-term capital outflows can occur to finance exports from Muslim countries. But accommodating short-term capital inflows will not be available to these countries. On the other hand, autonomous short-term capital movements can occur for reasons other than interest rate differentials between countries. Thus, interest arbitrage as an activity will be eliminated, but short-term capital flows can occur to take advantage of differentials in currency rates in the spot foreign exchange markets. Furthermore, the international banking system can offer a similar set of services to depositors from Muslim countries just as the banking system in a non-Muslim country provides for the Muslim community in that country. This will include all the non-interest-bearing services such as demand deposits to facilitate commodity and foreign exchange transactions and tourism.

Long-term international capital movements will be restricted to direct investment and portfolio holdings of stocks. But, financing of direct investment through long-term borrowing will not be available. Moreover, long-term capital inflows to the developing Muslim countries will be restricted to development finance available from those international financial organizations in the Middle East that lend at the zero nominal rate of interest and to grants from non-Muslim countries and international organizations such as the United Nations.

In brief, countries invoking the laws on ribā will limit their participation in international money and capital markets to the cross-section of activities that conforms with them. The net effect will be a shift in the pattern of import trade, as well as a reduction in that trade for countries which will be unable to obtain long-term interest-free financing of their import requirements for economic development.

3. The application of the laws on ribā to the foreign exchange markets imply several conditions. The conventional spot and forward foreign exchange markets will collapse into the spot market since the linkage between the two markets (interest arbitrage) will be eliminated. As indicated above, forward markets per se will be inoperative because under the laws on ribā forward transactions may be carried out only in terms of spot market prices. It will reduce speculative activity in the foreign exchange market to trading in the spot market simply to take advantage of differentials in bilateral or cross currency rates. Further, the elimination of the forward exchange market will remove hedging as an activity against risk in covering possible losses from receipts or payments in foreign currency and in the holding of assets in foreign currency whenever devaluations or revaluations take place. The absence of hedging will transfer the risk from commodity trading and foreign investment directly to the groups involved in these activities. It will limit activity in these areas since traders and investors will generally minimize risks and accordingly reduce the volume of their activity.

Whether the foreign exchange market consists of a system of flexible or fixed rates, the laws on ribā do not constrain trading in the spot market in general. The application of the interpretation of ribā faḍl to this market under either system may, however, involve ribā when the intrinsic and nominal values of currencies differ. The gold and silver standards exemplified the fixed exchange rate system, whereas the issue of differences in the intrinsic and nominal values of currencies under the flexible exchange rate system would arise when currencies are backed by gold or silver in different proportions that are generally not reflected in the market determined nominal exchange rates. The injunction, "do not exchange gold or silver except for equal quantity," precisely implies that metallic currencies and currencies backed by metals such as gold or silver should be exchanged at parity, reflecting their intrinsic values. Under current conditions, however, since gold and silver standards are only of historical interest and a return to these standards or the establishment of similar standards that may involve other commodities seems remote, pragmatically this difficulty in interpretation has no current relevance. Furthermore, the intrinsic values of currencies are generally below their nominal values. This means that under the flexible exchange rate system currently in wide use, even though currencies may not be exchanged at parity in terms of their intrinsic values, the question of ribā will not arise, since there will be no incentive for melting down currencies to obtain an increase over their market-determined unit values.

Notes

1. Reprinted with revisions from the *International Journal of Middle East Studies* 14, no. 1 : 3-17.

2. The injunctions against ribā in the *Holy Qur'ān* are contained in several verses: Sura II, 275-76 and 278-81, A. Yusuf Ali, trans. (3d ed.; Washington, DC: American International Printing Co., 1938), pp. 111-12; *Sahih al-Bukhari,* M. Muhsin Khan, trans. [rev. ed., 1976] Ankara: Hilal Yayinlari, III, 168-70; and Mohammad M. Pickthall, *The Meaning of the Glorious Koran* (New York: New American Library, n.d.), p. 59.

3. The study by Imam Fakhrudin Razi is "Mafatihu'l-Ghaile," cited in Anwar I. Qureshi, *Islam and the Theory of Interest,* 2d ed. (Lahore: S.H. Mohammad Ashraf, 1974), p. 45.

4. Cf. the translations referred to in n. 2 above.

5. Qureshi, *Islam and the Theory of Interest,* p. 70.

6. Ibid., pp. 46-47.

7. *Holy Qur'ān,* (3d ed.) Yusuf Ali, trans., p. 111, n. 324.

8. *See,* e.g., Shaykh M. Ahmad, *Economics of Islam: A Comparative Study,* 2d ed. (Lahore: S.H. Mohammad Ashraf, 1958); S.A. Ali, *Economic Foundations of Islam* (Calcutta: Orient Longmans, 1964); Qureshi, *Islam and the Theory of Interest;* Nejatullah Siddiqui, *Banking Without Interest,* 2d ed. (Lahore: Islamic Publications, 1976); and S.A. Siddiqui, *Public Finance in Islam* (Lahore: S.H. Mohammad Ashraf, 1962).

9. *Daawa* (Cairo), (April, 1980) : 50-51.

10. Qureshi, *Islam and the Theory of Interest,* p. 68.

11. Ibid., pp. 61-62. The Prophet Muḥammad mentioned six products in his statement on ribā faḍl: gold, silver, wheat, barley, dates, and salt. Some writers such as Yusuf Ali, trans. *Holy Qur'ān,* 3d ed. (p. 111, n. 324), would restrict the meaning of the Prophet's injunctions against barter to these

six products. The consensus is that the injunctions apply to all commodities. I adopt this interpretation. *See also* Qureshi on this issue, p. 64.

12. Qureshi, pp. 64–66.

13. On the prohibition of ribā the view may be taken that the Qur'ānic injunctions against ribā are absolute and thus the prohibitions must be accepted as they stand. Imām Razi and other Islamic scholars of Islamic law have pointed out a variety of arguments for these injunctions. In the final analysis they are reduced to the two types of loan transactions on consumption and investment, and the reasons attached to the prohibitions of ribā on these types of loans. *See* Qureshi, *Islam and the Theory of Interest,* pp. 45–48, and S.A. Ali, *Economic Foundations of Islam,* pp. 173–75.

14. While the injunctions against ribā apply to both parties in a loan transaction, they do not mean that borrowers can abuse borrowing privileges. There are reminders against abuse in borrowing and nonpayment of debt. Cf. Qureshi, p. 82.

15. Cf. S.A. Ali, *Economic Foundations of Islam,* p. 174.

16. On the theory of capital, *see* J. Hicks, *Capital and Growth* (New York: Oxford University Press, 1965).

17. E.g., D.B. Suits, "The Determinants of Consumer Expenditure: A Review of Present Knowledge," in W. Johnson and D. Kamerschen, eds., *Macroeconomics: Selected Readings* (Boston: Houghton Mifflin, 1970). M.J. Boskin presents evidence from U.S. data showing a positive correlation between the rate of interest and saving in "Taxation, Saving and the Rate of Interest," *Journal of Political Economy* 86 (Supplement, April 1978): S3–S27.

18. Siddiqui, *Banking without Interest,* sets up a model of banking that attempts to get around the basic question of charging interest on loans. His model basically refers to the practice of investment banking through which banks are direct investors as partners in business ventures. A second form of organization to which he pays a great deal of attention is called mudaraba ("joint enterprise") and is defined as that form of organization where "one party should provide capital and the other should transact the business under the agreement that he will receive a fixed percentage of dividend in the overall profit of the business" (p. 8). The latter type is a variant of the silent partnership. In both cases, active or silent partners share in profits and losses on the basis of prior agreements. But the problems of calculating profits, as noted above, and separation of ownership and control, a phenomenon common in modern corporate forms of business, are not explored. In other respects,

Siddiqui's book is of interest in showing how a banking system might work without fixed interest earnings and what the role of the central bank might be in such a system.

19. *See* Qureshi, *Islam and the Theory of Interest,* p. xviii.

20. For a survey of these and other arguments on interest *see* ibid., pp. 1-14.

21. Modern Library (New York: Random House, 1937), Book II, chap. 4.

22. Jon E. Mandaville, "Usurious Piety: The Cash Waqf Controversy in the Ottoman Empire," *International Journal of Middle East Studies,* 10 (August 1979) : 289-308.

23. Peter Gran, *Islamic Roots of Capitalism* (Austin: University of Texas Press, 1979), esp. pp. 3-34.

24. John Townsend, *Middle East Annual Review* (Essex, England: Middle East Review Co., 1979), pp. 121-47.

25. S.A. Ali, *Economic Foundation of Islam,* p. 168.

26. Ibid., p. 162.

27. E.g., on some aspect of the money and capital markets, *see* Siddiqui, *Banking without Interest,* pp. 49 and 79. For the commodity market, *see* Qureshi, *Islam and the Theory of Interest,* p. 88.

28. Some writers argue that the injunctions apply against all speculative activities without distinguishing between the various effects of speculation. *See,* for example, Qureshi, pp. 68-90.

29. *Daawa,* April 1980, pp. 50-51.

30. S.A. Ali, pp. 22-23.

II

Muslims in North America: Dynamics of Growth

The Canadian Muslim Community: The Need for a New Survival Strategy

Baha Abu-Laban

The Muslim community is a recent addition to the Canadian religious mosaic. Muslim immigrants began to come to Canada in small numbers around the turn of the century, and until the end of World War II, their in-flow was relatively limited. Since this period, there has been a progressive increase in the number of Muslim immigrants to Canada. The last 20 years, in particular, have witnessed a substantial growth in the Canadian Muslim community as well as a change in the type and national origin of Muslim immigrants. While the early Muslim pioneers came largely from the countries of the Arab world, the postwar Muslim immigrants represent a wide array of linguistic and national origins.

Like other Eastern religious groups, Muslims have had to adapt to the new Canadian milieu. Research evidence on Muslims' adaptive experience in Canada is rather limited and much of it tends to focus on acculturation or assimilation of Muslims into Canadian society, or on certain aspects of their problematic relationships with the host society, for example, coping behavior in relation to such requirements as praying five times a day and abstaining from eating pork or drinking alcoholic beverages.[1] The point stressed by many scholars is that the new socio-cultural environment hinders observance of some basic Islamic injunctions. Moreover, because of the secular legal system in Canada, Muslim institutions have no legal power to enforce Qur'ānic injunctions on their adherents. What these findings suggest is that the cohesion, even survival, of the Canadian Muslim community can not be taken for granted.

Immigration

The Canadian Muslim community is a product of two waves of immigration, one pre-, the other post-World War II. The latter wave of immigration is, by far, the larger of the two. The earliest record of Muslim presence in Canada dates back to 1871, when the Canadian census recorded 13 Muslim residents.[2] By 1901, Canada had from 300 to 400 Muslim immigrants, about equally divided between Turks and Syrian Arabs.[3] By 1911, the size of this religious group had risen to about 1,500, of whom over 1,000 were of Turkish origin and the remainder Arab.[4] The natural evolution of this budding Muslim community was disrupted by the Canadian government's earlier moves to restrict the entry of immigrants from Asia,[5] and by the onset of World War I, which witnessed the return of many Turkish immigrants (then classified as enemy aliens) to their country of origin.[6] Thus, from 1911 to 1951, the rate of growth of the Muslim community in Canada was very slow, based largely on natural increase (i.e., surplus of births over deaths). According to the Canadian census, in 1931, the mid-point of this period of restrictive immigration to Canada, there were only 645 Muslim residents. Most of these Muslims were Syrian/Lebanese Arabs and they represented a small fraction (six to seven percent) of the then well-established Syrian-Canadian community.[7] In 1951, prior to the heavy influx of postwar immigrants, Canada had from 2,000 to 3,000 Muslim residents. Today, it is estimated that there are about 100,000 Muslims in Canada representing different sects and ethnic origins, of whom the majority (about six out of ten) are foreign-born.[8]

Most of the turn-of-the-century Muslim immigrants were young males, with no capital and with little or no formal education. Upon arrival, many of them started as unskilled laborers or itinerant peddlers. Their entry status, in general, was at the lowest rungs of the occupational hierarchy. Most of them gravitated toward Canada's major urban centres (Toronto, Montreal) and from there they moved to different regions in search of business and job opportunities. The economic adaptation of the early Muslim pioneers was often linked with a keen desire for economic and occupational success. Through devotion to hard work, frugality, and reciprocal support, peddlers often experienced a steady rise in their economic fortunes and a broadening of their entrepreneurial functions.

The descendants of these early immigrants did not face as restricted a range of occupations as had the immigrant generation. Thus, as the Canadian-born generations entered the labor force, the early Canadian Muslim community began to experience further occupational differentiation.

The single most important characteristic of postwar Muslim immigrants is diversity. While they all share a common religious designation, they include immigrants from different parts of the Arab world (particularly Lebanon, Syria, Jordan, Palestine, and Egypt), and from Pakistan, Bangladesh, Turkey, Iran, Eastern Europe, East Africa, the Caribbean, and elsewhere. In addition, they include different Shi'a sects, particularly Ismailis (of Indo-Pakistani origin) and Druze (largely from Lebanon), although Sunni (i.e., "orthodox") Muslims are in the majority. In theory, differences based on sect, language, and national origin can result in cleavage and a corresponding reduction in communication between and among the different subgroups. This, in turn, would have implications for the cohesion of the Canadian Muslim community and for assimilation into Canadian culture and society.

Compared to the early pioneers, the postwar Muslim immigrants are more heterogeneous, educationally and occupationally. For example, about 40 to 50 percent of the postwar Muslim immigrants from the Middle East intended to pursue professional or managerial careers; about 20 percent intended to pursue white-collar or clerical careers; and the remainder had variable career intentions with a substantial portion aspiring to work in the manufacturing industry.[9] At present, the different generations of Canadian Muslims are to be found in a wide range of occupations across the occupational hierarchy, both in the public and private sectors.

Ontario and, to a lesser degree, Quebec and Alberta have attracted the majority of Muslim immigrants. The best estimate, based largely on Haddad,[10] is that about one-half of the Canadian

Muslim community, that is, about 50,000, live in Ontario, particularly Toronto (40,000); 15,000 live in Quebec, largely in Montreal; 15,000 live in Alberta (Edmonton, Calgary, and Lac La Biche); and the balance (about 20,000) are distributed elsewhere in Canada. The overwhelming majority of Muslims live in large cities and other urban centres, as evidenced by the intended destination of new arrivals[11] and by the location of religious and secular organizations established by different Muslim cultural groups. Geographically, they appear to be evenly spread, in relation to the inhabited areas of Canada, but with slightly more representation in Anglophone rather than Francophone Canada. Moreover, in the cities in which they have settled, they tend to be dispersed and there is no evidence of closely knit Muslim residential communities. This pattern of geographical distribution makes Muslims more susceptible to the acculturative and assimilative influences of the host society.

Factors in Immigration

According to a recent survey of the Pakistani community in Canada, economic and educational opportunities were major factors attracting immigration to Canada – accounting for 37 and 27 percent of the reasons, respectively.[12] The remainder of the responses were about equally divided among four additional factors: political pressure in the country of origin, adventure and travel, children's education, and family reasons. For Arab Muslims in Alberta, the reasons for immigration to Canada were structured differently: about 57 percent of the responses hinged on the pull of relatives already in Canada; 37 percent emphasized economic opportunities; and the balance of the responses referred to political alienation from the homeland and other factors.[13] In a broader study of Arab Canadians (including both Muslims and Christians),[14] of the 454 reasons for immigration to Canada given by the respondents, 45 percent involved the pull of economic and educational opportunities; 21 percent involved the pull of kin and friends already in this country; 12 percent involved political alienation from the ancestral land; and 9 percent of the responses focused on adventure and travel.

What is significant in these results is the absence of any religious motivation to immigrate to Canada. Like many other immigrant groups, Muslim immigrants came to Canada as individuals and families, not as corporate religious groups in search of a sanctuary. They hoped for freedom and prosperity in the new land. The fact that the religious factor was not an element in the motivational structure of these immigrants has important implications for their religious and spiritual adaptation in the new environment.

Institutional Development

The most pressing problem facing new immigrants to Canada is that of making a living while adapting to the new environment. Following an initial period of adjustment, which varies in length for different individuals and groups, immigrants tend to turn their attention to the founding of institutions and organizations to replace the ones they have left behind. Examples include religious, educational, social, cultural, and economic organizations, and newspapers. The institutional development of an ethnic group is always a matter of degree, ranging from a high level such as that characterizing Hutterites or Jews, to a low level such as characterizes immigrants from the United States.

The move to establish secular or religious institutions is determined by many conditions, chief among which are group size and inclinations, geographical distribution, and capacity or willingness to support such institutions. The Muslims in Canada provide an example of a relatively small, heterogeneous, geographically spread religious group which could not support certain kinds of institutions in Canada, such as parochial or private schools as distinct from language or "Sunday" schools. Nor could the early or postwar Muslim immigrants depend for their welfare on ethnically based economic institutions confining their services to their own kind. As individuals and as a group, they simply had to integrate with the host society in major institutional spheres such as the economic, educational, and political. The most prominent institutional symbol for Muslims in Canada is the mosque.[15]

If the history of the Canadian Muslim community is relatively short, the history of the mosque in this part of the world is even shorter. This is so because of the community's small size (particularly in the earlier period of immigration) and relatively even geographical spread. Another possible influence in impeding the institutional development of the Muslim community in Canada is inherent in Islam itself. Specifically, Islam does not have the priesthood that is both prevalent and elaborate in Christianity. This makes it possible for a given Muslim to be self-sufficient and discharge his basic religious obligations (for example, praying five times a day, fasting during the month of Ramaḍān, etc.) without having to have an intermediary between him and God. The leading of prayer in a group, say on Friday noon, which is equivalent to the Sunday service in Christianity, can be accomplished by the group's calling on any one of its members to act as imām (religious leader). Moreover, there are minimal restrictions in Islam on where an individual or group can pray.

Despite the above, the Islamic faith cannot thrive without institutional supports such as an imām, a mosque, and associated benevolent societies. In a non-Islamic environment such as Canada, these community resources are particularly important. Also, the arrival of children, that is, the second generation, and community growth often strengthen the need for the founding of institutions that would perpetuate the faith. Thus, to build a mosque and to select an imām for the group is to begin to develop the Muslim community and institutionalize the faith. The mosque provides a meeting place for the group and an imām is able to lead prayer, facilitate group solidarity, provide religious and language instruction, solemnize marriages, arrange for burials according to the Islamic tradition, and mediate in family and community disputes.[16]

Canada's first mosque, Al-Rashid Mosque, was erected in Edmonton, Alberta, in 1938. At that time Edmonton had approximately 20 Lebanese Muslim families who worked together on this project. For the Alberta Muslim pioneers, the Great Depression had its positive aspects. At that time, business was slow and Edmonton's Arab Muslims, who were in business for themselves, met regularly to discuss common problems and ponder the future. The idea of building a mosque crystallized in those meetings. A new association was formed under the name of the Arabian Muslim Association and a building permit was obtained in May 1938.[17] Also, a fund-raising campaign was launched and through the generosity of Canadian friends and other Arab-origin Canadians, both Muslim and Christian, in

Alberta and Saskatchewan, the mosque was completed in November 1938.

Further institutional development of the Arab Muslim community in Canada was not forthcoming until after World War II. In the 1950s and thereafter, the need for mosques and religious associations became pressing as a result of the arrival in Canada of large numbers of Muslim immigrants. Islamic mosques and/or organizations are now to be found in St. John's (Newfoundland); Dartmouth and Halifax (Nova Scotia); Montreal and Ville St. Laurent (Quebec); Ottawa, Toronto, Hamilton, London, Windsor, Kingston, Hespler, and Thunder Bay (Ontario); Winnipeg (Manitoba); Saskatoon and Regina (Saskatchewan); Calgary, Edmonton, and Lac La Biche (Alberta); and Vancouver (British Columbia). These mosques and organizations are usually managed by officers elected by their respective memberships.

The Council of Muslim Communities of Canada (CMCC) was founded in 1972. The CMCC grew out of a firm commitment to self-help, and the feeling that it alone could undertake a coherent, national approach to the issues facing the Canadian Muslim community. Affiliated with it is a large number of Muslim associations across Canada. The following list of committees organized within the CMCC gives some idea of the scope of its activities: Education, Youth, Women's, Religious Affairs, Public Relations, and Publications. The CMCC is a member of the Federation of Islamic Associations in the United States and Canada (with headquarters in Oldbridge, New Jersey) and works in co-operation with the Muslim Students' Association of the United States and Canada (with headquarters in Indianapolis, Indiana).

Several newsletters (mostly in English but also in Arabic and other languages), published by Muslim associations in practically all of the major centres, keep the membership informed of Muslim celebrations and holidays, on-going activities, programs, and future plans. A major quarterly magazine, *Islam Canada*, published by CMCC, has been in existence since 1972. It features a variety of articles dealing with religious, educational, and political matters; news of Muslim communities in Canada and around the world; and essays interpreting Islam and providing advice on how Muslims can best adapt to the Canadian environment.

The Challenge of the New Environment

Canada presents a challenge for most new immigrants. However, there are variations in the degree of adjustment required of them. For some immigrants (for example, those from Britain and the United States), similarities in appearance, dress, mannerisms, language, food, and customs may mitigate the difficulties of adaptation to the new environment. For other immigrants, these difficulties increase in proportion to the difference between themselves and native-born Canadians. Nor are these differences only in origins. Immigrants from the same country may differ. Some may find it easier or more appealing to acculturate or assimilate. A combination of factors, some reflecting the type of individual, some the characteristics of the donor culture, and some reflecting the state of Canadian society, have impact on immigrant adjustment.

Generally speaking, the problems of adjustment confronting Muslim immigrants to Canada have been enormous for at least three reasons. First, Muslim immigrants, on several important variables such as language, culture, and religion, bear little resemblance to the Canadian archetype. To survive, they have had to learn a new language, undergo change, and reconcile the old with the new way of life. For them, the adjustment process has not been easy, to say the least.

Second, Canada has experienced an ebb and flow in its receptivity to new immigrants. Around the turn of the century, the heavy influx of immigrants from Asia (whence most Muslims came) and eastern and southern Europe heightened concerns that this stream of immigration would have a negative impact on Canada's Anglo-Saxon heritage. These concerns meshed with existing stereotypes regarding the donor groups, resulting in a hierarchy of immigrant acceptability. Within this context, Muslim immigrants, as people of non-western extraction, found rising barriers against their admis-'sion. Today, while Canada's immigration policy is relatively free from discrimination, the stereotypes of Muslims that exist in Canadian society are not altogether complimentary.

For example, in a broad content analysis of 143 social studies textbooks used in Ontario schools, McDiarmid and Pratt[18] revealed that the five evaluative terms most often applied to Muslims are: infidels, fanatical, great, devout, tolerant. In contrast, the evaluative terms most frequently applied to Christians (the control group in the study) include: devoted, zealous, martyr, great, famous. For comparative purposes, it may be added that the terms most frequently applied to Jews include: great, faithful, just(ice), wise, genius; the terms applied to immigrants include: hard-working, enriched Canada, contribution, skilful, problem; the terms most frequently applied to Negroes are: primitive, friendly, fierce, savage, superstitious; and the evaluative terms most often applied to Canadian Indians include: savage(s), friendly, fierce, hostile, skilful. Commenting on the results of this extensive study, McDiarmid and Pratt note:[19]

> Prejudice still manifests itself in textbooks, but because it has been less respectable it is more subtle. Immigrants may no longer be called "shiftless and vicious," but there are still instances where they are referred to as "a problem" or "a swarm." It may be that these terms have a more immediate effect on readers' attitudes than would more obvious discriminatory references.

In a follow-up study of the treatment of the Middle East in social science textbooks authorized for use in Ontario schools, Kenny[20] confirms that Canadian textbooks tend to manifest biases and factual errors regarding Arabs and Islam. In one textbook examined by Kenny,[21] the author asserts that "Islam was born among the nomads of Arabia, who were 'wholly illiterate,' and for whom 'caravan raiding was a cherished pastime'." Kenny's study also shows that Ontario school teachers tended to reflect the same stereotypes and biases found in social science textbooks.[22] Similar biases against Islam are found in Sunday school textbooks used by the United Church of Canada and the United Methodist Church. In both of these church school programs, textbook presentation emphasizes the differences between Christianity and Islam and overlooks the common links between them; portrays Islam "not only in alien but also in negative terms"; and "lends to the interpretation of the Islamic faith as not just different but also inferior."[23]

Negative attitudes towards Muslims in North America have intensified within the past two years as a result of the Islamic revolution in Iran. Sometimes subtle and sometimes not so subtle, these negative attitudes, expressed in the media and by the general public, have been felt by many a Muslim in Canada.[24]

Generally speaking, minority group reactions to prejudice and stereotyping may take one of three forms: ignoring both the offender and the offence;fighting back (and thereby affirming ethnic identity); or assimilating into the host society (and thereby weakening or denying ethnic identity). All of these tendencies appear to be at work among Muslims in Canada.

The third reason why Canada has presented a strong challenge for Muslim immigrants concerns the widening cultural gap between them and their Canadian-born children. Members of the latter group have been born, raised, and educated in the context of Canadian culture and institutions. Research evidence, in addition to informed judgements, indicates that these children, compared to their foreign-born parents, tend to be more acculturated/assimilated into the Canadian way of life, and also less susceptible to control by ethno-religious institutions.[25] For these Muslim children, as for other children, the teenage peer group, the school, and the mass media are potent socialization agencies that may promote values different from, and possibly at odds with, those of the family. Muslim parents in Canada correctly perceive that they exercise less control over children than do parents in the ancestral homeland. This novel situation confronting Muslim immigrants suggests that their descendants' spiritual and psychological integration into Muslim institutions in Canada cannot be taken for granted.

Islamic Leadership:
A New Conception and Some Implications

The Canadian Muslim leadership faces a situation for which it has no concrete past experience to guide its activities in Canada. Given the spread of Islam, historically, throughout much of Asia, Africa, and parts of Europe, one would expect to find a few similarities between past situations in which Muslims found themselves and the current situation in Canada (or, more generally, North America). However, it is here argued that the Canadian situation is unique in terms of its essentials and details, and it has no clear historical parallel or precedent.[26] In brief, the new setting is highly secularized, with no trend in sight to change this dominant feature; there is a strong value placed on separation of religion (church) and state; religion is regarded as a private matter and there is a high degree of religious freedom; and the individual Canadian is under cross-pressures from many sectors, apart from organized religion, competing for his/her allegiance and commitment: for example, the state, the mass media, the school, and the peer group, not to mention professional and occupational groupings and voluntary associations. Moreover, Muslims in Canada encompass varied ethnic, linguistic, educational, occupational, and generational backgrounds. In addition, they are numerically and politically weak, geographically dispersed, more or less urbanized, and secularized, at best living a compartmentalized Muslim way of life with very limited community support. Finally, they are legally obliged to send their children to approved schools – usually public schools – which are highly secular in a predominantly Christian context, and where they may well be subject to stereotyping and somewhat negative social attitudes. Under these circumstances, the Muslim leadership must not only be creative, but also well informed about the socio-cultural conditions of the new environment.

North American Muslim leaders, in general, believe that their faith is good for all time and all places and any contradictions between it and the North American environment are more apparent than real. As one Muslim leader and scholar, Dr. Isma'il Al-Faruqi, observes, "failures in Islam today are due to the failure to put original Islam into practice."[27] In a similar vein Lovell goes on to say:[28]

> One can conclude that the Five Pillars of Islam can be observed easily in North America if the believer sincerely wants to do so and that the religion which has its origin in seventh-century Arabia seems flexible enough to be adapted to twentieth-century city life here.

There is ample evidence to suggest that Muslims in Canada share with their leadership the belief that Islam is capable of transcending the barriers of time and space.[29] While Islam is inflexible in matters relating to proscriptions such as drinking alcoholic beverages and eating pork, and on moral standards, it is believed to be flexible and pragmatic in the way it allows a Muslim to meet his religious obligations in the face of unusual circumstances. For example, in Canada, if a Muslim is prevented by his work from praying five times a day at specified intervals, he may combine these prayers at the end of the day. Also, if a Muslim is prevented by his work from observing the major weekly group prayer on Friday noon, he is allowed to make up for that either on Friday evening or Sunday noon. The latter group prayers, of which the Sunday noon one is more common, are aspects of Islamic adaptation to the new environment.

Important and necessary as these and possibly other adaptive changes may be, the basic dilemmas of Muslim leadership remain unresolved. These dilemmas will be illustrated by reference to three problem areas.

One of the most pressing problems confronting the Muslim leadership is relative inability to reach the new, Canadian-born generation of Muslim children, teenagers, and young adults. So far, Muslim leaders have directed most of their attention to the immigrant generation and its social and spiritual needs. This is understandable in view of the fact that the "lay" Muslim leaders are drawn largely from the ranks of the immigrant generation. More importantly, virtually all imāms in Canada (and the U.S.) are foreign-born, as well, and it is difficult for them to fully appreciate the totality of conditions in which the Canadian-born generation lives. While the "lay" Muslim leaders and imāms are bound together by having grown up in a strongly Muslim environment in their respective countries of origin, and by mutual understanding of traditional Muslim upbringing, they find it difficult to command the allegiance of the younger generation. According to some Muslim respondents, interviewed in the course of research on the Arab-Canadian community,[30] the most desirable type of imām is the one who combines high-level religious training with intimate knowledge of the North American way of life. It is generally believed that this type of imām could most effectively reconcile the Islamic faith with the new environment, particularly for those growing up in this different milieu. In reality, this type of imām is not frequently encountered for several reasons, including the fact that Islamic theological seminaries for the training of imāms are not available either in Canada or the United States.

The second pressing problem facing the Muslim leadership is the inability to weld into a coherent whole the diverse national and linguistic groups that comprise Canada's Muslim community. There is evidence to suggest that Islam in Canada is taking on an "ethnic" rather than the prescribed universal form. With reference to this issue, Haddad quotes a Pakistani leader who told her, "We worship together but then the Pakistanis go back to their curries and the Arabs to their kebabs." [31] Haddad further adds: [32]

> Thus the mosque provides an affirmation of the universality of the Islamic faith, but has not as yet provided for the social integration of the different national groups. Different ethnic allegiances tend to go to different mosques. This is true in Montreal where the Fatima mosque seems to attract a predominantly Arab congregation, while the Quebec Islamic Center appears to draw more Indo-Pakistanis. It is also true of the Ontario Muslim Association in Toronto which is predominantly Caribbean and West Indian. In other cities, it has been noted that after the Sunday services, groups tend to congregate according to ethnic identity.

The social integration of the diverse Muslim national groups, and even sects, cannot be left to chance. Accordingly, the Muslim leadership will do well to develop an integrative strategy emphasizing the commonalities of all these groups in their adaptation to the new Canadian environment. This will not only strengthen Muslim organizations in Canada, but also give a more concrete evidence of the universality of the Islamic faith and identity.

The third pressing problem confronting Muslim leaders concerns the need to elaborate Islamic law, in order to reconcile the Islamic faith with the new socio-cultural system. This need, based on Islam's professed transcendant qualities and flexibility, is felt not only in Canada, but also in many parts of the developing (modernizing) Muslim world. Indeed, as far back as the 19th century Muslim reformers called attention to the social and economic benefits of reinterpreting religious texts and reviving the spirit of theological inquiry.

For present purposes, it is sufficient to note that the two main sources of Islamic law are the Qurʾān, which is the Holy Book, and the Sharīʿa, which includes accumulated interpretations of Islamic law as developed by jurist-theologians. The Sharīʿa consists of three main elements: the sayings and decisions of Prophet Muhammad; *qiyās*, which involves utilization of the technique of analogy in weighing and assessing the teachings of the Qurʾān, the sayings and decisions of the Prophet, and juridical citations; and *ijmāʿ*, meaning consensus of jurists. The principle of independent reasoning as applied to religious texts is known as *ijtihād*. In the first three centuries of Islam's existence, ijtihād was the basis for elaborating Islamic law; since then, however, the spirit of ijtihād has declined steadily, to the point of almost complete disappearance today. As a demonstration of Islam's applicability in the new Canadian context, Muslim leaders need to revive the spirit of ijtihād. Examples of the areas that need to be addressed include women's and, more generally, the family's integration into the mosque; male-female interaction and rights and obligations in matters pertaining to personal status (for example, divorce, adoption, inheritance); economic relations in the modern world; and the role of Islam vis-à-vis modern scientific and technological development. In all these areas, and in many others, the spirit of ijtihād, or independent reasoning, would help better reconcile Islam, as a body of theological doctrines and beliefs, with the new Canadian environment as well as with changes in the traditional Islamic world.

Conclusion

About four out of every thousand Canadians are of Muslim background. The large majority of these Muslims came to Canada in the post-World War II period, from markedly different linguistic and national contexts. With the arrival of the second (Canadian-born) generation, social and economic differences within this religious group actually increased. These differences have acted as a centrifugal force, weakening Muslim religious organizations and the cohesion of the Muslim community itself. Moreover, in Canada, Muslims are absorbed by the educational, political, and economic institutions of the host society and this has further strengthened the centrifugal tendencies within the Muslim community. Given the social and demographic characteristics of Muslims and their status as a religious minority in Canada, there is need for an innovative survival strategy that facilitates community cohesion, on the one hand, and successful adaptation to the new Canadian environment on the other. Elements of this strategy include the need for Muslim leadership that is capable of addressing the needs of Muslim youth; integrating the diverse Muslim subgroups together; and considering, through the revival of the tradition of ijtihād, interpretations of Islamic law that would better reconcile the Islamic faith with the new environment. A main assumption underlying this strategy is that the Muslim leadership has a responsibility to recognize the social forces that impinge upon individual Muslims in Canada. With this knowledge, Muslim institutions are compelled to compete with other Canadian institutions for the allegiance of individual Muslims, an allegiance that cannot be taken for granted.

Notes

1. *See,* for example, Abdelmoneim M. Khattab, "The Assimilation of Arab Muslims in Alberta" (M.A. thesis, University of Alberta, 1969); Harold Barclay, "The Perpetuation of Muslim Tradition in the Canadian North," *Muslim World* 59 (1969): 64–73, and "The Muslim Experience in Canada" in Harold Coward and Leslie Kawamura, eds., *Religion and Ethnicity* (Waterloo: Wilfrid Laurier University Press, 1978), pp. 101–13; Sadiq Noor Alam Awan, *The People of Pakistani Origin in Canada: The First Quarter Century* (Ottawa: S.N.A. Awan, under the auspices of the Canada-Pakistan Assoc. of Ottawa, 1976).

2. The Canadian census provided no information on the origin or date of arrival of this small group of Muslims. Haddad adds: "the census for 1881 and 1891 lists their [i.e., Muslims'] number as zero"; *see* Yvonne Haddad, "Muslims in Canada: A Preliminary Study," in Coward and Kawamura (eds.), *Religion and Ethnicity,* pp. 71–100, esp. p. 95.

3. This is an estimate that places the proportion of Syrian Arab Muslims at about 10 percent of the total Syrian Canadian community. In the absence of official statistics, it is assumed that the Turkish component of the Canadian Muslim community at that time was approximately equal to the Arab component.

4. Official statistics show that the number of Turkish-born immigrants in Canada was 1,861 in 1911. Not all of these immigrants were of Muslim background. Also, between 1901 and 1911 the Syrian Canadian community experienced substantial growth; hence the assumed increase in the Muslim component of this community.

5. In 1885 the Dominion government imposed a $50-head tax on Chinese immigrants and in 1903 this was raised to $500; in 1907 Canada concluded a

"gentleman's agreement" with Japan, whereby Japanese immigration to Canada was held in check by the Japanese government itself; in 1908, two restrictive Orders-in-Council came into being: the first one excluded immigrants "who did not come to Canada by *direct continuous journey* from their homeland," and the second Order-in-Council, P.C. 926, imposed a stiff $200 landing fee requirement on immigrants from Asia other than Japan and China. *See* Canada Manpower and Immigration, *The Immigration Program,* Green Paper on Immigration vol. 2 (Ottawa: Manpower and Immigration, 1974); Freda Hawkins, *Canada and Immigration: Public Policy and Public Concern* (Montreal: McGill -Queen's University Press, 1972); David C. Corbett, *Canada's Immigration Policy: A Critique* (Toronto: University of Toronto Press, 1957).

6. According to the Canadian censuses for 1911 and 1921, the number of Turkish-born immigrants decreased from 1,861 in the former year to 401 in the latter year.

7. At that time, the overwhelming majority of Syrians in Canada were affiliated with the Maronite, Melkite, and Orthodox Churches.

8. This estimate is based on the combined judgment of many Muslim leaders in Canada; *see also* Yvonne Haddad, "Muslims in Canada," in Coward and Kawamura, eds., *Religion and Ethnicity,* pp. 71–100, esp. p. 73.

9. *See* Baha Abu-Laban, "Middle East Groups," paper prepared for the Dept. of the Secretary of State, Ottawa, 1973.

10. Haddad, "Muslims in Canada," p. 73.

11. As immigrants enter Canada, they submit to a fact-finding interview conducted by an immigration officer. Each immigrant is questioned about his/her ethnic (or racial) identity, citizenship, country of former residence, intended destination in Canada, and intended occupation, among other things. The information on intended destination in Canada, as well as on other characteristics of the respondent, is summarized in *Immigration Statistics,* which is published regularly by the Department of Manpower and Immigration, Ottawa.

12. Awan, *The People of Pakistani Origin,* pp. 2–3.

13. Based on previously unanalyzed data from Khattab's survey of Arab Muslims in Alberta. The larger study is reported in Khattab, "Assimilation of Arab Muslims."

14. Baha Abu-Laban, *An Olive Branch on the Family Tree: The Arabs in Canada* (Toronto: McLelland and Stewart, 1980), p. 77.

15. The present discussion is confined to the development of mosques and associated religious organizations and, therefore, no reference will be made to the development of secular organizations among different Muslim groups.

16. In addition to being a place of worship, the mosque in North America has been used for different functions, including community and Board of Directors' meetings, public lectures, dinners, and celebrations of religious holidays, weddings, and funerals.

17. Khattab, "Assimilation of Arab Muslims," pp. 22–23.

18. Garnet McDiarmid and David Pratt, *Teaching Prejudice* (Toronto: The Ontario Institute for Studies in Education, 1971), p. 41.

19. Ibid., p. 25.

20. L.M. Kenny, "The Middle East in Canadian Social Science Textbooks" in Baha Abu-Laban and Faith Zeadey, eds., *Arabs in America: Myths and Realities* (Wilmette, Ill.: Medina University Press International, 1975), pp. 133–47.

21. Ibid., p. 140.

22. For example, in response to a question about the characteristics most frequently associated with Arabs, teachers noted the following: "wild, uncivilized, nomadic, backward, disorganized, and militant against Israel" (ibid., pp. 138–39). While the terms Muslim and Arab are not synonymous, the target group, Arabs, is not totally irrelevant to the study of Canadian images of Muslims.

23. Sharon McIrvin Abu-Laban, "Stereotypes of Middle East Peoples: An Analysis of Church School Curricula," in Baha Abu-Laban and F. Zeadey, eds., *Arabs in America*, pp. 149–69, esp. pp. 160–61.

24. The Canadian Consultative Council on Multiculturalism, for example, in its "Submission by the Canadian Consultative Council on Multiculturalism to the Canadian Radio-Television and Telecommunications Commission on the Review of Canadian Content Regulations" (unpublished brief, 1980), was highly critical of the mass media's inadequate interpretive reporting "on the background events which have contributed to the frustration and hostility of the Iranian people towards the previous governments of Iran and the main supporters of those governments." The brief adds: "This type of journalism, as discussed in a recent article by Edward W. Said, does not provide balance. The media appears to have gone to war, presenting Islam and Iran as forces of darkness in a Manichaean clash between good and evil"; Edward W. Said, "Assessing U.S. Coverage of the Crisis in Iran," *Columbia Journalism Reviews* (March-April 1980). A recent report provides another example of negative social attitudes toward Muslims. According to the *Edmonton Journal* ("'Rude Bunch' Boos Plans for Mosque," *Edmonton Journal*, 18 December 1980, p. A9), about 300 residents of Burnaby, British Columbia, at a hearing held by their City Council, "booed and stamped their feet at the very thought of allowing a Moslem mosque in their neighborhood. . . . Those opposed

to the $5 million mosque [designed to serve Ismailis living in the Greater Vancouver area] said traffic congestion is the chief concern but many said the mosque would affect their quality of life. Laurie Feenie, president of the North Central Burnaby Retailers Association, said a mosque is not a church and could not be built as it did not fall within the guidelines of the municipal bylaw." Commenting on this situation, a Burnaby planner said "that residents' concerns about traffic were unfounded." The Burnaby Mayor was apparently shocked by the behavior of the crowd and was reported to have said: "I don't think you should boo your fellow man."

25. S. Abu-Laban, "The Arab-Canadian Family," *Arab Studies Quarterly* 1 (1979) : 135–56. esp. 135–36; and B. Abu-Laban, *Olive Branch on the Family Tree*, passim.

26. Haddad holds a contrary opinion in that she does not view the North American context as unique; *see* Haddad, "Muslims in Canada," p. 76.

27. Quoted in Emily Kalled Lovell, "A Survey of the Arab-Muslims in the United States and Canada," *Muslim World* 63 (1973) : 139–54, esp. p. 149.

28. Ibid., pp. 149–50.

29. This is reflected in the reactions of individual Muslims and in various articles appearing in *Islam Canada*, a major quarterly magazine published by the Council of Muslim Communities of Canada.

30. B. Abu-Laban, *Olive Branch on the Family Tree*, pp. 140–41.

31. Haddad, "Muslims in Canada," p. 80.

32. Ibid., pp. 80–81.

Islam in the United States:
Past and Present

Emily Kalled Lovell

Material for the following analysis is drawn from two questonnaires, the first sent out on 28 September 1970 to all the mosques in the United States and the Muslim Students' Associations in Canada. Of 28, some 25 eventually answered. The second was sent in the same period in 1980. Forty-three mosques were canvassed nation-wide, with a little better than 50-percent response. In addition, interviews with persons in a range of age levels were undertaken. [Eds.].

Although Islam has been spreading rapidly in the United States, it still has minority status and is often misunderstood in spite of the public relations efforts of various organizations – both of a formal and an informal nature. It is also the victim of religious prejudice because of these misunderstandings, for, as sociologists point out, the latter lead to the former.

Much of the growth can be attributed to Afro-Americans who have converted to true Islam from either the Black Muslims or other religions. They are now known as the Bilalians. This conversion is referred to as a "return to Islam" by Muslim writers such as Ali M. Kettani,[1] who says that conversion is responsible for three to four percent of the growth per year in the Muslim population in the United States.[2]

In addition to conversion, there are two other reasons for this rapid spread: natural increase by births and increase by immigration from Muslim countries.[3] Foreign students from those areas make up a large portion of the newcomers. The total number of foreign students in U.S. colleges and universities reported in the academic year 1969–70 was 134,959; this number rose to 286,265 in 1979–80.[4] The number from Africa and Asia, the two main sources of Muslim students, has increased more than two and a half times (71,918 to 181,270).[5] One writer estimates that there are over 750,000 Muslim foreign students.[6]

No religious census has been taken in the United States since 1936, and the figures that year did not include a count of Muslims (U.S. Department of Commerce), so no official government statistics are available on Muslims in the country. However, the Islamic Center in Washington, D.C., and the Federation of Islamic Associations (FIA) in the U.S. and Canada conducted a religious census during 1970. This has since been adjusted upward to include the increases previously mentioned, so that the figure now given is 2,000,000,[7] although Haddad estimates about 3,000,000.[8]

On 1 July 1980, the nation's population, estimated by the U.S. Census Bureau, based on the 1970 count, was 222,807,000.[9]

History

Some authors say that the first Muslims came to North America with the early Spanish explorers. However, the one who is most often named as the "first Muslim" was a guide – identified by Kettani as Estevanico – who arrived with Marcos de Niza in 1539 to explore Arizona. The next Muslim to be recorded was the cameleer, Hajj Ali – Hi Jolly – who was known in Arizona and California. He was brought to the desert to breed camels in an experiment proposed by government experts. After the failure of that project, he went to California where he prospected for gold.[10]

Others from the Middle East came after the Christians of that area had already been to the U.S. and returned to their homelands as wealthy men. Muslims had undoubtedly hesitated to come to a non-Muslim country but finally, in the 1860s, they started to migrate.[11] Muslims in Greater Syria (which included Lebanon at that time) came because they did not want to fight with the Turkish army. (My father was among them. He emigrated from Lebanon in 1911 when he was 15 years old. My grandmother, whose only other son was in a Turkish military prison because he refused to serve in that army, urged him to leave.) Waves of Muslim immigrants are noted in 1880, 1900, and 1910.[12]

The states attracting large numbers were Michigan, Ohio, Indiana, Illinois, Massachusetts, Iowa, Louisiana, New York, and Pennsylvania. The immigrants came mainly from Europe and the Arab countries at first and, later, from India (especially the Punjab) and Pakistan.[13] Kettani found that the Indians who had gone to California to do agricultural work found it easier to maintain their faith because they lived on farms and were not confronted with the demands of a metropolitan environment. He also stated that the Turks, as well as the Indians, have preserved their Islamic personality better than have the Arabs but that, among the Arabs, the Lebanese are more religious than those from the other Arab countries. Also, the more recent immigrants tend to observe the requirements of the faith more closely than the earlier ones.[14]

There was no organization of Muslim colonies before the 20th century. However, after World War I, a period of development at the community level began with believers in various cities organizing clubs or building mosques. It was not until after World War II, however, that development on the national level took place. The first such organization — the FIA — dates to 1952 (*see* "Mosques" and "Organizations" below). The Muslim Students' Association (MSA) is also described below in "Organizations." The MSA was an outgrowth of the marked increase in the number of students from Muslim countries coming to the U.S. to study during the 1950s.

Probably the most spectacular phase in the history of Islam in the U.S. was the conversion of Black Muslims to true Islam after pilgrimages to Mecca and visits to other Muslim countries by such leaders as Malcolm X. This conversion has resulted in their having 156 mosques, as listed in the *Bilalian News*, 24 October 1980, compared to 110 for other ethnic groups as compiled by the Islamic Center in Washington, D.C. (*see* Appendix II). Countries that have offered financial help in development are Egypt, Iran, Kuwait, Libya, Pakistan, Qatar, and Saudi Arabia.

Cedar Rapids, Iowa, has a history of Islamic life that merits special mention in any work on Muslims in North America. Although it has one of the smaller Muslim populations – 250 reported in 1980, which is an increase of almost 100 over the 1970 figure with most of the entire group having been born in this country – it has a story of continuous growth and activity. It is also the hometown of the young man who conceived the idea of the FIA (*see* "Organizations" below).

On 25 September 1972, a new Islamic Center and Mosque – the only one in Iowa – was dedicated. At that time it was one of about 20 in the country. The first Cedar Rapids mosque, however, had been built during the Great Depression and had been completed in 1934.

Syrian and Lebanese immigrants who arrived there during the early part of this century had rented a building in the early 1920s. Although they were fewer than 20 in number, they organized. Now their "congregation" also comprises Muslims from Afghanistan, Albania, Burma, Indonesia, Iran, Pakistan, Russia, Senegal, Turkey, and Yugoslavia. Students from six colleges and universities in Iowa are also served by the mosque.

The Sunday School, begun 10 years ago, is attended by 35 children at four levels of learning. The library was a gift from Egypt in 1959. The cemetery – the first independently owned one – was begun in 1948 on six and a half acres of land donated by one of their number, the late Hajj William Yahya Aossey, Sr.

A new monthly newsletter, *The Voice of Islam,* is being published by the mosque and center.

Full details of the activities of Cedar Rapids can be read in an illustrated booklet, *Fifty Years of Islam in Iowa 1925-1975.*

Minority and Prejudice

Unlike Christian immigrants who found churches that would welcome them, the Muslims, on their arrival, had to use their homes and find other places in which they could worship until they could afford to build mosques. Americans knew little or nothing about Islam in the early days so there was much discrimination reported – either against individuals in their jobs or against groups. In the latter cases, the building of mosques was at times prevented by zoning regulations.[15]

Muslims in America are best defined as the type of minority that wants to maintain its group identity based on religion but that also wants to give full allegiance to society. Yet even sociologists writing about religious minorities fail to mention Islam. They stress instead the "numerous varieties of Christianity and Judaism brought by immigrants from Europe and Mexico."[16]

For years, students in public schools and universities have been excused on Christian and Jewish religious holidays. Only recently have a very few universities asked professors to excuse Muslims on the two big feasts, Eid al-Fitr and Eid al-Adha. Arizona State University is an example. In 1976, at the urging of the MSA, the Dean of Students made this request.

The Muslims' lack of knowledge of the concept of public relations – probably based on the lack of any need for publicity in a Muslim country – no doubt had much to do with their early treatment. Many Americans seemed to believe that only Arabs were Muslims. Misconceptions from books and films contributed to misunderstandings of Arabs – and, thus, of Islam.

Since the Iranian revolution of 1979, the terms Arab and Muslim are no longer seen to be synonymous, and the word Islam is now in the vocabulary of more Americans. News stories, however, still reflect a lack of understanding, even though there are more of them. Television, too, helps to perpetuate the myths.[17]

Another reason for the hidden nature of Islam may have been that Muslims remained in what one author termed "sheltered obscurity" until their children had become successful in their chosen careers.[18] Responses to the questionnaires showed that Muslims tend not to live in ghettos but rather have their homes scattered around their cities. Yet they know where others of their faith live. Dearborn, Michigan, which has a heavy concentration of Muslims, could be considered the only exception.[19]

Now that Muslims from more than 60 countries are living in the U.S.,[20] that Afro-Americans are practising true Islam, and that such organizations as the Association of American-Arab University Graduates and Americans for Middle East Understanding are working for the improvement of English textbook materials, including religious materials, there may be less prejudice in future.

Efforts for better understanding are also being exerted by local mosques and centres, including the Information Service of the Islamic Center of Washington, D.C.,[21] the Task Force on Christian-Muslim Relations of the National Council of Churches of Christ, and the Duncan Black Macdonald Center at the Hartford, Connecticut, Seminary.

In 1957, the FIA national convention held in Detroit was "publicly snubbed" by that city's mayor. This action, rather than causing the association to be ignored, brought it nationwide publicity. The committee that had been created to plan the convention afterward continued to function as a public relations council.[22] Other small local organizations also function in this capacity. In addition, the Bilalians have an intensive, and extensive, radio broadcast program (see "The Bilalians" below).

Converts

The Conversion of Muslims to other faiths was not reported by any of those returning questionnaires. However, Haddad says that Muslims in Ross, North Dakota, where the first recorded group organized for communal prayers in 1900, have been integrated into the Christian community.[23] These Muslims had built a mosque in 1920 but abandoned it in 1948. The writer's research revealed one frank conversion to Catholicism and several instances of inter-faith marriages where the Muslim partner did not convert but did not prevent the partner from rearing the children in the latter's faith.

Persons converting from other religions to Islam do not present spectacular figures except in New York City and Washington, D.C., which listed more than 8,000 and almost 15,000, respectively. (These are also the locations of large numbers of Bilalians.) Former faiths were given as Protestant, Catholic, Mormon, and Jewish with women who married Muslim students making up the greatest number except for Afro-Americans.

Timothy Drew, who changed his name to Noble Drew Ali, has been named by Kettani as the first convert in the U.S. This was in 1913 in Newark, New Jersey.[24] However, the first known American

to convert to Islam was Mohammed Alexander Russel Webb, a jour-
nalist who entered diplomatic service in 1887 as the American Con-
sul in Manila. He was converted by Indian Muslims there. On his return to the U.S., he founded the Oriental Publishing Company in
New York City and published the first issue of *Moslem World* in
1893.[25]

Religious Observances and Assimilation

Since, to the Muslim, his religion is a way of life, he is responsible
for keeping the requirements of his faith even though he be alone in
a city. Islam has no clerical hierarchy responsible for propagation of
the faith. It is the consensus of those responding to the questionnaire
sent for this paper and for one written in 1971 that the Muslim in the
United States who truly wants to can easily fulfil his religious obligations, such as praying five times daily, fasting during Ramaḍān,
and abstaining from pork products and alcohol.

However, the most openly violated prohibition appears to be
abstinence from alcoholic beverages, followed by the one against
consumption of the meat of the pig. One cannot attribute these violations to years of exposure to these drinks and foods, as Muslim students in their first year of study can be seen purchasing beer or other
alcoholic beverages in stores or drinking them in bars. They also
give parties at which they offer a variety of liquors to their guest. A
Muslim student, filling out an application for an American host family, put only "ham and pork" in the diet restrictions blank. When
asked about alcohol, he replied that it was "different." One Muslim
wife, in her first year in the U.S., admitted to a fondness for beer.

In Toledo, Ohio, which has a Muslim population of approximately 1,000, most of whom are Arabs, Muslims own 127 of the city's
240 bars.[26] Kettani thought this "strange" because the Toledo Muslims are very active in Islamic work and have the only mosque outside of Washington, D.C., with truly Muslim architecture.[27] It was
built in the 1940s. Elkholy wrote that he had attended a wedding in
Detroit where many young people became intoxicated.[28]

Second-generation Muslim men who marry American girls seem
to eat pork and ham to keep peace in the family. Wives who did not
convert to Islam apparently do not want to prepare two separate

meat dishes. Some second-generation women, however, express a fondness for pork products as did one Muslim foreign student who said that ham was his favorite meat.

Yet most Muslims continue to observe prayer, fasting, and zakāt ("tithe") as the essence of their religion, in spite of the above violations. Moreover a number of the newer arrivals are openly demonstrative about their religious commitments and will pray in parks or in a public place and are credited with the swing to stricter adherence to religion during the past 15 years.

Muslims from most cities reported that the majority of their young people marry fellow Muslims, but, according to the Cedar Rapids respondent, some marry non-Muslims and attempt to convert them. Difficulty in finding Muslims in the same age group was given as the chief reason for inter-faith marriages. Both civil and religious ceremonies are frequently performed when the imāms are authorized to preside over the lay as well as the religious rites. Yet Abdo A. Elkholy notes that as Muslims in America are being assimilated as Arabs, Turks, and other ethnic groups, many do not see the religious wrong in mixed marriages.[29]

Some of the Islamic groups endeavored to adopt American culture completely—and quickly. They changed their Muslim names and gave their children Western names as well as Muslim ones.[30] One young woman interviewed for an earlier paper on assimilation among Arabs volunteered the information that she has never felt that the American name actually belonged to her. She thinks of herself by her Arabic name. Her two names are neither similar in sound nor are they translations. In discussing this naming phenomenon, Elkholy cited names used in one family. The list included Stephen, Dennis, and Churchill.[31]

Assimilation has led to a dilemma for some American-born Muslims who have non-Muslim mothers and an American-born father, as illustrated by responses in an interview conducted with three young women of the third generation. They were 29, 22, and 19 at the time of the first interview. Asked then if they claimed any religion, the eldest said it was Islam. The second said she considers herself a Muslim "once in a while." The youngest said she did, "usually." The two younger ones are married to non-Muslims and are mothers. Neither observes the tenets of Islam. The youngest even sends her children to a Protestant parochial school. However, the eldest, though once married to a non-Muslim, is divorced, still thinks of herself as a Muslim, and is even closer to her ethnic group than she was in 1970.

Mosques

The lack of organization among Muslims in the U.S. remained until the first large wave of 20th-century immigrants became settled. As stated earlier, meetings were held in homes and in rented or purchased halls. Detroit Muslims had purchased such a hall in 1912.[32] However, in 1919 they began what is believed to have been the first mosque in the United States, reference to the Ross one notwithstanding. Completed in 1922, it was later abandoned for a larger building.[33] Today it is a church.[34]

Through the years, churches have been purchased and converted to mosques and mosques have been sold and converted to churches. Mosques have been built in a non-Muslim way – by lottery or with wine as the source of the money. Completions of mosques have been celebrated with dancing and drinking in the buildings.[35]

Imāms have come mainly from Al-Azhar University in Cairo, Egypt, but others are from Turkey, Yugoslavia, India, Pakistan, Jordan, and even the U.S., this last reported by one respondent. Their ages range from 30 to 60.

The author was able to obtain names and addresses of 266 mosques, clubs, and centres, 156 of them Masajid Muhammad of the Bilalians, as mentioned above under "History." The other 110 are in 29 states and the District of Columbia. The one in Washington is considered the most beautiful. It was built in 1952 to serve the diplomatic community. Fourteen are termed models by Kettani,[36] three of which are in the Detroit area. Others are in Gary, Indiana; Cedar Rapids, Iowa; Toledo, Ohio; Washington, D.C.; Los Angeles and Sacramento, California; and Boston, Massachusetts.

The largest masjid in the U.S. is the Detroit Islamic Center, built between 1962 and 1968, and paid for by the congregation and the governments of Egypt, Saudi Arabia, Iran, and Lebanon. It is used by both Sunnis and Shīʿis.[37] In fact, most mosques ignore sects. The

Cedar Rapids respondent said, "After 60 years, there is no distinction." Mosque libraries contain books in both English and Arabic – often gifts from the Egyptian government. Two languages are often used in the services, one always being English.

The Afro-American Center in Washington has three floors: one for prayer, another for offices, and a third for women's clothes. Its founder studied in Medina.[38]

In Huntsville, Alabama, the president of the congregation built a hall connected to his home in 1970. It accommodates 40 persons and is used for weekly lessons.[39]

Three new centres in California were listed by the Sacramento respondent, but no addresses could be obtained before publication. These are the Lodi Muslim Mosque, Stockton Islamic Center, and the Chico Mosque.

Mosques are used for weekly prayer although some worshippers have found it necessary to hold the Friday noon prayer on Friday night or even on Sunday. Other uses are the observance of religious holidays, such as the two feasts, Birthday of the Prophet, the Isrā and Mi'raj, the Battle of Badr, and New Hijra Year. Marriages, dinners, and Sunday school are other events. Lectures are also scheduled in some.

Islamic education for children was given first priority by parents in two surveys conducted in 1973 and 1977.[40] Questionnaire responses showed that Sunday school is usually held on Sunday, but sometimes it is on Saturday. Teachers – both men and women – range widely in age. Of the mosques reporting, only Paterson, New Jersey, had all male teachers. Teachers were usually parents. The number of students varies from 30 to 250, most often with four levels of classes. The length of time Sunday school has been held was usually 10 years. The Detroit Center school, one of the best Kettani saw, is attended by 250.[41] The Dearborn school, which had 300 children enrolled at one time, opened in 1940 with the late Amerrie Kalled Zehra as first teacher. A set of books for classes in English by Dr. M. Abdul-Rauf, former director of the Washington Islamic Center, is available (see Appendix II under "Sources of Publications").

All respondents reported having burial facilities in cemeteries of their own or in sections of larger cemeteries.

Ethnic groups having mosques include Afro-Americans, Albanians, Arabs, Central Americans, Cubans, Egyptians, Indians, Iranians, Lebanese, Pakistanis, Palestinians, South Americans, Syrians, Tartars from the Soviet Union, and others from Poland, Turkey, Yugoslavia and Fiji.

The Bilalians

The Black Muslims of the "Nation of Islam," with their notion of Black supremacy, "were not Muslims at all by any definition of the word at first," but have recently adopted real Islam and in 1976 fasted Ramaḍān for the first time.[42] Now they are known as Bilalians, named for the Ethiopian who was the *muezzin* for the Prophet Muḥammad at the mosque in Medina. They are the "World Community of Islam in the West" with Imām Warith Deen Muhammad as their head. He is also leader of their American Muslim Mission, which sponsors educational programs on Islam. These are broadcast on 81 radio stations in 32 states.[43]

Some Afro-Americans have always followed Islam, with Noble Drew Ali founding the first Moorish-American temple in Newark, New Jersey, in 1913.[44] A "true Muslim club" was formed among Afro-Americans in Cleveland, Ohio, in the early 1930s. This group also built a mosque at that time.

Their 156 mosques are located in 39 states[45] (*see* Appendix II). The first Afro-American mosque in New York was started in Harlem by a student from the Caribbean in 1950.[46]

The original Black Muslim movement had basic beliefs that did not conform with Orthodox Islam. These were: There is one God, called Allah, and Elijah Muhammad is His last Messenger; Allah appeared to Elijah Muhammad in the person of Master Wallace Fard Muhammad in Detroit in July 1930; and God is not a spirit, but a man.

They also believed that heaven and hell are on earth at this time, that there is no life after death. Seven daily prayers and fasting during the month of December were other religious requirements.[47] Elijah Muhammad, the leader, outraged true Muslims with his statement that "Every white man knows his time is up."[48]

Therefore, it is easy to see why, as recently as 10 years ago,

Muslims in America considered the Blacks a great danger to Islam and to themselves.[49] One can also understand how the changes urged by Malcolm X caused the schism among the Afro-Americans.

However, in 1970 there were some Blacks who were true Muslims and were welcomed at the mosques of other ethnic groups. In the 1970 survey, the Washington respondent said that the Afro-American converts using the Islamic Center facilities were "dedicated and very active." Jazz pianist Ahmad Jamil was one.[50]

National Organizations

Two important national organizations have worked for a better understanding of Islam in the U.S. and have served to give Muslims a link with others of their faith throughout the country. One, the FIA, also has a junior affiliate, the Islamic Youth Association. The MSA is the second membership group. Both have individual dues-paying members.

The Council of Masjids in the U.S., formed to encourage the building of mosques, fosters their furnishing and maintenance and enables the many masjids to co-operate in various activities.

Imâms also have a council, organized in 1972, which helps them co-ordinate the observance of religious holidays and publicize publications on Islamic subjects.[51]

Abdallah Igram, a young Muslim officer during World War II, found that his religious classification was listed as X, residual category. He realized that there was a "lack of information and misinterpretation of the tenets of Islam" (FIA pamphlet). He hoped to form a national organization that would gain recognition for the American Muslim and give him a spokesman. It was founded, with a slightly different name, at a meeting attended by 400 Muslims in Cedar Rapids in June 1952. The second meeting, held in Toledo in 1953, attracted 1,000 persons.[52]

The objectives of the FIA are:[53]

To promote and teach the spirit, ethics, philosophy, and culture of Islam to Muslims and their children;

To participate in, and contribute to, the modern renaissance of Islam;

To establish contacts and strengthen the relationship with the

Muslim world community;

To expound the teachings of Islam;

To point out the common beliefs which other religions share with Islam;

To provide a media for religious, intellectual, and social needs of Muslims.

Wolf stresses that other faiths lacked the fifth aim in their objectives.

In June 1980, the FIA moved into new national headquarters, one of two buildings purchased with a $100,000 gift from King Khaled.[54] It is located in the Detroit area.

The FIA has two youth projects. One is a 137-acre summer camp once located at Chesterhill (near Columbus), Ohio, but recently for sale; it will be replaced by another site, preferably one on the shore of Lake Erie. The other project is a scholarship fund for high school students who will be attending college the year following receipt of the award.

The Muslim Star is the regular publication of the organization.

In 1963 the MSA was organized by Muslim students at the University of Illinois-Urbana with the assistance of Dr. Ahmad Sakar of Lebanon, Dr. Mehdi Bahdori of Iran, and Badia' Al-Qadu and Mundhir Al-Darwabi, both of Iraq. It now has chapters on 130 campuses and a press that publishes two magazines.[55] It also sells religious greeting cards, provides free literature, and operates an Islamic library for local and national use.

Three MSA alumni groups have been formed. These are the Islamic Medical Association, the Association of Muslim Scientists and Engineers, and the Association of Muslim Social Scientists.[56]

Students in Ann Arbor, Michigan, founded the Muslim Students' House, which has seventeen rooms available for students. Rents are used to defray operating expenses. A school for children is also held there. The house was paid for equally by Saudi Arabia and Libya.[57]

One respondent said that the Muslims in the U.S. had long been an amorphous body but that their disintegration had been halted and that Islam was being rejuvenated with the establishment of the MSA.

Haddad sees the rise in Islamic associations during the past 15 years as stemming from the increase and participation of students from Muslim countries and from the greater number of Muslim immigrants who are committed to an Islamic way of life.[58]

Conclusions

The Muslim feels Islam is not just a religion for Arabs, Africans, or other ethnic groups, but rather that it is one for all humanity. On his tour through the U.S., Dr. Kettani found that Muslims followed a pattern whenever they got together. In general he found: they tried to implement the basics of Islam and organized Friday prayer (usually held on Sunday, since Friday is a workday); they elected a leader, named a board, and set up a Sunday school for children; they made efforts to move away from the ethnic Muslim group concept and make their facilities available to any – whether they be Arab, Albanian, Indian, etc. He felt that the most important aspect was that they were teaching their children about Islam.[59]

The tendency to ignore sects has been mentioned as has the recent increased religiosity. These factors and the perpetuation of faith described above may help Americans who are born to the Islamic faith to combine their religion with the demands of everyday life in their native country. This combination may form an American Islam after all. The differences Kettani noticed may already be a blend of religion and culture.

Increased religiosity can also be attributed in part to the realization by second generation Muslims that their children were being assimilated by American Christians. They wanted their children to retain the faith so they started Sunday schools.

Yet, worldwide, Islam has changed a great deal in the 20th century with the West making the greatest impact in the Middle East. The late Philip K. Hitti believed that Christianity and Islam were very close and that "more and more in the future will the fact be realized that the realm in which they share is vastly larger than that in which they differ."[60] If the faiths do indeed grow closer, and if Islam can change abroad, one can expect more acculturation in the U.S., one source of the forces of the impact causing those changes abroad.

Whatever the development might be, Islam is getting more exposure through the activities of responsible non-Muslim organizations. Islamic groups themselves are also publicizing the faith and taking stands on current public issues. Some of the recognition and actions will merely be listed here.

- President Gerald Ford, in 1976, mentioned Muslims when listing the various faiths. It was the first time a President had done so.
- "The Mayor of Hartford, Connecticut, took an almost unprecedented initiative 9 September 1980, when he issued a proclamation of Islamic Appreciation Day" there for 13 September.[61]
- The Organization of Arizonans Supporting Islamic Studies (OASIS) was organized two years ago at Arizona State University. Its purpose is to "support programs which will provide Arizonans, students and visitors with opportunities to learn more about achievements of Islamic civilization, especially its religion, culture and art." Art and museum exhibits, lectures, and an international symposium on Islam have been sponsored. The symposium, held in January 1980, attracted 50 scholars from around the world.[62]
- The U.S. Congress adopted a resolution recognizing Islam in its fourteen hundredth year and pledged its efforts to a better understanding of this religion. The resolution was sent to heads of all Muslim states.
- The National Council of Churches of Christ in the U.S. sent a letter to Islamic organizations recognizing and honoring the fourteen hundredth year of the Islamic Era.
- The Middle East Institute in Washington, D.C., used the 1400 years of Islam as a conference theme.
- The Muslim World League met in Newark, N.J., on 26 January 1980, and condemned Russia's invasion of Afghanistan. The League also issued a press release urging Khomeini to release the American hostages in Iran.
- The National Council of Churches of Christ in the U.S. and the Duncan Black Macdonald Center of the Hartford Seminary have established a Task Force on Christian-Muslim Relations, an active group which publishes a newsletter and supports this religious understanding through various activities.

During her research the author found these to be some of the more impressive efforts in the U.S. where Islam is a minority; the *1980 World Almanac of Facts* cites the number of Muslims in the world as 546,025,000.[63]

Notes

1. Ali M. Kettani, *Al-Muslimūm fi Euroba wa Amrīka*, 2 vols. (Dar Idris: 1976). Kettani did the research for this work under a two-year grant from King Khaled of Saudi Arabia.

2. Ali M. Kettani, Lecture, University of Petroleum and Minerals, Dhahran, Saudi Arabia, Monday, 24 January 1977.

3. Kettani, *Al-Muslimūn*, vol. 2, p. 60.

4. Douglas R. Boyan (ed.), *Open Doors: 1978-79* (New York: Institute of International Education, 1980).

5. Ibid., p. 5.

6. Yvonne Y. Haddad, "The Muslim Experience in the United States," *The Link*, 12, no. 4 (September/October 1979): 1-12.

7. George E. Delury, ed., *The World Almanac and Book of Facts* (New York: Newspaper Enterprise Association, Inc., 1980), p. 351.

8. Haddad, "Muslim Experience," p. 2.

9. This figure was relayed by telephone on 29 October 1980 by the Government Documents Librarian.

10. Nadim Makdisi, "The Moslems in America," *The Christian Century* 76, no. 34 (26 August 1959): 969-71.

11. Umhau C. Wolf, "Muslims of the Midwest," *The Muslim World* 50, no. 1 (January 1960): 39-48.

12. Kettani, *Al-Muslimūn* 2, p. 55.

13. Ibid., p. 73.

14. Ibid., p. 60.

15. Haddad, "Muslim Experience," p. 10.

16. Robert Merton, *Social Theory and Social Structure* (Glencoe, Ill.: Glencoe Free Press, 1957), p. 45.

17. Jack G. Shaheen, "The Arab Stereotype on Television," *The Link* 13, no. 2 (April/May 1980): 1-13.

18. Abdo A. Elkholy, *The Arab Moslems in the United States* (New Haven: College and University Press, 1966), p. 29.

19. Barbara C. Aswad, ed., *Arabic Speaking Communities in American Cities* (New York: Centre for Migration Studies of New York, Inc., and Association of Arab-American University Graduates, Inc., 1974), p. 66.

20. Haddad, "Muslim Experience," p. 2.

21. *Al-Fajr* 2, no. 2 (March 1970): 16.

22. Wolf, "Muslims in the Midwest," p. 45.

23. Haddad, "Muslim Experience," p. 3.

24. Kettani, *Al-Muslimūn,* vol. 2, p. 62.

25. Makdisi, "Moslems in America," p. 969.

26. Kettani, *Al-Muslimūn,* vol. 2, p. 93.

27. Ibid., p. 94.

28. Elkholy, *Arab Moslems,* p. 31.

29. Ibid., p. 70.

30. Kettani, *Al-Muslimūn,* vol. 2, p. 60.

31. Elkholy, *Arab Moslems,* p. 63.

32. Wolf, "Muslims in the Midwest," p. 44.

33. Makdisi, "Moslems in America," p. 971.

34. Kettani, *Al-Muslimūn,* vol. 2, p. 62.

35. Kettani, Lecture.

36. Kettani, *Al-Muslimūn,* vol. 2, p. 67.

37. Ibid., p. 89.

38. Ibid., p. 86.

39. Ibid., p. 98.

40. Haddad, "Muslim Experience," p. 7.

41. Kettani, *Al-Muslimūn,* vol. 2, p. 90.

42. Kettani, Lecture.

43. *Bilalian News,* 24 October 1980, p. 26.

44. Haddad, "Muslim Experience," p. 6.

45. *Bilalian News,* 24 October 1980, p. 30.

46. Kettani, *Al-Muslimūn,* vol. 2, p. 75.

47. Ibrahim M. Shalaby, "The Role of the School in Cultural Renewal and Identity Development in the Nation of Islam" (Ph.D. diss., University of Arizona, 1967), p. 289.

48. "Races," *Time Magazine,* 10 August 1959, pp. 24-25.

49. Elkholy, *Arab Moslems,* p. 25.

50. Wolf, "Muslims in the Midwest," p. 44.

51. Haddad, "Muslim Experience," p. 5.

52. Kettani, *Al-Muslimūn,* p. 2, p. 63.

53. Wolf, "Muslims in the Midwest," p. 43.

54. *Detroit News,* 12 June 1980, p. 1.

55. Kettani, *Al-Muslimūn,* vol. 2, p. 64.

56. Haddad, "Muslim Experience," p. 5.

57. Kettani, *Al-Muslimūn,* vol. 2, p. 92.

58. Haddad, "Muslim Experience," p. 3.

59. Kettani, Lecture.

60. Philip K. Hitti, *Islam and the West* (Princeton: Van Nostrand, 1964), p. 94.

61. Task Force on Christian-Muslim Relations, *Newsletter* 10 (September 1980): 3-4.

62. Organization of Arizonans Supporting Islamic Studies (OASIS), Arizona State University, "Brochure" (n.d.).

63. Delury, ed., *World Almanac,* p. 351.

The Socio-Religious Behavior of Muslims in Canada: An Overview

Murray Hogben

Whether they know it or not, the Muslims in Canada are engaged in a socio-religious struggle for continued survival. If Islam and Muslims are to survive as a minority, either religious purism and cultural semi-isolation or a more liberal interpretation and cultural integration must succeed in protecting them from non-Muslim influences. The battle lines are not yet clearly drawn, but the skirmishing has been under way for more than a century. If they are to survive the campaign without much figurative bloodshed and literally considerable losses, Muslims will have to get the measure of the non-Muslims and gain their respect so that a pre-battle truce leading to a peace treaty may be decided upon as a better means of resolving differences. After all, as many of Islam's greatest victories have flowed from the pen, or have been brought about by the immigrant and the itinerant mystic or scholar, as have come from the blood shed of its warriors.

There are, initially, some problems in even defining and numbering the Muslim forces involved in this hypothetical campaign. Like their closest neighbors, the Jews, Muslims can be immigrant, native-born, or sometimes a converted element in Canadian society, although no doubt in differing ratios for all three categories.

To begin, what can be done to ensure we have correct statistics? The Council of Muslim Communities of Canada (CMCC) uses a general figure of some 100,000 Muslims when discussing the community it represents through the more than 30 member communities from St. John's, Newfoundland, to Victoria, British Columbia. Dawood Hassan Hamdani of Ottawa estimated as a result of his studies of immigration and other information, that there were about 70,000 Muslims in Canada.[1] This has been borne out by my own calculations. The basic problem of numbers is made more difficult by the fact that "Muslim" defines anyone who believes in God and His Prophet, Muḥammad, but since active membership or registration is not required, and because Statistics Canada ceased to count Muslims specifically after the 1931 census, only intelligent guesses can be made until the results of 1981 census are tabulated.

Then there is the problem of different ethnic groups. While most Muslims are from either the Arab-speaking countries of the Middle East, or from South Asia – Pakistan, India, and Bangladesh – there are those from North Africa, Black Africa, Southeastern Europe, and Turkey, Iran, Afganistan, Russia, and from Indonesia and Malaysia to the East. In addition, there are sizeable minorities from Fiji, Mauritius, Trinidad, and countries as disparate as England and China. Thus, each local community has a different mix of Muslims from various ethnic backgrounds, as well as different generations of "Canadians" of one ethnic background or more.

Also, there is the lack of manageable concentration as found in, say, a Little Italy, or a Chinatown. Muslims tend to be dispersed around all of our cities and towns, and are socially and geographically mobile, except for rare instances like Lac La Biche. Since they are not usually distinguishable visibly, except if of South Asian origin (which includes Hindus) and do not usually wear any distinguishing dress here, they are almost impossible to spot in a crowd.

On the question of piety or degree of adherence to the tenets of Islam, there is a complete spectrum of belief – from rare outright disbelief, through nominal or occasional observation, to the more or less full observation of the Islamic code. And since some Muslims still do not have any centres or mosques, and since they need not register at any of these, and since it ultimately comes down to personal belief and the recognition by God alone of one's piety, the calculation of numbers or depth of belief is extremely difficult.

Having defined some of the problems entailed in studying or categorizing the Muslims in Canada, one should note that Islam is, of course, both a religion and a culture. Many Muslims do not distinguish between the religion as explained in the Qur'ān and exemplified by the lives of the Prophet Muḥammad and his followers (and its later codification in Sharī'a law), and the vast collection of traditions and customs that one calls culture. These, of course, vary with time and space across the Muslim world and, in turn, influence the interpretation of the religion. In Canada, only a very personal application of Muslim civil law can be made in some cases, while the rest of the civil and criminal laws are inapplicable here. There is no place in Canada for the kind of expatriate communities or recognized minority situations such as existed in the Balkans or in the East. As much as some Muslims may want to see Muslim law brought here, others would have doubts about its usefulness or applicability.

What are some of the socio-religious issues in this campaign over the assimilation or integration of Muslims here? First, what are the demands of Islam and its culture which face the Muslim on the religious plane? Let us start with the observation of the well-known "five pillars" of Islam.

Muslims are initially defined as those who swear the oath of belief in one God, Allah, and in Muḥammad as his messenger. Those who say their prayers to some extent at least repeat this oath frequently every day. Some perform this obligation regularly and are rightly or wrongly called "good Muslims," while others neglect them for justifiable or unjustifiable reasons. There is a good deal of latitude in timing and degree and Muslims can take advantage of this if they are religiously inclined. The saying of prayers during work hours or even at the pre-dawn time, of course, raises problems they must live with on a daily basis. The obligation of attending Friday or *jum'a* prayers requires some sort of gathering, and the lack of concentration of population, available lunch hours, and gathering places causes problems for many Muslims. In some cities, a Sunday noon gathering is held that at least allows them an unofficial congregational prayer on the one day all Muslims are theoretically free to attend.

Eid prayers tend to draw much of the Muslim male population, at least, together these days, to such an extent that huge halls need to be rented in cities such as Toronto, Montreal, or Edmonton. But even then, many nominal or otherwise engaged Muslims fail to attend these special events although they might show an interest in the local festivities, and visit friends and relatives as is the custom in Muslim countries.

Then there is the question of zakāt (a tithe, or alms to assist the poor). Muslims here regularly give a few dollars each year per member of the family before the Eid-al-Fitr prayers as a bare minimum, and usually are generous with their money and aid to relatives, friends, and the wider Muslim community, especially to those in difficult minority situations, and even to those engaged in rebellions. Interestingly, in the true spirit of Islam, some individuals and communities send funds to non-Muslim organizations or victims of natural or man-made disasters but, of course, the tradition of concealment of generosity makes it hard to calculate the incidence and amount of charity given. The organization of zakāt giving is left to individuals and local communities.

The obligation of fasting during the lunar month of Ramaḍān again raises difficulties for some but not all Muslims. The pre-dawn to sunset period of abstention raises questions among the less religious of what to do about business and social meal obligations, children's lunches, of efficiency at work, or how to break the fast at work, etc. These are challenges that all interested Muslims grapple with if they are not among those who fast the full month, or make up for "lost" days by other fasts or financial contributions. As in the case of prayers, fasting divides the "good Muslim" from the less believing or less active one.

Finally, there is the question of hajj or pilgrimage to Mecca within a Muslim's lifetime. While in former times this was a rare, hazardous, and financially difficult hurdle for Muslims, a surprising number of them in Canada seem to make this trip by air, often when coming or going from their homelands to the East, and at a much earlier age than in the past. Modern travel arrangements such as charter flights and the availability of credit make this no longer the act of the pious old men, but of young couples as well. The growing numbers now flocking to Mecca each year are evidence of this. Of course, the slaughter of sheep and camels and the waste of meat in a world full of starving millions raises other questions, but money can be given instead.

Besides these "five pillars," there are obligations of reading the Qur'ān, and talking about and learning about Islam, all of which are part of the personal life of a Muslim. Under this heading it should be stressed that Islam emphasizes the family life as the good life, and here it frequently comes into conflict with the "Canadian" way of life and the ethics of the 20th century.

There is a strong tendency among Muslims both here and abroad to marry young, but because of Canadian law and changing world values, only once at a time. The old question of "four wives" is always posed, even thrown, at Muslims, but generally Muslims here adhere to the family unit and its morality, although a "double standard" may exist for some men. Certainly the overall Muslim practice of male domination places the burden of modesty in dress and behavior on girls and women, and often denies them equal opportunities in work, recreation, and education in more traditional families. "Barefoot, pregnant, and in the kitchen" is quite frequently the lot of Muslim women here, in direct contradition to the freedom and equality that prevails in most Canadian homes. Muslims continue to extol the great role of women in the past but this is questionable in the light of Muslim history. In fact it leads to questions and indeed rebellion among young and western-educated Muslims, both men and women, and is one of the more complex problems faced by North American Muslims.

There is also a history of large families among more traditional Muslims, reflecting their origins in the East and their reluctance to practise birth control, even though most "experts" say it is allowable, if not necessarily desirable. Hence the higher than average birth rate is one of the means by which Muslims, unconsciously perhaps, face the challenges of loneliness and self-imposed distancing from the mainstream of Canadian life. Of course, large families tend to be the custom among many minorities, recently arrived or at the lower end of the social and economic scale. "Zero growth" is not the way of the immigrant or of the family-oriented minorities.

Related to the conflict with the freer way of life in Canada is the strict Islamic code prohibiting pre-marital mixing of the sexes and sexual activity outside of marriage. While sexual freedom is gaining acceptance among Muslims abroad, it is much more prevalent in Canadian society, which causes problems between the more religious Muslims and non-Muslims. Thus, while girls especially are often still kept isolated outside school hours from the other sex, except for family members and relatives, those not married at a young age often question this aspect of Muslim law and tradition.

For example, Muslim teenagers at summer camps organized by the CMCC often object to the segregation of the sexes for sports, swimming, and even religious instruction when they can mix to a greater or lesser degree with members of other sex at home and at school the rest of the year. Many attend dances and parties and find it difficult to accept the arguments of camp instructors that they should at least experience the social side of Islamic life, as well as the traditional prayers, etc., while at camp.

Among adult, single Muslims, the problems of dating, cohabitation, or mate selection can be even more difficult unless they agree to "arranged" marriages with relatives or family connections here or from their homelands or parents' homelands. There is a fairly high incidence of Muslim men intermarrying with non-Muslim women, because they have met and fallen in love with an outsider and somehow missed finding or accepting a bride from within their community. While this is accepted by Islam for "the people of the book" – Christians and Jews – it is little tolerated in the case of their own girls marrying non-Muslims, unless the future husband converts to Islam. The "safe" marriage of daughters to Muslim men is a major concern of parents here as elsewhere.

There is also intermarriage with Muslims outside their own ethnic community, a rare, but growing practice. For example, someone from Lebanon or of Lebanese origin might marry a Trinidadian Muslim, and Albanian a Yugoslav, a Canadian convert a born Muslim, etc. There is a fast-growing number of Canadian-born who do not have the same reluctance to marry outside the clan. Islam in

Canada has both its own melting pot and its own multi-culturalism, as it has since its beginnings.

However, some Muslims feel that allowing male exogamy is also unrealistic, when Muslim males as members of a minority religion cannot always ensure the traditional upbringing of their children, and hence the wisdom or applicability of Islamic law is open to discussion on this point. While it is all very well for free individuals of whatever religion to state that they will practise their own religions – or not – the conflict comes when they marry and have children. And there are moments of crisis when a unity of faith would help keep families together and give spiritual support when one or other dies. In a number of cases non-Muslim and even nominally "converted" wives have reneged on earlier understandings or declarations and have had children baptized, or have hindered Muslim funerals for deceased Muslim husbands.

On the theme of death, Muslims in Canada have sometimes sent their dead back to their homelands for burial, especially recent immigrants or visitors. But in most major Muslim centres, there are funeral homes that will more or less allow the traditional Muslim funeral arrangements to be carried out, including ritual washing, winding in shrouds, plain caskets, all-night vigils, speedy interments, and who do not insist on embalming. And there are often parts of cemeteries, at least, where Muslims are buried in traditional positions related to Mecca, etc. Truro, Nova Scotia, has had such a cemetery for many decades. There is also a nice story about a Lebanese Muslim peddler and later merchant, who bought a piece of farmland in the Eastern Townships of Quebec for himself and his family, and ended up being asked to provide space for unbaptized children of Catholic parents! But many Muslims are still buried as most Canadians are and in cemeteries that have no connection with any Muslim community. And Islamic traditions of will-making and the division of estates are largely ignored here, since the laws are quite different and currently in a great state of flux.

Another area of personal life that causes difficulties for Muslims and often leads to a breach of the Islamic code concerns food and drink. Muslims are ordered to eat *ḥalāl* meat, avoid any pork products, and shun alcoholic drinks. Again, devout Muslims usually slaughter their own meat, buy from the *ḥalāl* butchers increasingly found in big cities, or kosher butchers, and avoid eating in public places. They also bake their own bread and pastries or buy from Jewish bakeries and carefully read all the ingredients now printed on most packaged foods. But for the majority perhaps, it is more a series of compromises and well-intentioned rationalizations or interpretations that allow them to buy and eat, though most still avoid pork products at least in meat form. As for alcohol, probably the great majority of Muslim Canadians abstain from alcohol in any form, although there are those less committed who may take a "social drink" with work mates, or at Christmas time, or in their younger years before settling down to become responsible "family men." It is always one thing to risk your own punishment, but fathers (who are more liberated from the home than their wives), still tend to want to set a good example for their children and be well-thought-of by Muslim friends and relatives. Of course, this may play havoc with being well-thought-of by their *non*-Muslim work mates and neighbors, as will be mentioned later on. With alcohol already banned to Muslims, it is possible that drugs are also much less in vogue among young Muslims, but I have no firm evidence of this. Several teenagers were expelled from a Muslim camp for the mere suspicion that they were smoking marijuana.

What sort of influences lead to the use of alchohol and drugs as signs of the acceptance of Canadian social customs; what sort of influences lead to this state of affairs? Obviously there is the everyday influence of society. But also there is the influence of the mass media—radio, TV, and the press—which show these and other aspects of North American life as desirable or undesirable, whether advertised or condemned as problems. Indeed there is a basic conflict between the maintenance of Islamic values and the active or passive acceptance of the messages received daily from the mass media.

Another area of possible conflict is with the educational system. Children and young adults are exposed to Canadian values, which are generally upheld, while the ways of others tend to be downgraded. Hence Christianity and Western traditions and culture are supported, and Islam with its non-Western traditions and culture are depicted as wrong-headed, out-of-date, or different at best. Contradicting these views are messages received through a Muslim edu-

cation, whether delivered in the home, at weekend classes and summer camps, or by speakers from the Muslim community. There are
difficulties here, in that these messages may not be strong enough to
counteract the subtle and overt lessons from the surrounding community, and hence there may be conflicts between parents and children over values and behavior. Generally, the older generation oppose the permissive society, while appreciating the religious, political, and social freedoms of the West.

One area of education of paramount importance to any immigrant community, and especially to one whose source of belief and
tradition is in a language other than English or French, is language
retention. Arabic-speaking parents encourage their children to
speak Arabic at least at home and to read the Qur'ān in the original.
Non-Arabic-speaking Muslims have a dual problem in that they
want to stress their own language, say Urdu, as well as have their
children learn Arabic – at least phonetically. They will want their
children to have enough Arabic to be able to recite the Qur'ān, if
not to read it. Hence, Arabic classes are usually part of the weekend
routine in urban centres, although whether an hour or two a week
without more constant exposure will have much effect is a worri-
some question for many Muslim parents.

Turning to the wider question of intra-community relations
between different Muslim groups, one can say that while in smaller
centres there is perhaps a real Islamic fraternity between ethnic
groups and individuals, in larger centres each ethnic group tends to
have its own small coterie. This is because language, customs, and
views on Islamic matters may clash when there are larger numbers
or one predominant group. This has often led previously mixed and
mutually tolerant communities to fall apart and reform into other
groups, often under the impetus of fundamentalism or militant
Islam. But there have been some positive effects of this tendency to
ethnic separatism too, such as the will to spend more money and
time on their "own" ethnic religious instruction.

On the question of inter-community relations, the Muslims of
Canada have had both good and bad times with the host community. In terms of work, in the early years – during the end of the last
century and the first half of this one – Muslims, still largely immigrants, were peddlers who were either welcomed to rural homes or

expelled at gunpoint! In factories, stores, and restaurants they were sometimes accepted and sometimes shunned. For example, it was impossible for the late Albanian imām of the original Muslim Society of Toronto to find a job at the time of the First World War because of his religion, and he was branded a Turk. Therefore self-employment was the only route for most Muslims, and indeed is still widely followed.

Socially, Muslims and the host community are often on terms of complete mutual isolation based on race, culture, and language differences, including the Muslims' unwillingness to drink or discuss sex freely with work mates or neighbors. Obviously there is some class connection here, as working-class immigrants have more trouble making friends with Canadians than do middle, upper-middle class, professional, and Canadian-educated or Canadian-born Muslims. Countless times I have heard about this inability of Muslims to bridge the gaps with their neighbors. Wives and daughters who are in semi-seclusion do not fit into the mixed-sex society of North America, and the husbands cannot relate to the beer-commercial sterotyped friendship with "the boys" seen so often on television these days. This, of course, is only a brief treatment of the question. Many exceptions do exist of good and frequent relations with the host community, but it is less prevalent among the religiously inclined immigrant group.

Of course, on purely religious grounds, there are more cases of mutual non-comprehension than of tolerance and interest. This results from more than a thousand years of armed hostility or sullen truce between Christianity and Islam, and from the ripple effects of the Arab-Israeli question, both of which lead to negative stereotyping in the press, schoolbooks, and popular mythology. It can only be hoped that the current wave of interest in courses in comparative religion, the problems of the Middle East, and widening horizons will help the host community to come closer to understanding and accepting the Muslims in their midst. Otherwise, the campaign for survival could become less a matter of words and more one of deeds if sparked by oil shortages or international incidents, such as have been seen in America as a result of the Tehran hostage drama.

Turning now to the question of economics, what can one say about the Muslims' concerns when faced with the economic life of

Canada? Firstly, as already mentioned, there is still much difficulty in being at all accurate about the Muslims' socio-economic condition or occupational distribution. However, Dawood Hamdani has estimated that between 46 and 47 percent of the Muslim population is employed in the work force. In 1976 about 32 percent was in the professional category, 19 percent was in clerical and sales, and 20 percent in manufacturing.[2] More research needs to be done in this area. Furthermore, discrimination may keep Muslims from achieving an even balance across the socio-economic scale; John Porter's *Vertical Mosaic* may apply to Muslims as much as to other immigrant groups, but again, evidence is still lacking.

Muslims also have some specific objections to the free enterprise system as practised in Canada, specifically to the charging of interest, and the lack of social responsibility among industrialists and business houses. There is a feeling that interest charges have been carried too far, and that society should be integrated and not just a platform for the elevation of the few.

With all these conflicts between Islamic beliefs and customs and Canadian ways, what have been the achievements of Muslims here?

There have been the establishment of mosques, Saturday and Sunday schools (the latter an unpopular day in that Muslims want to be distinctive), the recent organization of class curricula, Muslim camps for boys and girls, and regional and national conferences, open sessions on Islam for school teachers or the general public, a national umbrella organization, an Islamic magazine, *Islam Canada*, to name a few.

What needs to be done yet, I would suggest, is for Muslims to establish not only mosques but community centres, not only Saturday classes but regular day or boarding schools, not only Islamic associations but political and economic groupings, and a greater sense of unity and mutual co-operation. Many Muslims are not aware that they have a national organization like the CMCC, a magazine, a fledgling system of camps, a chance to organize their own schools and language classes using public money if numbers warrant, protection of their religious obligations (such as Friday prayers at least) or of religious holidays, or of their right to lobby politically. I once met a man who was presented with the alternative of attending prayers from 1 to 2 P.M. or keeping his job!

But besides these needs, I see some dangers to the Muslim community that should be mentioned. First, there is the previously mentioned rise of militancy and fundamentalism, which may discourage Muslim attendance at mosques or the observation of religious duties. Such a development would further alienate many immigrants who wanted to get away from this aspect of Islam at home, and also deter the Canadian-born and converts from becoming wholehearted in their observance of the faith. These are the possible losses mentioned at the beginning.

Then there is the danger of too heavy reliance on outside funding for the building of mosques or schools. The danger is that self-reliance will fall before the siren-song of petro-dollars and Middle-Eastern political interests. The examples of the early centre- and mosque-building that solidified communities should not be forgotten for the sake of grander "instant" Islamic structures.

Also, while it was necessary in early years to import brides and grooms from homelands across the sea because of shortages of suitable or related spouses here, the danger now is that this practice will further separate the native-born or mixed-origin Muslims from the more "ethnic" Muslims. If immigration is more sharply curtailed, as it might well be any time as a result of economic or political problems here or abroad, such a reliance might cause a sense of loss among some, but it could also lead to a consolidation among the groups here, making them more "Canadian." Reliance on outside sources of funds or population can be a sword that cuts both ways.

In conclusion, let me suggest that Canadian Muslims, like those in other New World or even non-Muslim World countries, are in a unique position to demonstrate that Islamic values and beliefs can survive successfully under very new circumstances, and that they can perhaps begin some necessary re-thinking of Islam which would be next to impossible at home.

There is also a chance to demonstrate that Islam can develop its own successful multiculturalism and become a melting-pot within the wider multicultural Canadian environment as it did in the past when Islam first swept much of the known world. After all, the conquests of Islam were not all a matter of the sword, but of ideas and people successfully mixing and adapting. A liberal interpretation may succeed in confirming the position and growth of Islam in Canada, as long as we do not "throw out the baby with the bathwater," as feared by the more militant or fundamentalist Muslims. I am certain, too, that in the long run, the clash of cultures can only be mitigated by positive thinking on the parts of Muslims and non-Muslims alike.

Notes

1. David Hassan Hamdani, "Muslims in Canada: A Century of Settlement, 1871–1976," Ottawa: Council of Muslim Communities of Canada, May 1978.
2. Hamdani, "Muslims in Canada," p. 58, table.

III

Muslim Immigrant Communities: Identity and Adaptation

Pakistani Canadians:
The Making of a Muslim
Community

Regula B. Qureshi and Saleem M.M. Qureshi

The research for this chapter has been part of an ongoing inquiry focusing on the Pakistani Muslim community. While dealing with an ethnographically specific topic, this inquiry is motivated by three general questions, which arise from, and reflect, each author's disciplinal background and concerns. The purpose of raising these questions is to enhance an understanding of the Pakistani Muslims in Canada, as well as to contribute to the continuing general discourse around these questions in their wider relevance.

The three questions are:

1. How does a Muslim community constitute itself in the contemporary North American version of Western society?

2. More specifically, how does the religious and socio-cultural identity of its members manifest itself in the process of adaptation to the North American context?

3. How, in investigating this process, is the conceptual dimension of religious and socio-cultural identity to be related to the domain of behavior in the process of adaptation?

Implied in these questions, as well as in their ethnographic focus, is the notion that the Muslim community should be defined and studied at the level of a socio-cultural or ethnic entity, assuming a common regional and linguistic background. This contrasts with the concept of a larger Islamic community, so defined in contrast to non-Muslims, specifically in the non-Muslim North American context.

The argument for choosing the particular concept – without, however, denying the reality of the universal one – requires touching on the fundamental question as to the nature of the umma, the community of the faithful. The concept of umma is built into the very creed of Islam; hence the umma is a conceptual reality for all Muslims. But it is more than that; the umma is also an experiential reality, confirmed each time one Muslim encounters another, anywhere, anytime. The umma as a fact of real life is experienced most vividly and intensely where no links are perceived other than that of the common faith, and where the common Muslim identity alone acts to bridge geographic and cultural distance.

In Canada, this bond between Muslims has operated and continues to operate mainly at two levels. The first is the level of the individual Muslim, especially the individual not surrounded by those with whom he shares other bonds of a socio-cultural or linguistic nature. Thus, during the early period of largely individual immigration to Canada – as well as in small Canadian communities today – groups of Muslims came to be linked into what may loosely be termed "incipient Islamic" communities, based on their members' shared identification with the umma of Islam. This type of community, however, has today been largely superseded in Canada, due to much more massive Muslim immigration enlarging various Muslim groups and thus giving the individual Muslim the opportunity to link up with those with whom he shares a socio-cultural and linguistic, as well as a religious identity. This is largely true for the major urban centres of Canada, although smaller cities still harbor groups of "Muslims at large," spanning the wider community of Islam.

The second level at which the bond between Muslims operates is the supra-personal or institutional level, where diverse individuals or groups join under the banner of Islam to further the interest of Muslims in general, especially within the larger Canadian context – the socio-cultural and political context of their non-Muslim host country. This second level is represented by two institutions; one purely religious in orientation – the mosque – the other having more of a socio-political and cultural focus – the Muslim associations, most particularly an umbrella association such as the Council of Muslim Communities of Canada. This institutional level, however, already presupposes the existence of individual Muslim communities of diverse geographic and socio-cultural origins; indeed, it represents the distillation of these communities' common ideology, Islam.

As real as the bond of Islam is at these two levels, the fact is that today, Muslims in Canada are constituted into communities at an intermediate level where individual Muslims share not only a religious but a socio-cultural and linguistic identity as well. Given the fact that Muslims in Canada are largely immigrants, it is obvious that bonds of common origin have acted most strongly to link them into rather distinct communities as soon as numbers permit. Increased immigration has resulted in these communities becoming, if anything, more differentiated. Even mosque organizations, the pan-Islamic institutions par excellence, have come to reflect this differentiation, as much as they are ideologically committed to supersede them. Of course, mosques are still able to invoke the all-encompassing religious bond, but to extend the efficacy of this bond beyond the realm of religious observance and belief necessitates dealing with the realities of social and cultural differences between Muslims of different origins so that gaps can be bridged. In Canada, the emergence and vigorous expansion of the Council of Muslim Communities in itself constitutes evidence that the need for such efforts is being recognized within the Muslim community at large, as do discussions and attempts at creating a dialogue among Muslims of differing socio-cultural backgrounds.

There is a further, powerful motivation for Muslims of different groups or socio-cultural communities to join hands: their common situation as immigrants in a non-Muslim, Western host society, and their common need to adapt to it. Here too, however, the common belief system is inextricably linked at the level of its actualization with the social norms and cultural practices particular to the home traditions of each group. Hence, adaptation is often seen from different perspectives, especially when it comes to the particulars of practice.

In order, then, to be able to gain an understanding of North American Islam it is ultimately of central importance to investigate the dynamic inherent between the two levels, and to do so in terms of both perception and reality. One level is the universal ideology of Islam, the other the particular socio-cultural version of Muslim life in the immigrant's home country. The Islamic ideology accounts for much commonality in the community life of Muslims from different regions. But allowing a common ideology to overshadow what nevertheless are real differences will severely limit the chances for achieving an understanding; at the same time it will not eliminate differences.

In the light of this reasoning it is of primary importance to inquire into the reality of particular Muslim communities or groups and explore their particular social and cultural identity together with their universal Muslim identity within Canada. The starting point is not so much an ethnographic account of the community's life-style or adaptation, as an investigation of the premises that underlie that life-style or motivate that adaptation. Such an emphasis seems particularly relevant where, as in the case of a majority of Muslim Canadians, immigration is recent and community life still in flux, lacking norms established over time. To study such communities presents a very real problem of evaluating behavioral diversity over place and time. Reporting such diversity statistically may obscure the common base, while selecting a particular pattern as the norm may distort it. We, therefore, propose a third approach, that of interpreting the behavioral diversity in the light of the concepts that underlie it. For behavior, we believe, is guided and motivated primarily by concepts or principles which are learned as part of socialization and shared by members of one community. Hence, an understanding of these concepts — or conceptual framework — is a necessary prerequisite to interpreting the observable domain of behavior.

This chapter, therefore, attempts to isolate the social rules that motivate, guide, or inform social action for Pakistani Canadians, thus laying the groundwork for studying particular communities or groups of Pakistani Muslims in Canada. Applying such an approach to this particular Muslim group is promising inasmuch as it consists entirely of immigrants who have brought with them a conceptual framework based on their own socialization in their home community where long-established common norms prevailed. This framework serves them as a guide in establishing their communities; and it is this framework, therefore, which may be considered as a key to the interpretation of Pakistani-Canadian community life, governing the interaction between individuals and society.

All this is not to imply that Pakistani-Canadian concepts are static and their behavior unchanging. Their established conceptual framework may act as a guide to behavior, but in the light of actual social experience, that framework inevitably undergoes a gradual process of modification – which in turn affects the behavioral sphere. However, this dialectical process is as yet in a state of flux and therefore difficult to analyze; indeed it can be expected to take on a more manifest shape only in the socialization of the second generation. The foundation for following the process of adaptation is now to investigate how the first generation is establishing itself as a community on the basis of concepts and ideals acquired back home.

The data for this inquiry consist of two kinds of information. First, there is the background knowledge of Pakistani concepts and principles of social interaction, and this was accumulated during the course of extensive field research on aspects of Indo-Muslim society and culture. This research has been supplemented and informed by the study of socio-religious and cultural issues pertaining to both India and the Islamic world.

The second kind of information pertains to how Pakistanis in Canada apply the conceptual framework acquired in their childhoods in their new life and is based on close contact with particular Pakistani-Canadian communities in Edmonton since 1963, supplemented by more structured inquiry among such communities in other parts of Alberta, primarily Calgary, as well as in smaller centres. Informal observation and questioning (using primarily the Urdu language) provided much data on social processes, which ultimately motivated the search for an explanatory model. To the extent that both data and analysis attempt to capture a social process very much in flux – as indeed do all studies dealing with recently immigrated groups – they are not as readily accessible to verification or objectification from within the community as are studies of long-established cultural groups. At the same time, there are individual Pakistani Canadians who, taking an observer's stance, concur with this presentation of their community's social dynamic.

Who are the Pakistani Canadians?

In accordance with the scope of this paper the term Pakistani Canadians is here used in a sense which is both normative and expanded. Normative, because it refers to Muslims, arbitrarily excluding non-Muslim Pakistanis in order to avoid introducing the entirely new variable of a religion other than Islam. Expanded, because it includes Muslims from India with whom considerable socio-cultural bonds continue to exist. Indeed, Pakistan is a recent political entity, as before independence in 1947 its population formed part of the larger community of Muslims within British India.[1]

Muslims have constituted a major group within the larger South Asian immigrant community living in Canada and the U.S. for some years but little separate attention has been paid to it other than through unflattering epithets. Yet this group has a very distinct socio-cultural identity among Canadians of East Indian origin, founded in its religious affiliation with Islam. It originates from all over the Indian subcontinent, for even many Pakistani Canadians hail originally from other parts of India, having migrated to Pakistan to join that country on its independence. At the same time, Indo-Muslim and Pakistani society was always characterized by a dominant supra-local élite that had much in common across the regions, including, primarily, religious ideology and practices, a common language (the Muslim élite language and *lingua franca,* Urdu) and a shared body of cultural and social ideas and traditions. This situation had resulted from the nature of the Muslim presence in South Asia which may be broadly characterized as feudal and highly stratified. Hence, a Muslim ruling class and its supporters set general socio-cultural standards and provided a normative component for South Asian Muslim society in general. This élite focus was long centred in Delhi, locus of imperial Muslim power; later, under the British, the focus spread to secondary centres of Muslim local rule, and today it resides among the upper and middle class in major cities. It is this élite and its standards that are relevant for this chapter for they continue to represent a point of emulation or at least orientation even for the lower strata of Pakistani society.

The Indo-Muslim or Pakistani élite identifies itself on the basis of descent. Collectively called ashrāf (noble), it traces its descent either from early Islamic nobility (*sayyid* from the Prophet, shaykh from the Prophet's tribe), or from Muslim conquerors (*Mughal* from Turkestan, *Pathān* from Afghanistan), and it also includes upper-caste Hindu converts (e.g. *Rajputs*). Accordingly, Indo-Muslim élite culture has been characterized by a blend of traits drawn from Islamic-Arab culture, "which has always been valued by the Muslims as the ideal way of life";[2] traits left by Turko-Iranian culture, "represented for quite a long period in India by Turk, Afghan, Moghul rule as well as by the landed and military aristocracy of the time";[3] and Indian socio-cultural traits. Together these have, in the words of an exponent of this culture, produced "an entirely new and typical social pattern: Indo-Islamic culture."[4]

There is no doubt that in basic respects Indo-Muslim social organization shares traits with Hindu society; at the same time there are clear differences. Particularly important among the differences is socio-economic mobility, based on an essentially egalitarian ideal inherent in Islam (as opposed to the religious basis of caste in Hindu society). Education and religious commitment have been traditional avenues of social advancement in Indo-Muslim society. Recently, the concept of mobility has found increased practical realization in Pakistan where changes of population and the need for new institutions have allowed scope for individual achievement independent of ascribed social status. At a more fundamental level of social structure, this concept is also reflected in a rather flexible system of marriage anywhere within the ashrāf category. On the whole, however, mobility does not encompass the lower classes of Pakistani society, so that there remains a fundamental division between what amounts to two major strata, quite in accordance with the traditional concept of Muslim social structure.[5]

Immigration into Canada has very largely come from the élite strata of upper- and middle-class Pakistanis. Most Pakistani Canadians come from urban centres and very few indeed have a low class origin. For the purpose of this chapter, there is no need to go into details of immigration history beyond the following generalization: after the limited individual immigration under the 100-per-year quota, the removal of the racially biased immigration policy in the late 1960s resulted in what may be termed the formation of Pakistani-Canadian communities in and around major cities of Canada.

The main point here is that on the whole these communities are no more than 10 to 15 years old.

As for characterizing members of these communities, a few important points need to be made regarding the immigration pattern. Most immigrants initially have been males who came to Canada during training or early in their career. The majority came married or married soon after, under traditional arrangments; hence most wives are also Pakistani. As a result of this youthful immigration, today few Pakistani Canadians are past middle age. The majority are within a generation of each other in age and most have small or growing children. Recently, a small but increasing number of aged parents have joined the community permanently or for extended visits.

Concepts of Social Grouping

The central concept is that of kinship. It provides an individual with identity and status as well as with a personal support system. The kinship sphere is set against society at large. This is expressed in terms of two dialectically opposed categories, represented by the Urdu adjectives *apnā* (one's own) and *ghair* (strange, foreign). Apnā denotes family, intimacy, the personal sphere (which can also include close personal friends). Ghair denotes outsiders, the public sphere, impersonal relationships. To a Pakistani Canadian, the relevant sphere is the kinship or family sphere, even though he, especially if he is a male, also learns to deal with the outside sphere successfully. But he considers his first obligation to be his family, a commitment which has a strong Islamic foundation as expressed in the Qur'ān as well as in both sunna and ḥadīth.[6] Indeed, his personal social universe is conceived of in terms of the kinship sphere. It is for this reason that in this paper the focus will be on concepts of family, for we consider them to be of primary importance as forming the core of the Pakistani-Canadian model for a social structure.

Within the kinship sphere, or as it will be termed henceforth, the family, *membership* is defined on the basis of two principles of social structure. Both have Islamic sanction and are distinctly Muslim in origin, though not exclusively so. The first one is patrilineal descent with a patrilocal household as a nucleus that may, but need not, be extended. Reckoning descent through the male line is clearly evidenced in the Qur'ān, by way of patrilineal inheritance rules (IV: 11ff). Further reinforcement comes from the ḥadīth and sunna, referring to these Qur'ānic laws and to early Muslim practice. The second principle is lineage endogamy, not as a rule but as a principle of preference. This means that marriage among kin as close as first cousins is not only permitted but even encouraged. The practice is sanctioned by the Prophet's own example – he married his daughter Fatima to his paternal cousin, Ali – and reinforced by the traditional Arab concept of *bint al-ʿamm* (preferential marriage to father's brother's daughter).[7]

In concrete terms, the two principles of patrilineality and lineage endogamy result in a concept of kinship that is characterized by strong ties of descent. At the same time, it implies flexibility as regards membership. For endogamy implies the absence of any exclusion principle that would categorically separate a husband's and a wife's kin groups. An individual's family group can therefore extend bilaterally, in the manner of a kindred.[8] This in effect means that any kin tie on either the mother's or the father's side can be activated, depending on the amount of close and frequent contact. Finally, the nucleus of the social group is the household (*ghar*), usually – but not necessarily – consisting of a father with sons and their families, but there is no concept of a joint family as a corporate unit (as there is in Hindu social organization).

In sum, the Pakistani Muslim brings with him a concept of social grouping that identifies a personal sphere of intimacy, identification, and mutual support, rooted in his experience of his own family and reinforced by a strong Islamic emphasis on the centrality of the bonds of the family. At the same time, this concept of a strong family group is characterized by a unique flexibility, again rooted in the Pakistani-Muslim experience of a relatively closely knit household surrounded by a larger kin group that extends bilaterally.

Concepts of Social Structuring

Pakistani Canadians consider two structural principles basic to the family sphere: one is seniority, the other sex role. Both principles have their foundation directly in Islamic ideology; they are set forth in the Qur'ān itself, expounded in the ḥadīth and reinforced by early Islamic practice.

The seniority principle is fundamental; at the most primary level it governs the relationship between parents and children, as expressed in the Qur'ān (XVII: 24f), while in a wider context it is applied across the generations generally. Within generations, the principle is specifically extended to siblings, by means of analogy with the parent-child relationship.[9] In fact, the entire kinship sphere is permeated by the seniority principle. The cumulative result, in the case of Pakistani Muslims, has been a hierarchical concept of social structuring generally; this, however, is also due to the ubiquitous contact with the highly hierarchical Hindu social reality.

In terms of operation the seniority principle means that juniors defer to seniors and accept their authority. Obedience is expressed in the form of politeness (ādāb).[10] Seniors in turn exercise authority and personal domination, but they also bear responsibility for juniors. Both in substance and form the operation of the seniority principle reflects Islamic tradition.[11] The seniority principle has a dynamic quality inherent in it: over time every junior becomes a senior, so that submission eventually leads to authority, confirming the notion that playing one's part in the system will in time be rewarded by the system. The general assumption underlying the practice of the seniority principle is that "the individual submits to authority until he assumes it himself."[12] There are two corollary notions to this assumption: submission to authority in no way detracts from an individual's dignity — indeed, it is enjoined by the Qur'ān (IV: 59) — nor is the free exercise of authority considered presumptuous; for "not to make use of authority is interpreted as weakness."[13]

The principle of structuring society according to sex roles is enshrined in the Qur'ān and runs through the entire fabric of Pakistani-Muslim society. It is of course unchanging and as such serves as the true mainstay of the Islamic concept of the family.[14] Two components characterize this principle: one is the assumption of a fundamental complementarity between male and female (II: 189), the other is the assumption of ultimate superiority of men over women (IV 33ff). Male superiority means that men are characterized by assertiveness, leadership, authority, and responsibility, while women by submission, dependence, and the acceptance of domination. Complementarity, the more significant component of the sex-role principle, means that men and women have separate spheres of action and control. Men operate in the public sphere and control interaction with the outside world. In operational terms, this means earning a living, building a standing in society, etc. Women operate in the private sphere and control the home. In operational terms, this means managing the house and raising children as well as managing relations with relatives.

Taking both aspects of the sex role principle together, there is an implication of team work between both sexes, but it is of a fundamentally asymmetrical quality, for it is assumed that the male, outside sphere is ultimately dominant over the female, private sphere, because ultimately the inside sphere exists with reference to – and in dependence on – the outside one. In that sense, the home sphere is seen as an extension of a man's public social identity; hence it is his wife who represents his social standing and "holds the good name and honour of her husband in the hollow of her hand."[15]

It may, as an aside, be well to consider female seclusion, practised by many in Pakistan in the light of the above: whether conceived of and practised literally, in the form of physical veiling, or by other means of enforcing social distance, female seclusion as a concept reflects the separation of spheres between men and women within a framework of male dominance; as a practice it serves to realize the separate allocation of these spheres. Thus seclusion or *purdah* is not just an isolated concept regarding physical living arrangements, but is a social structuring device and as such is a functional part of the sex-role principle of Pakistani Muslims.

Concepts of Social Interaction

Within the kinship sphere interaction is based on bonds of solidarity and mutual support. The commitment to kinsmen is a concept stated in the Qur'ān (xvii: 28) and made further explicit in the ḥadīth.[16] Indeed, kinship ties represent "given" ties that need only be called upon to be activated. The concomitant notion is that in the family one gets what one needs from relatives as a right; equally, one owes support to relatives as a duty. This constitutes an ideal that clearly goes beyond reciprocity, for it obviates debit and credit.[17]

This concept of free give-and-take within the bonds of kin solidarity becomes manifest in two types of interaction: individual to individual, and individual to family group.

Interaction from individual to individual is conceptualized according to the structuring principles outlined above and within the role models defined by seniority and sex. The ideal individual stance within the family is epitomized by devoted, selfless women — a nurturing mother, a supportive wife, a serving daughter.[18] As for interaction between the individual and the family group, the concept is to share one's bounty and good fortune by distributing it within the family. This is expressed principally in the very important ideal of hospitality, primarily through the social gesture of giving food. More generally, it is assumed that individuals capable of it will provide material support wherever it is needed within the family. Certainly, this ideal is practised on the small scale at the everyday level of sharing food or any other bounty within the family group.

In sum, interaction within the family is conceived of both in terms of realizing the structural relationships, that is, seniors versus juniors and males versus females, and in terms of transcending the established norms of reciprocity that are implied within those relationships, that is, giving without expecting a return, and taking without fear of obligation.

A last point needs to be made for the purpose of setting the family into the perspective of the individual Pakistani, since it is at the level of the individual that this concept becomes a tool for community building in Canada. Here, an obvious distinction exists between men and women. For the individual woman, the family sphere is primary and the concepts governing that sphere constitute the rules according to which she orients herself — although she, of course, also has dealings with the outside world, but those are considered to be secondary. For the individual man, on the other side, dealing with the outside world is essential. There he is expected to operate within a stratified social structure, validating his status and maximizing his opportunities mainly by means of a "credit system" of reciprocity.[19] Ideally, this requires constantly controlled behavior, self-presentation, assertion, and role-playing. It is in contrast to this that the family sphere allows the individual to be "himself," for there his self-definition is given, he receives acceptance and need not assert and control himself. In a very real way, the family concept is at the base of an individual's sense of identity and strength.

Having now outlined the conceptual framework that governs the family sphere for Pakistani Canadians, a last point needs to be emphasized regarding the relationship between concepts and the actual social practice of Pakistani Muslims. Whereas in fundamental respects Pakistani society reflects these concepts and Pakistani Muslims see them reinforced by social practice to an extent, they are nevertheless ideals, a set of guidelines rather than inflexible custom. It is precisely in their capacity as guidelines, reinforced by the explicit ideology of Islam, that this conceptual framework acquires its significance as a tool to be applied to the immigrant situation.

How do Pakistani Canadians Apply the Conceptual Framework in the Canadian Situation?

The issue central to this question is that of portability: how is the conceptual framework transferable into a totally different socioeconomic and cultural context? The ideological portability of this framework has already been established. Of equal, if not greater practical relevance is the structural portability which is built into the concept of a personal family sphere, set in clear opposition to the domain of public interaction represented by the larger society. The entire framework is thus transferable from one society to another, since a new country simply means a change of outside sphere.

Managing the new outside sphere has not required major conceptual adjustments for the Pakistani Canadian for he has the advantage of training and language institutions modelled by British colonial rule. However, the new inside or family sphere is far from intact in the new country; after all, the immigrant usually has at most the nuclear family around him. For a man this means he can practise the standard interaction pattern vis-à-vis the outside world, but finds the family support structure missing. For a woman, her entire home sphere is severely truncated. What is needed, for both, is to create a group that can take the place of the missing extended family, so that the family sphere can be put into operation. It is on this basis that ultimately a community emerges, but the primary concern is to establish a network of personal social interaction. Impersonal community identification as such appears to be of secondary importance.

Applying Concepts of Social Groupings

The first, crucial concern, then, is a search for group members to substitute for "missing" relatives. The basic criterion of selection is that of shared assumptions. Pakistani Canadians can draw on two aspects of identity held in common with other immigrants: one is religious, the other geographic-cultural. Thus they can activate the common bonds of language and culture with Canadians of South Asian origin, or those of religious background with other Muslim Canadians. The goal is, of course, to narrow down the association to those who share the same religion as well as the same language and regional background. The process of reaching this goal has generally been gradual for Pakistani Canadians, since increased immigration allowing a greater choice of association is a very recent development, and one which has generally been confined to the largest cities.

The actual process is likely to begin with a scrutiny of the telephone directory for familiar names, Muslim names, but also names suggesting non-Muslim East Indians/South Asians, particularly those belonging to the same linguistic region. In this way, an individual Pakistani Canadian may have found his first friend based on a common Muslim or Indian identity. Initial bonds of socializing would develop with any available Muslim families, especially those of Arab origin who already had established communities in Canada earlier. Likewise, non-Muslim Indians would likely form part of such an incipient personal network, simply because of their far greater percentage among immigrants from South Asia. Once large-scale immigration was bringing greater numbers of Muslims from the subcontinent, this initial network would gradually be expanded and eventually replaced by relationships based on more immediate common ties. With more people to choose from, such ties have quite naturally been further refined into a closer and intensified association with fellow Pakistani Canadians, who often share the same regional origin in the subcontinent. While the concrete process may vary considerably the point being made here is simply that any perceived bond of common association or of shared assumptions is put to use as a criterion for membership in the new "family" group being established in Canada.

There is, however, yet another factor which begins to operate at this point. The very presence of a larger "pool" of potential group members sharing the same socio-cultural and religious origin allows for a further process of selection. This process is initiated and carried out, quite naturally, in accordance with the concept of a stratified élite society. There is no doubt that the factor of social status has come to play an increasing role in the formation of social ties among Pakistani Canadians, serving both as a selecting criterion and as a structuring device. Initially, status tends to be assessed in terms of Pakistani social norms, which form part of every Pakistani Canadian's larger conceptual framework. However, there is also the Canadian component of status comprised of the material and social standing a Pakistani immigrant has in Canada. Where the two are mutually reinforcing, the validity of the status concept itself is reinforced as well. However, that is not always the case, and indeed, status ambiguities are a major cause of group instability within Pakistani-Canadian "family" groups. But this becomes an aspect of group structuring and as such will be considered further below.

Applying Concepts of Social Structuring

The first point to be made is that the application of social structuring is general rather than specific, that is, little need is seen to emulate the pattern of particular kin relationships. Thus the two principles of social structuring are applied in an overall flexible sense. Across generations, seniority is self-evident and considered as "given"; this principle is therefore applied as a matter of course. It is within the same generation that the seniority principle is difficult to apply, since absolute age differences between first-generation immigrants are generally not major enough to establish who is senior to whom. Also, there is a general reluctance to grant others in the same generation seniority and what is implied in it in terms of deference. Yet, the natural tendency for Pakistani Canadians is to structure their personal circle around an axis of seniority. As a result, attributes other than physical age are sought as additional or substitute criteria for seniority ranking. These are principally criteria representing patronage ability such as socio-economic standing as well as such recognized status attributes as family background, education, or occupation.

An example of the seniority principle operating on this basis would be the relationship between two nuclear families of similar ages, but with one man of a distinctly higher professional status. The two families develop a senior-junior tie; the senior's wife becomes like an elder sister, etc. There is, however, a serious complicating factor: the status of new immigrants is often in flux, there is upward mobility, and seniority attributes brought from the home country may be superseded by status acquired – or lost – in Canada. Thus status assertion within the community, inasmuch it affects the seniority structure of the group, does contribute an element of structural instability that has to be dealt with at the interactional level.

The sex-role structure introduces stability because criteria for sex identity are both biologically given and socially very clearly defined. Within the Pakistani-Canadian family, husband and wife each continue to accept their traditional role models and strive to realize the complementary relationship so strongly sanctioned by religious teaching. Thus, both operate on the assumption – as they did in Pakistan or India – that the husband leads and provides, controlling relations with the outside sphere, whereas the wife follows, supports and nurtures, managing the inside sphere and accepting his ultimate dominance in return for protection and rewards – which traditionally take the form of personal adornments (clothes, jewelry) or an extended visit with her natal family.

The Canadian situation, while hardly imposing on the male sex role, does affect the implementation of the female role model in several ways, most of all as regards the establishment and maintenance of the "inside" family sphere. Traditionally, this sphere is established and maintained through the support of related women, in fact it thus forms part of a network of such spheres. However, the position of most Pakistani-Canadian women as wives of nuclear families is characterized by considerable initial isolation from other women, since kin-related women are absent. Furthermore, the strong patrilineal bias causes women to identify themselves socially through their husbands even once a social network with other Pakistani Canadians is established, so that contact with other wives continues to be defined – and limited – by the relationship between the husbands.

If she stays at home, the Pakistani-Canadian woman suffers isolation; if, as is often the case, she works outside the home to increase the income or escape isolation, lack of time and energy make her home role difficult to fulfil. Yet, many Pakistani-Canadian women do study or work, while also running a family in accordance with traditional expectations, including time-consuming cooking and hospitality. Such a *tour-de-force* is based on ingenuity and hard work as much as on strong traditional values, which a good many women maintain in the concrete form of religious observances such as prayer.

It is significant to note that the outside contact engendered by a job does not normally affect the traditional female role; by mutual agreement is it simply bracketed, so that the Pakistani-Canadian woman generally continues to limit herself to only indirect input – through her husband – as to the family's dealings with the outside sphere. An exception are matters concerning the children's upbringing.

Obviously, there is a need for Pakistani-Canadian women to have close ties with other women for mutual support. Once family-type relationships are established, this is achieved more easily than closeness between men, mainly because no question of direct status arises between women. Social status between families is reckoned through men, and thus even where women themselves are highly educated or have well-paying jobs, these "outside assets" are quite easily disregarded in interaction between women.

As for interaction between non-related men and women, it is generally confined to minimal contact, except where a large age difference creates a natural distance. Men mediate their wives' relationships with other men.

Applying Concepts of Social Interaction

Obviously, a basic sense of kinship obligation cannot be assumed within what amounts to a non-related group of Pakistani Canadians. Uncertainty about basic relationships results in a limited sense of what the duties and rights between members are. Where the relationships are clearly structured on seniority lines, especially between children and adults, traditional interaction patterns are of course easier to follow. In addition, in extreme circumstances such as illness or death when the uncertainty regarding social relationships is temporarily superseded by the certainty of the human condition; then group members always extend a supportive hand unasked and regardless of particular relations, much as they would within their own families at home.

In interaction between individuals, free giving and taking is limited along given axes of seniority and sex roles. Most of all, children can be made the recipients of free giving, since as juniors they may accept freely, even though their parents may not, feeling obligated to return.

As for interaction from individual to group, the generalized sharing of bounty is such a basic concept that it is indeed practised in Canada; it is furthermore also a religious requirement for Muslims. Such sharing requires a group, and it is therefore one of the means of activating group ties. Hospitality is its principal form, most of all through formal dinners, celebrating birthdays – a child's birthday party always includes a dinner party for the adults – anniversaries, or moving to a new house. Of great importance are religious festivals and commemorations such as Eid or *Muharram*. Casual bounty is shared more informally, for example, by asking the "family" over to eat homemade mango ice cream, to listen to special records from home, or to watch an Indian film on video-cassette rented for the weekend – always together with a sumptuous dinner. What should be noted especially is that occasions such as birthdays or anniversaries are not formally announced to the guests so that an implied request for a gift does not cancel out the sharing act.

In summing up the general method of realizing the family interaction concept, it may be said that a firm basis of solidarity to govern informal, everyday life is absent in the recreated family sphere, precisely because it recreates relationships whose basis of seniority and status is at times tenuous. Importance is therefore given to formalized interaction in ceremonial or celebrational contexts, which leave no room to compete for improved positions of seniority or status. Such formal occasions provide a structured situation for acting out the family model very freely, yet leaving the individual participant's autonomy intact. Religion provides an important framework for such interaction, through its shared ideals and forms. This is manifested in the practice of religious festivals, but also in the marking of personal life events, from a childs *aquiqa* and *bismilla* (shaving the head of a baby and introducing a child to Islamic teaching respectively) to a parent's death anniversary. Such events, also including the inauguration of a new home, are often provided a religious reference as well, usually in the form of *Qur'ān-khwani*, a reading of the Qur'ān, thus social and religious concepts are applied in a mutually reinforcing way.

Implications

This chapter has so far identified the building blocks for the making of the Pakistani community in Canada. It has also demonstrated that the principles of operation, both as to structure and dynamic, are workable in the Canadian context. The level at which this process has so far been demonstrable is that of the individual and individual nuclear families, resulting in the establishment of a personal sphere of interaction which first and foremost serves to satisfy personal needs. Thus Pakistani Canadians have succeeded in putting into realization their "family model" with the result that the individual and the nuclear family receive a support structure.

This process constitutes the initial stage of community-making practically from scratch – it is not a process of reconstitution or adaptation of a community that was already in existence. Given this fact, what has been built so far can only represent a first stage. This first stage satisfied the individual's need for community so long as he was otherwise adrift in an alien society. It has been superseded by the reality of larger numbers of Pakistanis, with whom there exists an identification of ethnicity and religion, but not of the personal sphere.

Can the conceptual framework, which has worked in the initial stages of community making, also serve equally effectively in the context of expanded numbers of Pakistani Canadians? Can the "family model," which has enabled Pakistani Canadians to reconstitute the family sphere, be extended to the entire ethnic and religious group? The fact is that the family model evolved as part of a social universe of two spheres – apnā and ghair – a conceptual division of inside and outside which could be applied successfully in Canada during the inital period of community formation when numbers were small and the outside sphere could clearly be identified with non-Pakistani, non-Muslim Canada. This harmony of a dual social universe now has been disturbed by the emergence of a third sphere, that of the Pakistani ethnic community at large which is "outside" as far as the family sphere is concerned but "inside" vis-à-vis Canadian society at large.

Because of the commonality that exists beyond the personal sphere between all Pakistanis, this third sphere does constitute an integral part of the Pakistani-Canadian identity. Attempts to apply the family model at a larger level of inclusiveness, mainly through community organizations, bring into focus the difficulties of extending a personal model into what amounts to an impersonal sphere. Indeed, Pakistani Canadians themselves are often frustrated by the problems they face in attempting to generate and maintain such formal community associations, as much as they consider them necessary tools to integrate their community vis-à-vis the non-Pakistani, non-Muslim outside sphere.

However, there appears to be a growing awareness among some Pakistani Canadians of the limitations inherent in the attempts to extend the "family model." Some new approaches are being explored, significantly in the area of socializing the younger generation, and significantly with reference to Islam. But it is yet too early to evaluate the efficacy of such social innovation and the role Islam will play in it as an ideological base. What can be said, on the basis of this study, is that Islam does occupy a place of great significance in the process of community-building. This is so because Islam is so very much integral to the traditional conceptual framework of Pakistani Canadians, and indeed of all Muslims. As such Islam serves to reinforce and reify that framework and the sense of identification with those participating in its actualization. Since Islam is a highly developed and formalized belief system, and it is also highly portable, it has always offered – and continues to offer – a solid foundation for social organization and continuity of identification for Muslims wherever they are. Thus, in situations where departures from traditional socio-cultural bases are unavoidable, Islam will continue to play the vital role of providing legitimization to such departures, linking them to traditional meaning.

Notes

1. Muslims from Bangladesh as well as communally organized sectarian groups like the Ismailis (cf. chapter in this volume by Nanji) are excluded from consideration here, because they are culturally and linguistically different to a considerable extent.

2. Abul Hasan Ali Nadvi, *The Musalman: Social Life, Beliefs and Customs of the Indian Muslims* (Lucknow: Academy of Islamic Research and Publications, 1972), p. 41.

3. Ibid.

4. Ibid., p. 42.

5. Reuben Levy, *The Social Structure of Islam,* 2nd ed. (Cambridge: Cambridge University Press, 1962), ch. 2.

6. Abdullah Allahdin, *Extracts from the Holy Qur'ān and Authentic Traditions of the Holy Prophet Muhammad,* 11th ed. (Secunderabad, India: n.d.), pp. 158ff.

7. Robert Murphy and L. Kasdan, "The Structure of Parallel Cousin Marriage," *American Anthropologist* 61(1959): 17–29.

8. Ibid.

9. Allahdin, *Extracts,* p. 160.

10. Nadvi, *The Musalman,* p. 18.

11. Donald Wilber, *Pakistan, Its People, Its Society, Its Culture* (New Haven: HRAF Press, 1964), pp. 153ff.; Ishtiaq Husain Qureshi, *The Pakistani Way of Life* (London: Heinemann, 1956), pp. 117ff.

12. Wilber, *Pakistan,* p. 122.

13. Ibid.

14. Ali Musa Raza Mujahir, *Islam in Practical Life* (Lahore: Sheikh Muhammad Ashraf, 1968), pp. 128ff.; Wilber, *Pakistan,* pp. 153ff.

15. Nadvi, *The Musalman,* p. 52.

16. B.A.B. Wakf, *Islam, An Introduction* (Karachi: n.d.), p. 28; Allahdin, *Extracts,* pp. 158ff.

17. A manifestation of the principle of the "free gift" as espoused by Mauss (1967).

18. Mujahir, *Islam,* p. 99.

19. Zekye Eglar, *A Punjabi Village in Pakistan* (New York: Columbia University Press, 1961).

The Nizari Ismaili Muslim Community in North America: Background and Development

Azim Nanji

North American society has increasingly become the subject of detailed study by those interested in examining its various ethnic and religious minority groups. As yet, very little significant research in the humanities has been focused on immigrant Muslim minorities attempting to develop and maintain their religious values and identity in a secular North American environment. This chapter studies the development of the Nizari Ismaili Muslims in North America and the ways in which they are seeking to cultivate a community defined by their religious heritage.

The Shiʿa-Ismaili Legacy

Though at present the Nizari Ismailis constitute a small minority within the wider umma of Islam, they have played a significant role at various points in Muslim history and made an important contribution to its intellectual and cultural life. After the death of the Prophet Muḥammad in 632 C.E.,* the Muslim umma evolved a variety of groupings exemplifying different understandings of the

---

* Christian Era

primal message of Islam, and of how this message, based on the Qurʾān and the example of the Prophet, could best be fulfilled or realized in the practical life and organization of the umma. The Ismailis are one such group. Their roots go back to the foundational period of Islam, when, after the death of the Prophet, a group of Muslims gave loyalty to the Prophet's cousin and son-in-law, Ali. They believed that before his death, the Prophet had specifically designated Ali as his successor. This group of Muslims, generally referred to as Shīʿa, also believed that the succession was to continue in the Prophet's family, through the offspring of Ali and his wife Fatima, the daughter of the Prophet. The function of the imām (as the successors came to be called) was to ensure that the Qurʾānic message was preserved and interpreted to the followers in accordance with changing times and circumstances. The imām, according to Shiʿite belief, was endowed by God with a special knowledge and capacity to enable him to carry out these tasks. In addition, the imām, while caring for the spiritual well-being of the community, was also to be continuously concerned with its safety and material progress. The Shīʿa developed the practice of *taqiya* or pious dissimulation to guard against persecution.

In the course of Shīʿa history a number of splits took place over the issue of succession to the position of imām. After the death of Imam Jafar al-Sadiq in 765 C.E., a body of followers gave allegiance to his son Ismail and came to be called Ismailis; those who accepted a younger son as heir are known as Ithna Ashari and today form the largest group of the Shīʿa. The Ismailis themselves later split into two further groups, the Mustali Ismailis and the Nizari Ismailis. This chapter discusses the Nizari Ismailis, who at present give allegiance to H.H. Aga Khan IV, Shah Karim, the 49th imām, whom they believe to be the successor and direct descendant of the Prophet and Ali. There are Ithna Ashari Shīʿa and Mustali Ismaili communities in North America as well, but their history and development is beyond the scope of this chapter. However, to avoid a cumbersome repetition of the term "Nizari Ismaili" in what follows, I have merely used Ismaili, trusting to the reader to bear in mind that it is the Nizari Ismaili who are under discussion.

With this background in mind, we can now study the specific Ismaili experience in North America. Because they are still in a state of transition and development, this chapter is only a preliminary study of what promises to be a fascinating and complex field of inquiry.

The preliminary field work for the study was done in 1975 and 1976 during my tenure as Killam Fellow at Dalhousie University. Since then I have had occasion to do additional work during the summer of 1978. I am grateful to the various officers in the U.S. and Canada of the National and Regional Councils and the Associations for their co-operation and for making available data on the community's history and development.

The Home Country Experience

The 1972 expulsion of Asians from Uganda, which included a large number of Ismailis, and the subsequent settlement of about 6,000 of the refugees in Canada and the U.S., drew the first large-scale attention to the presence of an Ismaili community in North America. However, immigration had started some time before that. The present community consists of immigrants from many parts of the world. The largest number is from the East African countries of Tanzania, Uganda, Kenya, the Malagasy Republic, and Mozambique. Others have come from Zaire (formerly part of Belgian Congo), Pakistan, India, Bangladesh, Burma, Central Asia, and more recently from other already established centres in the West, such as Great Britain. The majority of all Ismailis in North America trace their origins back to those parts of the Indian subcontinent, primarily Sind, Punjab, Gujarat, and Cutch, where their ancestors were converted to Islam and Ismailism from the 12th century onward. It is this stock of Indo-Muslim Ismailis that migrated to the East African coast in growing numbers during the 19th and early part of the 20th centuries. Since it would be helpful in understanding the present community in North America to grasp something of the essential home-experience of these migrants, I have chosen to dwell on the East African experience as a case study of the background and traditions these migrants brought with them.

The earliest Indian Ismaili immigrants to East Africa were attracted by the prospect of a better material life and the opportunity to participate in the opening up of the East African hinterland. They were primarily traders and entrepreneurs who also sought to escape the restricted economic conditions in parts of British India in the late 19th century. The imām of the time, Hasan Ali Shah, Aga Khan I (d. 1881), had moved his seat from Iran to British India in 1843 in the face of adverse political conditions in Iran. The imām also induced his followers living in economically disadvantaged parts of British India to emigrate. Thus by the end of the 19th century, there were at least a thousand Ismaili families in Zanzibar alone. Successive migrants helped the community grow, and when most of them moved into the interior, they helped greatly in opening up the hinterland to trade and greater contact with the coast and the Indian Ocean. At its height in the 1960s the community in East Africa numbered over 50,000.

Perhaps the most remarkable feature of Ismaili history in East Africa was the total transformation of its material and social life effected by Aga Khan II, Sultan Muhammad Shah, who was imām from 1885 to 1957, at three complementary levels.

In cultural and social life, the imām's policy de-emphasized the Indian social and cultural habits of the immigrants. He explained, "They [the Ismailis] arrived there with Asiatic habits and Asiatic patterns of existence, but they encountered a society in process of development which is, if anything, Euro-African. To have retained an Asiatic outlook in matters of language, habit, and clothing would have been for them a complication and in society an archaic dead weight for the Africa of the future."[1]

In educational and economic life, the commercial and entrepreneurial talents of the immigrants were harnessed to create communal institutions that would provide many Ismailis with the opportunity for modern education, housing, and material and economic sufficiency, if not wealth.

In religious life, the imām's guidance was focused on strengthening the centre of spiritual life among the Ismailis, the jamat khana, literally "house of assembly," which served as a place both for prayer and worship and for congregational activities related to all aspects of Ismaili life. Owing to persecution and other adverse conditions in the Indian subcontinent over a large period of their history, the Indian Ismailis had adopted elements of traditional Indian culture and practices from the communities in which they found themselves. The imām was able gradually to eliminate such traits and to bring community practice and custom into conformity with that of other Muslims in East Africa, thus creating a unified framework of practice and observance in the jamat khana. The Ismailis, however, maintained the exclusivity of their specific *tariqa* or way of practising Islamic observances. That is, at the level of religious life the community remained exclusive, but particular efforts were made to establish a common purpose with indigenous Muslim groups. The imām established and funded an East African Muslim Welfare Society in 1945 to promote educational and economic development among indigenous Muslims. The society built both mosques and schools and offered scholarships for advanced study to African Muslims.

At the time of Imām Sultan Muhammad's death in 1957 a strong corporate community, linked by several administrative structures to the imām, had been established. Ismailis received the benefits of the growing educational and economic institutions established in the community, and most centres in East Africa had at least one jamat khana. Though the majority were still traders and business people, a variety of professionals manned newly established health, educational, and economic institutions. Most Ismailis spoke the local African languages, communicated with each other in Gujarati or Sindhi, and were learning to master the administrative language of East Africa – English.

The overall process of change had not been without its problems. Particularly in its earlier phase, the imām's authority and policies had been challenged. Dissension, however, did not take root, and the community at large remained faithful to the imām and his policies.

The new imām, Karim Aga Khan IV, assumed leadership at a time when most of Africa had already entered an era of change. During the early 1960s three independent East African nations emerged – Tanzania, Kenya, and Uganda. In pre-independence East Africa both imāms guided their followers to identify their aspirations with those of the newly emerging nations and to seek to become full nationals at the time of independence. But the Ismailis, as indeed other Asian groups in East Africa, were perceived in some national circles as an economically privileged group, generally unintegrated into the mainstream of new African society. Asians found themselves in a dilemma. As civil servants, traders, and entrepreneurs under British or French rule they had acted as a middle group between the colonizer and the colonized. With independence and increasing nationalization they were called upon to revise and adapt their roles to the changing situation. A combination of fear, insecurity, and the pressures of a changed situation led a large number of these Asians to leave East Africa. At this early stage in the 1960s, however, most Ismailis stayed and applied for citizenship in the new nations. This attempt to make a constructive transition was fraught with problems, some of which the Ismailis could not control.

In summary then, the period of the 1960s marks a major shift in several spheres of Ismaili life in East Africa. Though the strong religious and spiritual base continued, there were major changes in the economic and political context to which the community had to respond. One response was to intensify the educational effort, so that younger Ismailis, through higher education, would be better prepared to meet the needs of a more competitive, modernizing national trend. A second response of the community sought to develop a broader economic base in conjuction with the new national governments by establishing Industrial Promotion Services, whose function was to assist Ismaili business men to establish industries in East Africa with government and non-government participation. These services came to be established in all three new East African countries, as well as in other areas of the world where Ismailis were involved in trade, such as Pakistan and Bangladesh.

Through the 1960s and the early part of the 1970s the Ismaili community in East Africa experienced tremendous economic growth. This was in part a reflection of the growth experienced by the countries themselves. The level of educational attainment also grew so that the Ismailis constituted the largest among Asian groups at the three East African universities by the end of the 1960s. The overall pattern of development, however, was not the same in all three countries; political and economic development gradually diverged as each sought to establish differing priorities and strategies for growth. The economic and education growth in the Ismaili community had created a greater international and global awareness within it. This in turn caused both business and professional Ismaili people to look beyond East Africa, and precipitated the first emigrations to North America, but it took a drastic political event in Uganda to move large numbers to emigrate. It might be useful here to take a general look at the major influences that motivated emigration to western countries.

The first influence was obviously political change. Some Ismailis were unable to make the psychological transition of accepting independent African rule. A small number, retaining their status as British subjects, migrated to Great Britain and eventually to North America. A second influence was the limitation of economic and professional opportunity. As greater pressure was put on non-citizens to allow "Africanization" in trade and commerce, some of those who lost their jobs or businesses left. Another small number migrated because they had developed professional competencies in areas where they were in unequal competition with local African citizens or were without opportunities to practise their professions. In Tanzania, for example, the redressing of economic and social balance through the practice of *Ujamaa* or African socialism, reduced the opportunity both for entrepreneurship and for advanced education. Thus by 1970 the combination of economic and political factors had induced a small number of Ismailis to leave East Africa for Europe and North America, but it must be emphasized that until then, a majority in the community had chosen to stay. The ambiguities and tensions of being a minority, in new nations that were seeking to modernize themselves and trying to create a unified society, still remained. In 1972 in Uganda these tensions exploded and led to the expulsion of all Asians from that country.

Later events in the country revealed this particular episode as the action of a megalomaniac and irrational dictator, but at the time Idi Amin so cleverly played upon the feelings of hostility towards the Asian population that he was hailed as a hero for his action in some African countries and elsewhere. The impact on the Asian population, including the Ismailis, citizens and non-citizens alike, was devastating. In a space of less than six months they were refugees seeking new homes in India, Pakistan, Great Britain, Europe, and North America. The international effort to find homes for the refugees was co-ordinated through the UN High Commission for Refugees. A few Ismailis went to India and Pakistan; however, a larger number sought homes in the West. Several thousand Ismailis made their homes in Canada and the United States, and joined with the several hundreds already in North America to develop what by the end of the 1970s had become a new centre of Ismaili settlement in the world.

The Ismaili Community in North America

The first Ismaili families to migrate to North America arrived in Canada in the 1950s from Pakistan. Through the fifties and the early sixties only a handful of families came here to make a permanent home for themselves. This early group consisted of professionals and their families: engineers, lawyers, doctors, and teachers who for the most part were the only ones who could find admittance as immigrants to Canada or the United States. Most lived in isolated centres, including, interestingly enough, the Queen Charlotte Islands off British Columbia. Communal life as such was unknown.

In the latter part of the sixties the number of both permanent residents and students increased, so that small groups of Ismailis emerged in cities such as Vancouver, Toronto, and Montreal. Occasionally, these families would get together to say their prayers and commemorate religious festivals among themselves, as well as with other Muslims. The families came from various countries, Pakistan, India, East Africa, the Republic of Malagasy, and South Africa. The new groups ultimately constituted a significant international Ismaili presence in North America. Their professional backgrounds and education prepared them to communicate in English or French, though they spoke differing mother languages. By 1968 the groups in Vancouver and Toronto each had organized themselves into a jamat and met once a week in either a rented hall or a residence for prayers and communal activities. Beyond this loosely structured jamat there was no other form of organization. Daily religious practice, as I was able to determine, was carried on individually or within a family; ties were maintained with Ismailis in the home countries, but by and large the groups expected to remain a fairly small, isolated community in North America. The total Ismaili population of North America probably numbered around 600 until after the Ugandan expulsion took place in 1972, when the number rose drastically. The majority were Ugandan Ismailis who had been directly accepted as immigrants into Canada and the U.S. in October 1972; others subsequently joined families or migrated from the several refugee camps in Europe that had been set up in 1972 and 1973 to house those who had been rendered "stateless" by the sitution in Uganda.

The events in Uganda also triggered migration from Tanzania. A few Tanzanian Ismailis had been among those already resident in Canada or the United States before 1972. Partly as a result of the impact of the Ugandan expulsion and partly because there was a feeling that henceforth North America was likely to become a major settlement of Ismailis, a significant number left Tanzania. A slightly lesser number also left Kenya, though the Ismaili community there did not face problems of economic shrinkage or lack of educational opportunity as in Tanzania. At about the same time, political events in Zaire and the Malagasy Republic induced the Ismailis there to leave for North America. Because most of the Ismailis in these two countries were business people functioning in French, they chose to make their homes in Quebec. By 1975 this steady influx of Ismailis, refugees and others, had swelled the community to 10,000 strong. It was increasingly necessary if this growing community was to be organized, that new institutions be developed for them. This task was accomplished between 1975 and 1978 when the present imām visited the community in Canada. During these four years, the number of Ismailis migrating to North America continued to increase. Existing centres also acted as an attraction for those from India, Pakistan, Bangladesh, and Burma who wished to leave their home countries but dreaded the prospect of being isolated from other Ismailis.

A rough estimate indicates that the current Ismaili population in North America is about 25,000, approximately 20,000 Ismailis in Canada and 5,000 in the United States. More than half those in Canada live in Ontario, Quebec, and the Maritime Provinces; metropolitan Toronto accounts for over 70 percent of these, with Montreal, Kitchener, and Ottawa as other centres. However, Ismailis are to be found in at least 45 other cities and towns across eastern Canada. In western Canada, the greater Vancouver area accounts for the largest number, with Edmonton and Calgary as other important centres. But in both eastern and western Canada some Ismailis are to be found in most major cities. In the United States, Ismailis are scattered in small groups in about 22 states from Spartanburg, South Carolina, to San Diego, California. The major centres are in the New York City area, in Greater Los Angeles, Chicago, Dallas, and Houston.

For a community still in a state of transition, it is difficult to be specific about socio-economic activity, but some general trends can be discerned. Those who came as refugees included both business and professional persons. Most business people had lost their capital and arrived with nothing to invest; many professionals found jobs hard to get at a time of economic recession; those who were unskilled or unable to speak either English or French (primarily elderly persons) were at the most serious disadvantage. For those who were not refugees, the situation was a little better. Some had capital to invest or start small businesses, others found their professional qualifications in demand and already had jobs prior to emigration. The overall economic situation of the community has improved greatly since 1972. Like most other immigrant groups with a commercial or entrepreneurial background, the Ismailis have fared well in adapting to a highly competitive business context. Some 10 to 15 percent are now engaged in business that they own solely or in partnership. The most common business ventures are general retail stores, laundry and dry-cleaning operations, import and export agencies, restaurants and catering, and increasingly, motel and hotel ownership, as well as real estate. Ismaili Business Information Centres established in Vancouver and Toronto render a professional consulting service in capital investment to Ismaili businessmen. These centres have worked with major Canadian banks to obtain financing for new business ventures. No centres have been required for the economic activity of the professionals in the medical, legal, business, and industrial fields. Moreover, some professionals who came here as teachers or civil servants have retrained themselves in more profitable fields such as computer programming and business administration. Those who came without professional or vocational qualifications are employed in unskilled or semi-skilled jobs. Overall then, a variety of economic situations exist among the first major generation of Ismailis living in North America.

It must also be noted that over half the current Ismailis are of school or university age. There is a tremendous emphasis on acquiring education and this is reflected in the number of Ismailis, male and female, currently receiving higher education. At a rough estimate approximately one thousand young Ismailis are studying in universities or colleges across Canada and the United States. The bias seems to be towards professional faculties such as Accounting, Business and Commerce, Engineering Sciences, Medical Sciences, and Nursing. There is no corresponding trend to acquire a technical education or trade skills. The Aga Khan Aid Fund for Higher Education has been an important source of financing for some of these students.

As the social characteristics of the new migrants vary with their countries of origin, it would be helpful to outline certain general characteristics here. Most African Ismailis had already been exposed to western culture and had as part of their experience adopted Euro-African modes of social life. For them the transition to North American living did not represent a major adjustment. In modes of dress, language, and to a certain extent, lifestyle, African Ismailis and in particular the younger generation were already prepared to face life in new lands. For some of the older generation the transition was not as easy. The different climate, especially in Canada, lack of familiarity with the pace of city life and its exigencies, and the transition to a more self-reliant home life (without the domestic servants available to them in Africa), created stress in the process of adjustment. The existence of a wide variety of Asian ethnic groups in North America was helpful in terms of the availability of ethnic foods and other items, since most African Ismailis had retained some of their traditional Indian or Pakistani eating habits. For Ismailis from the Indian subcontinent, the difficulties of the initial period of social transition would to a large degree be similar to those faced by other South Asian Muslims. Social adaptation is a long-term process and one must await the collection of more data over a longer period of time to be able to evaluate this process satisfactorily.

The demographic and social characteristics cited above provide the background for a study of the development of institutions within the community to reinforce specifically its religious and corporate identity. Among these institutions the two key ones, referred to in the East African case, continue in the North American context to form the focal points of community development and identity. They are the jamat khana and the administrative structure embodied in the Councils.

The Jamat Khana

All specifically religious activity in Shi'ite Ismailism is centred around the jamat khana. It serves much the same purpose as a traditional mosque among other Muslims, but in addition is also the place for religious observances specific to the Ismaili tariqa of Islam. Early in their history, the Ismaili immigrants had no jamat khana. When the local groups increased in number, informal centres were formed, as gathering places for prayer. These may loosely be termed the first jamat khana(s). As with other Muslims, it is not incumbent for Ismailis to pray in a mosque or in congregation, except on Fridays. In East Africa and elsewhere, however, the jamat khana had become a vital gathering place for daily congregational prayers in the morning and evenings. Thus for the early migrants, one important element in the reinforcement of their religious identity was missing. In time, as numbers increased in larger cities, school halls, or similar locations were rented so that at least once a week there could be a congregational prayer. When the large influx of Ismailis took place after 1972 only a small number of such jamat khana(s) existed in any organized capacity.

Since 1972 however jamat khana(s) have been established in each growing centre, so that at present most places where Ismailis are settled have at least one meeting place. In larger centres such as Vancouver and Toronto there are several jamat khana(s), as many as 10 in the case of Metropolitan Toronto, where the Ismailis number over 5,000. Most of them are open every morning and evening to allow for daily prayers. Like other Shi'a, the Ismailis combine some of the daily prayers. In most Ismaili centres in Africa and Asia these were said at three standard times – dawn, sunset, and evening, and this practice has continued in North America.

Statistics for attendance are hard to pinpoint, but on the average the congregation is larger on Fridays and weekends and on important commemorative occasions such as Eid Moulid (of the Prophet, Ali and the present imām), and on Imāmat Day, which commemorates the day of accession to the imāmat by the present imām. On some of these occasions the community may hire a hall or other larger facility and meet in one place. The jamat khana also serves as a place for those who wish to participate in very early morning *dhikr*, the practice of personal meditation which is an important part of Ismaili religious observance. This takes place usually in the hour preceding the recitation of the dawn prayer. The practice is not *fard* (obligatory), and hence only those who choose to do so visit the jamat khana at that time.

The jamat khana also acts as a focal point for social activity which may be linked to religious observance. An interesting illustration is the practice, continued since Indo-Muslim times, of bringing food items to the jamat khana. These are auctioned off and distributed among members of the congregation. The origin of this practice probably goes back to early *Sufi* organizations and their tradition of hospitality (from which, it has been suggested, the founder of Sikhism, Guru Nanak, adapted the open-kitchen system). In North America this practice serves the students and single people well since they would otherwise not have easy access to traditional food. In addition the jamat khana also serves as a centre for other rituals specific to Shīʿa Ismailism, such as payment of zakāt, *khums*, and ṣadqa. All of these are traditionally submitted to the imām in trust for the community, support of community institutions, and needy individuals. Activities in the jamat khana are co-ordinated by individuals called Mukhi and Kamadia and their female counterparts. (Among Ismailis, women and children participate as actively as men in religious practices.) These officials act as overseers of the place and maintain cleanliness, order, and decorum for the proper observance of religious practice.

So far most places that function as jamat khana(s) in North America have served as centres during the period of transition. New construction of jamat khana(s) is planned, and the first North American one to be built incorporating Islamic architectural values is scheduled for construction in Burnaby, British Columbia.

The Ismaili Councils and Associations

A major feature of organization of Ismaili communities in Africa and Asia was a system of councils created to serve the various centres and to provide an efficient means for relating the guidance and policies of the imām to the followers. This system has now been extended to North America, and an overall framework links all centres in Europe, Canada, and the United States. The breakdown of the organizations is as follows:

1. A Supreme Council for Europe, Canada, and the United States of America that provides guidance and effects general policy, under direction from the imām. The members are drawn from the three areas.
2. Three representative National Councils for Europe, Canada, and the United States, responsible specifically for the community in each area, oversee all other national organizations and make recommendations to the Supreme Council and the imām.
3. Regional Councils for eastern and western United States in New York and Los Angeles, and for eastern and western Canada in Montreal, Toronto, and Vancouver. Their jurisdiction extends to regional institutions and their work is related to the policies determined at the National Council level.
4. District Councils, in most major district centres such as Calgary, Edmonton, Winnipeg, Ottawa, Kitchener, Miami, Chicago, and Houston.

In addition to the above Councils there are other organizations such as grants councils in each of the North American countries to provide for financial assistance to the needy, students, and those refugees who are still in the process of establishing themselves.

The councils thus act as extensions of the imām's authority and function primarily to provide a means of implementing and continuing development in the material life and organization of the community. Their sphere of influence extends to social, educational, health, economic, and cultural activities. The task of preserving and cultivating the specifically religious traditions is assigned to national Ismaili associations, which function on more or less the same pattern as the traditional da'wa institution of earlier Ismaili history. In concept and organization, however, they have adapted to the newer circumstances by realigning religious curricula and teaching modes. For this purpose, the associations train honorary teachers, from among university students and others who are willing to commit time, who run classes for children and adults in the jamat khana after the daily prayers are over.

During the period of settlement, the jamat khana, the councils, and the associations have played a critical role in helping the migrants to adapt to their new lands. By providing traditional anchoring points and serving as a focus of religious and social identity, they have succeeded in retaining to a large extent the concept of a defined and well-organized religious community. In due course the North American Ismailis hope to have a formal constitution, as in other parts of the Ismaili world, to consolidate more fully the institutions that have developed.

Concluding Remarks

In summing up this preliminary survey of the background and development of Ismailis in North America, several general points need to be considered, which may help to throw some light on the Muslim experience and the immigration experience of specific ethnic or religious groups in general. In the Ismaili case, much of the experience is rooted in past history as well as present circumstances. This makes it necessary to take into account the specifically Ismaili understanding of Islam and the role played by a living imām in their material and spiritual life. Their experience in Africa and Asia represents an attempt to order the totality of life in accordance with their traditional values. The crux of the experience is the creation of a society which, while providing the best of all possible material conditions, can also act as a context in which to practise the faith. In times of crisis or political and social change, this may not always be easy and it remains to be seen if the Ismailis can successfully effect their vision in North America. There are obvious underlying tensions that have not been treated in any great detail in this chapter. Some of these have to do with whether there will be continuous acceptance of the imām's authority and guidance and of the structures created by the community. The East African experience revealed a tendency to adapt well, though often in isolation from other Muslim and Asian groups. Can the North American community play an important role in conjunction with other Muslim groups, or will it remain exclusive? Certainly if the activities of their imām in the field of Islamic Architecture and Education are any indication, then the community here can do much to contribute to the total Muslim effort.

At the level of general immigration experience in North America, the Ismailis have faced almost the same set of problems encountered by other non-white minorities in a western society. The fact that they were in some cases better prepared for the task has not prevented problems in obtaining facilities for jamat khana(s) in certain areas because of racial prejudice or, on rare occasions, acts of violence against individual members because of their race. To this extent any successful adaptation and integration into the mainstream of society will depend on various factors such as the proper implementation of multi-cultural policies in Canada or affirmative action procedures in the U.S., the attitude of major elements in the host societies towards increasing pluralization in North America, and finally the effort made by immigrant groups to contribute their specific talents and values in a North American context.

The first decade of Ismaili history in North America has certainly been eventful. The next promises to be even more so, since the present Ismailis have now established permanent roots in the two countries, adopted Canadian or American citizenship, and been visited by the imām, whose increasing contacts with civil and religious leaders and institutions in North America indicate a continuing effort to consolidate the Ismaili Muslim presence on this continent.

Note

1. Aga Khan II, Sultan Muhammad Shah, *Memoirs* (London: 1954), p. 30.

The Impact of the Islamic Revolution in Iran on the Syrian Muslims of Montreal

Yvonne Haddad

From 1976 to 1979 I was engaged in a study of Syrians in Montreal. I examined the process of development of social institutions among recent immigrants from Syria in order to assess the role and function of those institutions in the building and maintaining of an ethnic group identity.

As a charter member of three clubs – The Syrian Club, The Federation of Arab Women of Quebec, and the Federation of Arab Women of Canada – I had a special vantage point from which to observe the interaction of the members of the group. I attended numerous meetings of the several organizations as they attempted to articulate their goals and define their purposes, and was thus able to record the discussions of draft constitutions and attempts to articulate group identities. The members' observations on group interaction were cross-checked with other participants in an attempt to gain access to the motives and perceptions of the various members of the community. I had extensive conversations with Syrian Muslims in various circumstances. (For the purposes of this chapter, the word Muslim designates one who is born into a Muslim family.)

When the Iranian Revolution occurred, the social dynamics of the community as well as the existing patterns of behavior of some of the individuals changed dramatically. Most obvious was the Muslim members' loss of interest in the clubs.

First of all it must be recognized that hatred of the Shah was not restricted to Iranians; it was shared by Arabs who have long considered him a "stooge of imperialism and Zionism" in the heart of the Muslim world. Perceived as a traitor, he headed the list of those reviled for co-operation with Israeli interests in the area. MOSSAD[1] had trained SAVAK[2] forces in security techniques and means of extracting information from political prisoners, and through co-operation between the two countries Israel had received a sustained provision of oil for its armed forces.

Furthermore, the Shah over the years had come to personify "the collaborator" who for reasons of self-aggrandisement, malice, or misguidance had consistently frustrated Arab efforts at revival and ascendancy. The doctrine of Arab nationalism developed at the turn of the century had consistently attributed the fall of the Islamic Empire in the Middle Ages largely to the passing of the leadership of the Muslims to non-Arab hands (Turks and Persians). The Shah had accentuated this mistrust of Persians by emphasizing the Persian aspects of his rule (over against the Islamic), by grounding his rule in Persian history (Cyrus the Great), and celebrating the Persian year (rather than the Islamic).

The joy expressed at the passing of the Shah's regime was shared by Muslims I interviewed from 18 different countries then residing in North America. For most of them (85 percent), the most significant aspect of the revolution was that it demonstrated the ability of a people to withstand the pressures of the "greatest power in the world" and to be able to affirm its will in designing its own destiny. The Islamic nature of the revolution was seen by many as the guarantee of the search for indigenous answers to local problems. Normative definitions of what it is to be human or relevant need not have a foreign origin or stamp of approval, nor be validated by their appeal in the American context. The Iranian revolution appeared, to its supporters, to affirm that questions of identity and purpose in life can be defined by the people involved.

All Muslims questioned about their reaction to the Iranian revolution said that it enhanced their pride and provided them with a positive affirmation of identity. This was especially true of Muslims residing in North America who have encountered negative responses to their Islamic identity by the host culture. The Iranian revolution, since the taking of the hostages, has engendered a flood of information about Iran and Islam in articles, books, and on television. A substantial amount of this material is full of error, leading some Muslims to despair of the ability of North Americans to ever understand Islam. Others, however, find it hopeful that Islam is being taken seriously, and not dismissed as insignificant, irrelevant, and obsolete. Several Muslim leaders in North America have expressed satisfaction to the author that Islam is getting free exposure, its teachings are reaching homes, factories, businesses, and schools without the expense of an extensive missionary effort.

That the American press has sometimes been hostile or derogatory in its attitude toward Islamic peoples has had the effect of reaffirming Muslim identity in some otherwise lukewarm Muslims. An official of the Muslim Student Association in a meeting with the National Council of Churches in Detroit in 1979 cited tolerance as a major enemy of Islam in the United States. It has led students from Muslim countries to neglect their faith and opt for a secular lifestyle, assuring them integration into the mainstream of American life. The Association leadership hopes that prejudiced reports about Islam will unmask the intrinsic evil of Western culture and restore the students to their Muslim heritage by casting it in the light of a superior identity that God has willed for humanity. This, however, does not in any way mean that Muslim leaders seek these negative depictions of Islam; rather, they attempt to capitalize on them hoping that they will confirm their perception of North American culture as corrupt, racist, and pornographic, and elevate Islam to a superior status by contrast.

Meanwhile, more and more Muslims in North America take the view that the hostile attitude of the press toward Islam is engendered by Zionist interests intent on the elimination of any gains Arab or Muslim causes may elicit among North Americans. The majority of those interviewed believed that the hostage situation in Iran was deliberately exacerbated by President Carter for his own political gains. All of his statements on the subject were dismissed as "grandstanding" aimed at increasing his ratings in the polls. Not one Muslim interviewed believed that President Carter's stance came from his concern for the hostages. The majority believed that his main concern was oil and the control of a strategic area of the world.

To committed Muslims in North America, the victory of the Muslim forces in Iran had a special significance. They believed it fulfilled the Qur'ānic promise that God will give the victory to the believers if they unite and strive to bring about an Islamic order in the world. It appeared to vindicate the 20th century Muslim revivalist belief that Muslim reverses in the world in the face of colonial powers were not due to the inadequacy of Islam for modern life or the inferiority of Islam vis-à-vis Christianity or Judaism, but were the result of a slackening of the zeal for the faith and the appropriation of alien values. Thus, the Muslim revolution in Iran was perceived as a moral drama: the mightiest army in the world could not protect the oppressor from the justice of God. That a people willing to be martyred in the name of God were able to stop the tanks, missiles, and jets that the Shah assembled was seen as evidence of God's power over the forces of the world and the fulfilment of the Qur'ānic promise that God will give the victory to the believers if they but take Him seriously in His promise.

It is obvious that Syrian Muslims in Montreal welcomed the fall of the Shah because they viewed him as a friend of Israel and an enemy of the "Arab cause." The victory of the Islamic revolution was also perceived to enhance their pride and dignity. A close look at the community shows that it was deeply affected in the way its members perceive themselves and their future, an impact intensified by the nature of the group.

The Syrian Muslim community is a tiny minority that numbers about 150 people. Most of them are recent immigrants who arrived in the sixties and seventies from the larger urban areas of Syria, including Damascus, Aleppo, and Latakia, in search of a better life. A few are political refugees who had belonged to national parties in Syria prior to the socialist takeover, while several come from the land-owning class that was dispossessed by the Baath regime. Some of the males came to Canada to study, others to evade the draft. The majority come from the middle and upper middle classes of that country. Their educational standards are above average for both Canada and their home country. A substantial number are professionals or self-employed.

Efforts to locate second- and third-generation Syrian Muslims in Montreal led to the discovery that only three had come at the turn of the century. Because they were so few in number they attempted to integrate with Christians from Arab countries. One, a Druze, was a member of the Antiochian Orthodox Church for a while, but joined the mosque in Montreal when it was organized. He contributed to the construction of mosques throughout Canada and became a noted figure in the Arab community of Montreal. Another early immigrant has held tenaciously to the faith as an identity. Although he and his family do not appear to be practising Muslims, he has raised a closely knit family·and has instilled in his daughters the necessity to marry within the Muslim faith. The third immigrant has remained a Muslim, but his two daughters are married to French Canadians. These precedents are a source of consternation to the more recently arrived immigrants who are anxious to avoid the experience of the earlier settlers.

The recent immigrants reported that they experienced a feeling of joy upon arrival in the new land at having achieved a dream that is the envy of many left behind. This was accompanied, however, by a certain bewilderment at being in an alien culture. Initially they sought other Arabs for companionship and guidance, and in no time a network of relationships was developed as they attempted to integrate within the group. The ability to be discriminating in the choice of friends became contingent on the availability of a pool of immigrants from which to choose. Several factors appear to be operative in the selection of friends and the determination of one's circle of social interaction.

The closest associations are reserved for immediate relatives and members of one's family. This is followed by associations with those who come from the same region in Syria, especially those who were previous acquaintances and friends. The rest of the friendship network appears to be regulated by a definition of class and status. (It is not unusual for people to ask, "Whom do you associate with socially?") The definition seems to be determined by level of education, type of employment, and assessment of wealth, as well as the status of the family in the home country.

As a minority group in Canada the Syrian Muslims of Montreal have three foci of identity. They are Syrian, and as such constitute a fraction of the immigrants from that country, most of whom are Christian (about 4,000). As Arabs, they are a small group among other Arabs in the Montreal area, including an estimated 60,000 Lebanese and 40,000 Egyptians. Finally, as Muslims they are a tiny minority among the 15,000 Muslims in the city, most of whom are of Pakistani background.

It became quite clear in the course of this study (1976–80) that the community is attempting to define its identity and its priorities. Most of the members talked about the search for stability and a focus in life. They appeared to be experimenting with a variety of life-styles, seeking an integrating factor that would provide a feeling of well-being.

The majority have been indoctrinated in the precepts of Arab nationalism. Their original hope was to join the social and cultural activities of the other Arab communities in Montreal and foster a homogeneous Arab identity that transcends regionalism, factionalism, and religious differences. They were frustrated in these efforts by the earlier established immigrants, mostly Lebanese, who had based their institutions on ideas of Lebanese identity. They were also rejected by the Egyptian immigrants, predominantly of Coptic Christian background, whose social activities centred around the Nile Club. The exclusive nature of the two groups and their allegiance to regional identities led the Syrians to refer to them in derogatory terms as the "Phoenicians and the Pharaonics."[3]

The allegiance of all immigrants from Syria (both Christian and Muslim) to the ideas of Arab nationalism and the search for stable institutions led to the formation of the Arab Club. This club aimed at fostering and maintaining an Arab identity among the members, combatting prejudicial literature about Arabs in the Canadian press, providing assistance to new immigrants from Arab countries, and providing a framework for social interaction among the members.

The club foundered because of the struggle for leadership among the various members. "Everyone wanted to be boss" is the way one veteran of the club's internecine fights put it. Other factors aggravated the regional incompatibilities. The club had a large number of students at the various campuses in Montreal. The presence of the students lent a transient character to the club because of the high rate of attrition as members returned home after the completion of their education. The Syrian immigrants, as settlers, were anxious to develop stable social relationships and institutions for their families. There was some concern among parents of teenage daughters about the preponderance of young men at the club; there was also some apprehension over the militant nature of some of the students, which led to the fear that their activities might jeopardize the status of the immigrants who now have a stake in their new country.

By 1977 the Syrians began to think of forming their own institutions. They started the Syrian Club, organized by Christians and Muslims in the hope of maintaining the identity of Arab nationalism as well as the ideals and values that make life worthwhile. Two other clubs started at this time by the Syrians were the Federation of Arab Women of Quebec and the Federation of Arab Women of Canada. All these institutions appealed to the middle-class immigrants from the various Arab countries. They emphasized the social dimension, holding parties and gatherings, and they all felt the need for a centre for recreation as well as for affirmation of inherited value systems. All the clubs were aware of the discrimination against Arabs in the press and textbooks of Canada; they hoped that their united efforts could lead to a better understanding between Arabs and Canadians.

The constitutions of these clubs show a great concern on the part of the parents to have their children remain knowledgeable about the Arab world. They hoped to teach language and history lessons to the second- and third- generation members of the group as well as to interested Canadians. Besides the educational and social concerns, the constitutions show political awareness. The rights of the Palestinians to their homeland were supported by the group.

The constitution developed for the Syrian Club stressed the Arab character of the group, while restricting membership to a maximum of 40 percent of persons from non-Syrian background. This reflected the fear that should the club recruit members from other countries they might dominate the club and wrest the leadership from the Syrians.

The majority of Syrian immigrants are of Christian background. Their primary identity has been fashioned by Arab nationalism; however, their most important institutions have continued to be the ethnic churches which they appear to have successfully imported and established in the Canadian environment.[4] These churches have been the main socializing institutions for the group for several centuries. They not only have preserved an ethnic language, but have also fostered a different identity vis-à-vis other churches through education, the dissemination of denominational literature, and the control of the lives of their members through the implementation of church law in the areas of personal status. A survey by the author among Christians shows a marked decrease in church attendance in Canada as compared to Syria. This was attributed by those questioned to the need of corporate reassurance and mutual support necessitated by the minority status of the group in Syria. The "Christian" character of Quebec and the availability of other social institutions decreased the importance of church attendance in the life of the immigrant Christians.

For the Muslims, the mosque in Syria had not functioned in a similar manner. Many had not attended mosque services regularly in their country of origin, nor had they been diligent in maintaining the rituals of Islam. Few had practised the ṣalāt on a regular basis or had tithed the proper amount. As members of the majority in Syria, Arab Muslims had found Arab identity and Islamic identity interchangeable and had not thought carefully about the distinction.

In the Canadian milieu the question of identity becomes a focus of attention. The immigrant is constantly queried about his country of origin. The Canadian's ignorance about Syria necessitates a refinement of definition in which Syrians are differentiated from other Arabs, Christians distinguished from Muslims, and, since the Iranian revolution, the differences between Sunni and Shiʿa Islam clarified. Furthermore, the Canadian environment provides a testing ground for ideologies held dear in the home country. For many, the emotional commitment to Arab nationalism slowly disappears before Maronite ridicule and the awareness that despite the shared history, language, customs, and culture, other Arabs are different and difficult to co-operate with.

Another ideology that is strained by the test of reality is the commitment to pan-Islamism which assures the believer that Islam is one and does not discriminate among members of the umma. It affirms that all Muslims are equal regardless of race, color, or national origin. The only discrimination among people is their measure of piety. However, the different ethnic backgrounds and languages of Muslim immigrants in the Quebec Islamic Center have raised questions for some about the practicality of the ideology.

The situation in Syria today has a strong impact on many Syrian Muslims in Montreal. Because of the war economy due to the intervention in Lebanon, Syria appears to be thriving. Several members reported after a visit to the homeland that their friends have become millionaires. The availability of jobs in the Gulf area, the affluence of those left behind, and the inflation and recession in the Canadian economy have caused them to question their decision to emigrate. The Arab world, not Canada, appears to have become the land of opportunity. The sacrifice in separation from family and friends, the agony of compromise in the pursuit of adjustment, and integration in the Canadian environment have become painful. The members of the community constantly discuss the feasibility of returning, and some of them even maintain homes in Syria for such an eventuality.

Some members of the Syrian Muslim community in Montreal were among the charter members of the Quebec Islamic Center. They organized social gatherings which included community meals and folk dances. The women also participated in fund raising activities for the mosque. In recent years, members of the Jamaati Tableegh (a conservative missionary movement started in India) have taken control of the mosque. They put an end to social meetings and kept women from participating in cooking meals for community affairs. Some of them took up residence in the mosque, forcing the more liberal members to go to another mosque (the Fatima Mosque). A substantial number ceased to go the mosque until the victory of the Iranian revolution, which reversed the trend of non-attendance.

Other ethnic differences among Muslims surface over trivial matters. Some Pakistanis, for example, have insisted that during prayer men should roll up their trousers and others think it necessary for them to cover their heads. Neither custom is practised in Syria. Thus Syrians are accused of being negligent in their practice of Islam. On the other hand, the Syrians consider the Pakistanis too rigid, with a tendency to adhere to regional customs and confuse them with prerequisites for proper Muslim practice. Furthermore, for several years the Pakistanis did not allow Arab Muslims to make political statements in the mosque. Several years ago an Arab was carried away by several Pakistanis as he was making a speech supporting Nasser against Israel.

In 1978 politics became part of the Islamic message. This was due to several factors, including the assumption of the position of secretary to the Council of Muslim Communities in Canada by a Palestinian and the support of the Muslim World League for all Muslim causes throughout the world. The Lebanese civil war has had a great impact on the consciousness of group identity of Syrian Muslims in Montreal. Several incidents were reported in which Lebanese Canadians villified the Syrians at parties and public functions. These incidents, combined with the situation in the Arab world, have led to doubt concerning the practicality and efficacy of the ideology of Arab nationalism. Syrian Muslims now seriously question the loyalty of Arab Christians to Arab causes. For example, they ask: Can Muslims trust Christian fellow countrymen in the future, given the collusion of the Maronites with the Israelis in Lebanon?

Most specifically, however, politics has become part of the Islamic message as a result of the Iranian revolution. As it became quite evident in the closing months of 1978 that the revolution in Iran was gaining the support of the masses and that its leadership was able to muster the co-operation of the merchant class and other sectors of the Iranian population, the Syrian Muslims of Montreal displayed a heightened interest in the events as they unfolded in the streets of Tehran. This interest manifested itself in an obvious change in their lifestyle, some of it conscious and deliberate, engaged in for the purpose of bringing about change in the conditions in Syria.

There was a heightened sense of an impending revival of Islam in the world that demanded the attention of every Muslim. That the revolution in Iran began to succeed under the umbrella of Islam gave it, for many members of the Syrian Muslim community in Montreal, cosmic dimensions. It was perceived as moving beyond a coalition of various forces trying to remove the Shah from power to become the beginning of the end of the tyranny of Western colonialism and its surrogates, and the initial victory of the Muslim people, the People of God, against the forces of darkness and evil in the 20th-century world.

The success of the revolution in Iran and the return of Khomeini to that country was described by several members of the group as equivalent to the return of the Prophet to Mecca to cleanse it from all its previous ignorance, its adulation and worship of false gods, and its commitment to profit and materialism, and to restore it to the worship of the true God. According to this view, the faithful have finally taken control of their destiny under the leadership of God and can now implement His way in the world.

The changes that took place in the Syrian Muslim community in Montreal became apparent during the Christmas season. While several families had decorated Christmas trees and exchanged presents during the 1978 season, none of these (to the best of my knowledge) did so in 1979. Furthermore, while a substantial number of Syrian Christians were invited by Muslims to a New Year's Eve party in 1978 (in fact, the Christians outnumbered the Muslims there), only one such family was invited in 1979, and reportedly several Muslims questioned their presence at the event.

The impact on change in lifestyle became evident in other areas. There was a dramatic rise in regular attendance at mosque services. The revolution in Iran was perceived to have confirmed the efficacy of such practices in bringing about desired change. There was also a substantial rise in the number of those in the group who began to take seriously the practice of the ritual prayer five times a day. The majority had never been faithful observers of this tenet of Islam. However, the hope that their participation in ritual acts and obedience to religious law might hasten the day of divine victory in the world appears to have encouraged the Syrian Muslims in Montreal to become more committed to observance of the faith. In fact, their zeal appears to have resulted in a novel way of fulfilling this duty. Several observers reported to this author that members of the group began to hold corporate prayers whenever they gathered if they were together at the appointed time for prayer. This occurred, for example, when a group assembled for a dinner party were summoned to pray by one of the members. All those present performed ablutions, the women borrowed covers for their hair and the whole group performed the prayer together. It was observed that a woman in her ninth month of pregnancy was performing extra *rak'as*. When she was asked about the propriety of such activity given her condition, her answer reflected the hope and commitment of the group to the cause of bringing a change in the political situation in Syria. She is reported to have said, "In my condition, the merit is multiplied 70 times; this will hasten the victory of the Muslim forces in Syria."

This belief in the efficacy of living a correct Islamic life led to the intensified concern over raising children in a non-Muslim environment. The demand for religious instruction brought about a substantial growth in the number of Sunday schools organized to teach Arabic language, the fundamentals of Islam, and the tenets of the Islamic life. Thus the education of the children was decentralized and several new Sunday schools were organized in various sections of Montreal, again as a specific result of the pride and self-identity engendered by the Iranian revolution.

Muslim Syrians in Montreal became interested in sharing in the struggle of other oppressed Muslims. Donations for Islamic causes in the Philippines, Ethiopia, Syria, Lebanon, and Afghanistan among other areas of the world have been collected. The members gave generously without hesitation or reservation. One member explained to me that besides the special satisfaction he receives in knowing that this money is spent in the cause of God, he is glad to know that it will aid Muslims struggling to bring about justice in the world. He also feels sure for the first time that the money will reach its destination and will not be pocketed by middle men, government agencies, or fraudulent leaders. He believes that leaders in Islamic causes in the various areas are dedicated and honest men who do not seek personal aggrandisement, ensuring that the cause of Islam can remain pure and noble.

Islamic solidarity and identity also became evident when a few members of the group began to grow beards and their wives to wear scarves when outside the home. The zeal to imitate the life of the Prophet and fulfil all the requirements of the Shari'a has led some to purchase the *siwāk* (available at the Quebec Islamic Center) and use it instead of a toothbrush.

The success of the revolution in Iran led the Syrian Canadian Muslims to believe in the possibility of a similar occurrence in their homeland. Phone-ins were initiated to keep members abreast of the latest developments in Syria. Members deemed interested were contacted and apprised of the situation as it was perceived from several sources. Information was gleaned from recent arrivals from Syria who were asked for assessments and reports. Other sources of information included broadcasts received over shortwave radios from "Voice of America" or from radio stations in the Middle East. Middle East journals and Arabic newspapers were studied for any details that could be added to the story of the Islamic revolution in Syria. A few members had access to the publications of the Muslim Brotherhood revolutionary command in Syria, *al-Bashir,* which arrived by mail from Washington, D.C., and *al-Nazeer* from Detroit.

The emotional involvement of the group became very intense. Great concern was shown when word was received of reverses. News of the execution of Russian advisors or government collaborators by the revolutionaries elicited expressions of pride and satisfaction, and word about deaths among the anti-government forces brought forth ululation or the affirmation of *Allahu Akbar* (God is Great), as for martyrs to the cause. Conversation at social gatherings often centred on the issue, and there was obvious joy at any information suggesting that the victory of the cause was both imminent and inevitable.

This concern for an Islamic revolution – achieved in Iran and expected in Syria – manifested itself in other notable changes. There was a heightened concern for the ethical and moral upbringing of children, which has led to exploring the possibility of starting a school run by the group. Much discussion has taken place over the question of whether to call it Arab or Islamic. In any case, the aim is to provide an environment that will not condone drinking, narcotics, or sexual promiscuity. A great deal of attention is given to the importance of implementing the Islamic teachings in everyday life. The majority of the Syrian Muslims in Montreal who might have taken or offered an occasional drink have now stopped, and do not refrain from rebuking the few who still do. Friends enjoin each other to be more firm in adherence to such practices as the daily prayers and attendance at the mosque and Sunday school. The roles of wives and husbands, of children and parents, of Muslims in a non-Muslim society, are discussed and elaborated on. Members of the community are urged to write wills that specify the implementation of Islamic inheritance laws as prescribed by the Shariʿa.

Also evident is a growing separation by the members of the group from the Syrian Christians. In fact, a major re-orientation appears to be taking place. There is a notable decrease in participation in ethnic activities and a rejection of Canadian customs practised with enthusiasm only a few years ago (such as exchanging gifts on Valentine's Day). In fact, discussion has been initiated about organizing a definite network of social interaction that would maintain this group in its chosen identity. This would be a replica of a social custom that exists in Damascus and other Syrian cities where certain days of the month (such as the first Wednesday or the second Monday) are designated as reception days by the various families. Members of the community would be apprised of the schedule and would then visit one another accordingly.

Despite all of these developments, it is also the case that the delay in the solving of the hostage issue, the disputes among the various Muslim groups in power in Iran, and the apparent decrease in the number of Muslim Brotherhood successes in Syria have led to an attrition in the number of supporters of the Islamic revolution and a slackening of the enthusiasm of a large number of others. Most Muslims continue to experience a special therapeutic satisfaction in the Islamic victory in Iran as it has restored self-confidence and faith in the efficacy and validity of the Muslim way of life. However, a substantial number have made it quite clear that they do not share the excitement of the core group of zealots. They are less diligent in their efforts to maintain an Islamic identity, and have reentered the mainstream of Canadian life. A substantial number among this group came to Canada when young, married Canadian women, and are more fully integrated into Canadian society. Others have a network of Canadian friends, having spent their formative undergraduate years of study on Canadian campuses. Although they may have Syrian wives, they appear to have more friends outside the Syrian community. It is this group, then, whose members are the most socially, professionally, and economically integrated into the Canadian culture.

The rest of the Syrian Muslims in Montreal, however, continue in their efforts to affirm Islam as a total way of life and in their conviction that the Islamic cause will triumph. They trust implicitly the leadership of Imām Khomeini. His revolution is perceived as pure (compared to that of Pakistan, whose attempts since 1948 to define an Islamic state have resulted in fratricide), since he is seen to support the oppressed and the poor, to emphasize egalitarianism, and to attempt to keep away from sectarian schism. Furthermore, Khomeini promised a delegation from the Council of Muslim Communities in Canada that he would exert all efforts to free Jerusalem from Zionist occupation, and would support the establishment of a Palestinian state. This is considered by the majority of the practising Muslims as a commitment that he will carry through just as he freed Iran from bondage to the Shah's rule. "He will be true to his word," said one member of the group, "not like Nasser who used Palestine for propaganda purposes and as a masquerade." A survey of the members of the core group revealed a profound faith that the preaching of Islam and the commitment to the practice of the law will bring about the conversion of the whole world. The conversion of some North Americans to Islam is seen as evidence of God's continued favor.

Not surprisingly, perhaps, the membership of the group committed to Islamic practice appears to be least integrated into Canadian culture. They include those who have no university education, or those who have a swarthy complexion or other recognizable Middle Eastern features. Among them are also those who have pursued their undergraduate studies at Arab universities prior to coming to Canada. The members of this group tend to consider their stay in Canada as temporary, and continue to hope for the time when they will return to the Arab world. Some have even refrained from purchasing a house since it implies permanence (others refuse to do so on religious grounds, believing that paying interest on a mortgage loan is usury and banned by the Qur'ān). In the meantime they continue to look to the revolution in Iran, and the movements in Syria, as vindication for their conviction that beyond all national and cultural identities lies the unifying force of Islam, and that that force will ultimately succeed.

It is clear that the success of the Islamic revolution in Iran provided a motivating force for the redefinition of identity for a group of Syrian Muslims in Montreal. The durability of this new identity cannot be assessed at present because of the continuing influence of events in the Middle East and in Canada on its formation. That the events to date have had a cathartic effect on the group is evident in the significant behavior modification that has taken place. Members of the group have exhibited a definite reorientation of their activities and social relations, channelling them towards the achievement of what they see as a higher goal.

The group is currently defined by commitment to the practice of the Islamic way of life, religious zeal, and the willingness to sacrifice for the common good. This supersedes the older definitions of cohesive groupings that were formed on the basis of social distinctions defined by professional, economic, educational, and social achievements. Such distinctions appear to have become irrelevant as the emphasis is placed on responsibility for fellow Muslims and for Islam in the world.

Such changes are not due, of course, to the Iranian revolution alone. They have been made possible by the failure of the experiments of Arab nationalism, socialism, industrialization, Westernization, and modernization to provide a feeling of relevance, worth, and power in the modern world. This failure has been accentuated by the feelings of impotence in dealing with the problem of Israel and the shock of Christian collusion with Zionism in the Lebanese civil war. In North America, this new identity is nurtured in Islamic circles through the publication of Muslim Brotherhood and Jamaati Islam material in English. (Writings of Abul Ala Maududi, Sayyid Qutb, and Muhammad al-Ghazzali are made available through the Muslim World League and the Muslim Student Association.)

In the Canadian milieu this identity is enhanced by the hostility of the host culture. Faced with rejection, the immigrant seeks an alternative integrating system for his life. Furthermore, Islam's ethical teachings are perceived as a superior system. They give the Muslim a feeling of stability and assurance in the face of what he sees as the moral bankruptcy of the Canadian society evident in its economic, social, political, and ecological problems. Islamic identity will guarantee the preservation of the family and prevent the children from total integration into the host culture. Such identity, affirming the authenticity and validity of the Islamic way of life, ensures that marginality in the Canadian culture can be perceived as a choice rather than a necessity. In this way, they are able to maintain perspective in relation to the cultural mainstream of Canada and to affirm identity with a wider Islamic community.

Notes

1. The Israeli intelligence agency.

2. The Iranian intelligence agency.

3. Unlike other Arab Christians, the Maronite and Coptic communities do not adhere to the ideology of Arab nationalism; rather, they ground their identity in earlier civilizations and express pride in such a relationship. The Maronites claim that they are the remnants of the Phoenicians, while the Copts insist that they are the descendants of the Pharoahs.

4. Montreal has several Arab Christian churches including: the Syrian Orthodox Church, the Chaldean Church, the Antiochian Orthodox Church, the Melkite Catholic Church, the Maronite Church, the Armenian Catholic Church, and an Evangelical Protestant Group.

IV

Islam and the Educational Establishment

The Development of
Islamic Studies in Canada

Charles J. Adams

The real history of Islamic Studies in Canada begins in the period
following World War II when there was an awakening in North
America generally to the need for more knowledge of the vast non-
Western portion of the world. There is something of a history, or
perhaps a pre-history, however, that stretches back into the 19th
century. In Canada as in other places on the continent, there has
been an indirect, almost accidental, kind of attention to Islam
through concern for the Arabic language. Wherever biblical studies
have been pursued along with their sister disciplines, comparative
Semitics and ancient Near Eastern history, Arabic has inevitably
had its place. For Arabic is not only the richest of the Semitic family
of tongues in its literature and cultural heritage, it is also the one
among the group whose history is best documented, and which, as a
still-living language, is the most accessible. Arabic has thus provided a reference encyclopaedia for students of Semitics, and much
in the linguistic traditions of the ancient Semites would never have
been deciphered without the hints garnered from the study of
Arabic usage. It was but a short step from interest in the language as
a tool for understanding other languages to interest in Arabic for its
own sake and thence to interest in the content of the documents

written in the language. As far back as the mid-19th century in the departments of the University of Toronto known as "Orientals" and "Near Eastern Studies" a certain amount of attention was given to Islam, because of the connection with Arabic. It was indeed in Near Eastern Studies at the University of Toronto that Wilfred Cantwell Smith, the most distinguished native-born student of Islamics this country has produced, received his basic training. This pattern of progression, from comparative Semitics to Islamics, is familiar from numerous examples in Europe and represents the path which many of the foremost names in the field, for example Goldziher, have followed.

To my knowledge the first step in Canada towards the creation of a fully-fledged program of work in Islamic studies per se was the founding of the Institute of Islamic Studies at McGill. The Institute was established in 1951 and, after one year spent in planning, recruiting staff, and making other preparations, opened its door to students for the first time in the autumn of 1952. In every sense the Institute was the creature of its founder, Wilfred Cantwell Smith. The conception was his, his the enormous effort that convinced university authorities and raised the initial outside funds, his the driving spirit in the difficult early days, and his the Directorship of the Institute, as well, for its first 13 years. Some words concerning Wilfred Smith are in order, therefore, for his views and contribution shaped the Institute. Smith did his undergraduate studies in Toronto, then went on to Cambridge in Britain for higher studies and thence to India for doctoral research. The years of World War II Smith spent in the sub-continent teaching in various missionary institutions and pursuing the inquiry that eventually led to the publication of his first major work, *Modern Islam in India*. Initially the work was presented to Cambridge as a basis for a doctorate but was rejected on the grounds of its tendentiousness. The Marxist perspective that provided the framework for the study and its explicit praise for "progressive" points of view and the Soviet Union were apparently not consistent with the examiners' view of scholarly objectivity. Smith, however, was not to be denied; after the return from India, he enroled at Princeton as a candidate for a doctorate where, incidentally, he worked with another eminent Canadian who was also a product of Near Eastern Studies in Toronto, T. Cuyler Young. His doctorate having been completed in record time despite the problems attendant upon the appearance of twins in the family in the crucial dissertation-writing stage, Smith became Professor of Comparative Religion in the Faculty of Divinity at McGill in 1949, where he very soon took up the dream of founding an institution for the serious study of Islam on the North American continent.

It cannot be emphasized too strongly to what extent the Institute of Islamic Studies is the creation of one man. The organization institutionalized many of the insights that Smith had won from his long stay in India and from the unsettling experience of Muslim hostility towards *Modern Islam in India.* He determined that the Institute should be a joint Muslim-Western enterprise, an effort to interpret Muslim faith and civilization in a manner true both to the faith itself and to the Western critical university tradition. Islam was to be discussed in the presence of both Muslims and non-Muslims by a staff and a student body that were to be similarly composite. It was hoped in this manner to institutionalize the conditions for communication and to avoid the negative aspects of the "outsider's view" that had been so characteristic of much of Western orientalism. The very heart of Smith's concern was the Islamic faith, and this was reflected both in his own work as well as the structure of the Institute. There was no doubt something of an anomaly that an Institute of such a nature should be set up in Montreal, in French Canada, where there was little knowledge of the Muslim world and even less interest in it. When a former principal of McGill, just after his appointment as chief executive officer of the university, made a visit to Islamics as part of a process of becoming acquainted with his new domain, he expressed his wonderment by comparing the Institute to the city of Regina. One travels across the vastness of the Canadian prairies for miles, he remarked, and then suddenly there is a city. Having passed through the city, one is plunged back once more into the sameness of the prairie landscape, and says to oneself, "Why is it here?" You may be sure that this remark was not particularly comforting to members of the Institute who heard it, but it is one whose substance has been often repeated in other contexts. The answer to the question, however, is clear. It is there because of the vision, the energy, the determination, and the hard work of one man. The origin of Canada's first major Islamics program is thus a sharp contrast with the birth of the second one in the University of Toronto in 1958, which was much more the natural outgrowth of a vigorous department seeking to respond to new demands made upon it.

In its first year the Institute enrolled 11 students. W.C. Smith delighted in pointing out that they were evenly divided; there were five Muslims, five Westerners, and one Lebanese Christian whom Smith considered to be half-and-half. The largest number of students the Institute has ever enrolled in its history is 65 in the current year (1982); well over half are Muslims from a variety of countries. This number will almost inevitably decrease in the future because of the inability of a diminished staff to deal adequately with so many graduate students. That development will not, however, be entirely unwelcome; the growing public interest in Islamics and the increased number of applications for graduate studies will permit the use of more strict criteria for admission and for degree standards. The Institute of Islamic Studies in its own right functions only at the graduate level. It has no programs for undergraduates; however, for many years, by an ad hoc arrangement with the Faculty of Arts, it has taught courses in Arabic, Persian, Urdu, Islamic history, and the Islamic religious tradition in conjunction with undergraduate departments and programs. The situation of the Institute – lacking a base in an undergraduate faculty and working wholly at the graduate level – is anamalous and a source of problems.

In its first year there were five staff members, two of them visitors; at its peak staff strength in the early 1970s the Institute employed 10 persons. The history of the staff has been one of considerable change with many different individuals having served for longer or shorter periods of time. At the same time there has been an enduring core of scholars who have given continuity to the Institute's life and program. There has been only one retirement from university service in the Institute's history, that of the distinguished Turkish scholar, Niyazi Berkes, and only one death among members of staff, that of Keith Callard. In 1980–81 there were eight staff members.

When the Institute of Islamic Studies first opened its doors, its library was all but non-existent. Apart from offices, one small room was assigned to the Institute in Divinity Hall on University Street, and that room served as seminar room, student lounge, and library. Such books as had been acquired were ranged on shelves along one wall of this general-purpose room, and the Divinity Hall Librarian, whose primary responsibility lay with the theological library, was in charge of the collection. Those of us who were students had little choice but to borrow from the personal libraries of our teachers, and the choice of material available to us was obviously quite small. The McGill Islamics Library now numbers approximately 80,000 volumes, and the library staff includes three professional librarians and five non-professional people. In terms of its size, the McGill collection is perhaps inferior to that of Toronto, which has been more blessed financially, but it is, nonetheless, one of the significant North American research libraries in Islamics. The McGill collection, furthermore, is more readily accessible than many. Indeed, one of the aspects of the Institute of Islamic Studies that is often envied by others is the existence of a separately housed Islamics collection next to staff offices and student study areas. However, the growth in the library over recent years and its location at the top of a tower-like building have created over-crowding and inconvenience for library users. In consequence the university has decided to relocate the Institute of Islamic Studies along with its library into refurbished quarters on the McGill campus. Perhaps appropriately, at least in W. C. Smith's terms, the building that the Institute will occupy is the former Presbyterian theological college.

The development of Islamic Studies in Canada's second major centre has followed quite a different course from that at McGill. As noted above, Toronto has a tradition of interest in Arabic and the wider Islamic world stretching back well into the last century. For the most part, however, that interest concentrated upon the Islamic past and the more classical expressions of Islamic civilization, especially literature. In 1957 the Department of Near Eastern Studies under the chairmanship of F. V. Winnett, one of the great scholars of the ancient Near East, expanded its activities to comprehend aspects of the modern Near East. The first appointment for the purpose was Michael Wickens, who was later also to be the first chairman of the separate university department of Islamic studies. Other appointments quickly followed, that of Michael Marmura in 1959, and that of Roger Savory in 1960, bringing the Islamics or Middle Eastern group within Near Eastern Studies to a strength of four.

The distinct University Department of Islamic Studies was created in Toronto in 1961 with the four Islamics specialists from Near Eastern studies as its initial members. Professor Michael Wickens, to whom goes the credit for taking the work in Toronto through its planning and maturing stages, was the first chairman. The department came into being largely under the influence of the awakening to the political and economic importance of the Middle East that followed World War II, the founding of the State of Israel, and Canada's role in the peace-keeping efforts in the region. The department quickly flourished, establishing co-operative arrangements and making cross appointments with a considerable number of other branches of the University of Toronto. At the height of its strength during the expansive days of the 1960s the department had 16 members. Financial stringency, however, has forced a certain retrenchment in more recent times. The death of 'Aziz Ahmad in December 1978, which was a major loss to the department and to all of Islamics scholarship, was felt the more because his position was allowed to disappear from the department's roster. At the present time the department has 11 members and two cross appointments with the Royal Ontario Museum (ROM) in the field of Islamic art and architecture. The presence of the ROM on the Toronto campus and the department's strong connection with it makes Islamic Studies in Toronto the one place in Canada where the artistic heritage of the Muslim community can be studied in depth. As may be seen from the figures cited, the department in Toronto is the largest centre of its kind in this country; in comparison with centres elsewhere it is also unusually strong in the quality of its personnel and its publication record. In 1976, following a public controversy over the department's teaching of Islam, the name was changed to Middle Eastern and Islamic Studies, which more accurately reflects the activities and purposes of the department and conforms with university terminology in other places.

In the beginning the program in Islamic Studies in Toronto bore a close resemblance to oriental studies in British universities and to the general pattern for honors and general courses at the University of Toronto. Emphasis was placed upon the acquisition of Islamic languages at the undergraduate level, two languages being required along with a certain amount of Islamic history, literature, and the study of an European language. The wholly laudable purpose of the program was to erect a firm specialized foundation upon which graduate study could properly be built. As a result of integrating this preparatory specialized training into the undergraduate curriculum, Toronto has been able to avoid many of the problems that the lack of such undergraduate possibilities have created at McGill. It has also been able to a far greater extent to recruit properly trained persons for graduate study from its own undergraduate population.

An additional advantage, and one whose importance it would be difficult to overemphasize, lies in the fact that it is a department of instruction alongside and like others in the university, drawing the whole of its finances from the normal budgets of the university in the way that other teaching units do. Thus, not only has it been unnecessary for members of the department to expend major portions of their energy raising money outside the university, but the department has been spared the uncertainty and the bother of the variety of special arrangements that have been so important to the continued existence of the McGill Institute.

Somewhat to the disappointment of at least some members of the department, it has not proven possible to hold to the ideal of specialized programs in Islamic Studies at the undergraduate level. An initial difficulty arose because of the all but complete absence of anything pertaining to Islamics in the pre-university schooling of most students, quite unlike the situation in some other fields of inquiry such as history or modern languages. The department, like similar enterprises everywhere, also found itself under pressure to develop less specialized programs to satisfy the demands of those without professional ambitions who wished simply to know more of the Islamic world. Accordingly, it has given close attention to developing social science oriented, comparative, and other non-specialized studies that have allowed some innovation in its work. The department is aware, however, that the newer non-specialized directions of its development, as interesting as they may be, have been bought at a price. Inevitably, the developments have meant some diminution in the emphasis given to the more specialized work and to graduate study, the areas from which advance in scholarship is most likely to come.

Outside of Toronto and McGill the principal advances in the Islamics field have occurred in departments of religious studies such as that at the University of Alberta. When departments of religion began to appear in North American universities as a regular feature of the academic landscape after World War II, they were at first slow to emphasize Islamics. Most students of religion on the continent simply had no opportunity for a serious encounter with Islam. In contrast, departments of religion demonstrated great avidity to launch programs and to hire personnel specializing in the religions of the Indian sub-continent and of the Far East. To what we should attribute this preference I am not certain; it accorded, at the least, with the widespread fascination for the exotic that characterized the counter-culture of the 1960s. The imbalance now appears to have been recognized, and a number of departments both inside and outside of Canada have either already brought Islamic specialists to their staffs or are planning to do so. In these difficult days in the academic marketplace the announcement of posts and the inquiries about personnel that most often come to my attention are those from departments of religion, followed by those from traditional departments of language and literature. In Canada there are persons with special training in Islamic Studies associated with the teaching of religion in at least the following institutions; the Université de Montréal, Carleton University, Concordia University, Queen's University, the University of Alberta, the University of Calgary, and the University of British Columbia, and, of course, McGill and Toronto.

A related development of some considerable importance is the growth of the program in Middle Eastern History conducted by the Department of History at Simon Fraser University. The department has three full-time staff members working in the Middle Eastern field, and there are others elsewhere in the university with strong interests and publications in Middle Eastern Studies. The program offers both a minor in Middle Eastern History as well as graduate work leading to the M.A. degree. The program's offerings, which are weighted on the side of modern studies of the Middle East, also include two levels of instruction in Arabic. One course of the group is devoted primarily to the Islamic tradition in the Middle East, and several of the courses that deal with modern developments also give attention to religious matters. Student enrolment in these courses has been consistently high over the past years.

There is also a scattering of individuals, either themselves Muslim or having a special interest in Islamic matters for other reasons, who are distributed through other departments across the country. Most are concentrated in the social sciences – in political science, economics, and anthropology – though there are others such as an eminent historian of Islamic Art in the Department of Fine Arts at the University of Victoria, and musicologists at different places.

In sum, however, it would appear that departments of religion are our brightest and best hope for any greater recognition or expansion of Islamic studies on the Canadian scene, at least for the moment. They are the points of entry through which the grandeur of Islamic civilization may be made known to a larger audience and through which, by a gradual expansion we may eventually hope to see broader programs of instruction in language, literature, and history introduced, and research facilities created.

Some brief comment is also in order concerning the development of Islamic Studies in the universities of French Canada. Despite a long-standing interest in the field, and a desire, encouraged at times by government, to see a greater development of studies, the Francophone institutions have experienced difficulties in creating viable programs. For many years, Laval had as a member of its staff an Arab scholar who was engaged in lexicographic work supported by the Canada Council, and Laval also began as early as the 1950s to stage courses and seminars on the Near and Middle East. In its desire to foster relations with other countries that it considers as Francophone, the government of Quebec has encouraged exchange, technical assistance, and the like between the French universities of Quebec and those of the Maghrib and of former French colonial West Africa in particular. Overtures have been made in other directions as well. Premier Robert Bourassa made an official visit to Iran during his last year in power; while there, he visited the small research branch that McGill's Institute of Islamic Studies maintains in Tehran, the one Quebec-based cultural organization functioning in Iran. He took that occasion to announce the intentions of the government of Quebec to establish a chair of Persian Studies, not at McGill as one might have thought, but at Laval. Even so, sadly enough, the promise was not fulfilled. The Université de Montréal now has a program of Arab studies whose emphasis falls largely on politics and recent developments in the Arab world. The program also offers instruction in Arabic and opportunities for the study of Islamic history. There have been difficulties, however; symptomatic of these troubles is the fact that the person charged with teaching Arabic and Islamic history has the status of a *chargé de cours,* that is, she is not a regular full-time member of the university staff and receives only a minimal compensation for her efforts. In the Université du Québec à Montréal there has been an effort to set up a program of Arab studies with a strictly practical focus. The program was intended principally to serve the needs of business men hoping to improve their performance in economic relations with the Arab countries. It envisaged a diploma or certificate program giving some minimal instruction in language, a series of fairly elementary courses on the culture and recent history of the region, and courses on business opportunities in the area. This proposed program was evaluated by the Quebec authorities recently and apparently rejected. Thus, although UQAM has for several years possessed a program on paper, it has not been able to translate this program into the reality of studies open to its students. Surely one of the most desirable developments to be sought in Islamic Studies in the Canadian scene is the emergence of a strong program of instruction and research in one of the Francophone institutions. It is to be hoped that such a program could be developed in co-operation with and not at the expense of the work already done in English in the province, but in any case it is vital that students in French Canada should have access to disciplined and rigorous means of gaining more knowledge of the Islamic world. Their exclusion from such studies on linguistic grounds is likely only to perpetuate the problems of the Anglophone institutions in gaining adequate support for Islamic Studies from the government of Quebec.

We who follow the profession also face a number of issues and problems. The first and perhaps the most fundamental of these is the indifference in Canada generally – in academia, in government, and among the general public – towards Islam and the Islamic world. In spite of the role that the Middle East and its people have played in world affairs for many years now, and despite a developing world crisis which centres upon the social situation, the political stability, the economic power, and the energy resources of the largely Muslim Middle Eastern peoples, awareness of Islam and its meaning are minimal in the Canadian situation. As many observers have remarked, such awareness as may exist is often accompanied by negative feelings toward the Islamic faith and the persons who profess it. All of this has changed to some extent because of greater Canadian exposure to the Islamic world in such activities as peace-keeping and business enterprises and through the presence in our midst of large numbers of Muslim immigrants, but there remains for us in Islamic Studies a massive task of persuading our fellow citizens of the importance of what we do.

A second basic problem that arises in part because of the indifference to Islam of which we are all aware, is the matter of finance for university programs in Islamic studies. As we all know, the ability of colleges and universities to mount and maintain specialized programs depends mainly on the sums of money available for investment in those programs, and no problem is closer to the heart of any department chairman or university administrator than that of money. I should like to suggest that we in Canada face certain special difficulties because of the way in which our university finances are provided throughout most of the country. These difficulties arise from two facts in particular: that education, including that at the university level, is considered solely a provincial responsibility; and that the massive development of Canadian universities as a whole is a relatively recent phenomenon owing its existence almost exclusively to support from the public sector of the economy.

The first of these facts, i.e., provincial responsibility for education, is one of the major reasons for the indifference to Islam and its implications that we noted above. Even in the highly decentralized federal system characteristic of Canada, provincial governments do not normally have direct relationships with governments and peoples in distant places. With the sole exception of Quebec, with its Ministry of Intergovernmental Affairs and its propaganda efforts abroad in the Francophone world, provincial governments do not maintain ministries of foreign affairs or make much effort to respond to the situations and concerns of people in other parts of the world. On the whole their principal concern is with the people and the problems of their own province and beyond that with the relation of the province to the other provinces and the central government in the federal system. Such an outlook makes the Islamic world seem very far away in the eyes of most provincial politicians or bureaucrats in provincial educational establishments. Islam may be important in its own right, but from a Canadian provincial perspective it is something exotic, not directly related to what are seen as the real and pressing problems of daily life. In the circumstances it is only to be expected that educational authorities should hesitate about investing major resources in matters that seem to have little direct relevance to them and their constituents. In this situation the constitutional bar against the federal government's being directly involved in educational programs is highly damaging to Islamicists and to others like them who want to conduct study programs having to do with eras, areas, peoples, or cultures that do not immediately touch provincial life. The federal authorities who might be expected to be more responsive to the claims of our studies are debarred from measures that can help us directly. In short, one of our greatest public relations jobs is to convince the provincial governments that it is of basic importance to support what we try to do.

Although some of the older Canadian universities possess sizeable endowments, there is to my knowledge no major institution in the country that is not directly dependent upon a provincial government for the greater part of its funds. This is true in particular of the relatively new institutions that gained their real significance in the great growth period of the 1960s. This fact makes the university community necessarily responsive to the views of government and also, as has often been noted with some alarm, leaves it highly susceptible to government control of one kind or the other. Where governments are unwilling or unable to underwrite studies in Islamics, it might seem that there is a possible solution in the appeal to private resources outside the university. Unfortunately, however, the prospects in that direction within Canada are not promising. There are Canadian foundations of some size but none with really massive resources and none that has shown interest in developing and establishing studies of the kind that concern us here, indeed, none that has evidenced willingness to initiate or underwrite major academic programs in the way that Ford, Rockefeller, and Carnegie did in the years after World War II. Where there has been success in getting money from "outside", that, is, non-government sources, the money has come from outside the country entirely. In

Islamics the notable example is the Institute of Islamic Studies at McGill, which has been supported almost entirely from outside. The vast majority of these funds have come from the much maligned Americans with lesser contributions from governments in the Islamic world. With the academic year 1982–83 there was also substantial assistance from His Highness, the Aga Khan. If there are untouched sources of help in Canada for our field, they most probably lie among corporations with developing business interests in the Middle East and among wealthy private individuals. To extract such money would require an incalculable expenditure of time and effort, and such activity is not really the business of scholars. In my view private resources are not truly the answer to our financial problems, as welcome as they may be when we receive them. The true solution lies in gaining acceptance for our studies from the educational authorities and in persuading them that despite the unusual costs and all the elements of exoticism, our concerns are of national and, indeed, human importance. In dealing with our governments, however, we have to face squarely the fact that serious studies of non-Western cultures and areas are extraordinarily expensive and of little immediate practical consequence. Not only do we have to admit these disquieting facts, but we have also to be prepared to defend our studies, even given these disadvantages.

In must also be pointed out that there are undesirable aspects of dependence upon money from private sources. Not only do scholars have to divert themselves from their proper work to do the job of raising money, liaison, report filing, and so on, but such money is often short-term, is frequently restricted in the purposes for which it may be spent, and not uncommonly has certain strings attached or the expectation of a quid pro quo. Also, donors of outside funds do not always keep the promises they make, and I personally know from bitter experience the embarrassment that can ensue when funds that have been promised and committed do not actually appear. If it is necessary to seek outside money to maintain our activities, we should press for permanent endowments that assure support over a long period; and we should strive for conditions that permit the flexibility and freedom for our studies to develop in accord with the best of emergent academic insight. In no case should we be guilty of accepting money with conditions attached that compromise our academic freedom or tie us to the support of special causes.

Some remarks also seem to be in order about the kinds of money we in Islamics require to have, or rather, the purposes for which we require to have it. Broadly speaking, in North America any good scholar with a well-developed research project or plan of study can, with a bit of ingenuity and persistence, find the means for carrying out what he wishes to do. There are agencies ranging from the Humanities and Social Sciences Research Council to a variety of foundations, government agencies, and the graduate faculties of our own universities that will assist us in valid works of research. I do not wish to appear to speak against making available even more research money than we may now have access to, but in my view our great need as Islamicists does not lie in that area. What we require most urgently are ongoing funds for building the basic structures of our institutions and ensuring their continued operation. The difficulty lies not in finding some thousands of dollars for a visit to the libraries of Cairo or Istanbul but in finding some hundreds of thousands, year after year, to pay the salaries of specialists who can mount a balanced program of instruction and research, to build and maintain libraries, to provide for graduate students, and the like. In the parlance of the economists, Islamics in Canada is still a "developing country," and what must be created before the final flowering of research and study will occur is the infra-structure of well-manned departments and well-stocked libraries. This type of on-going money is obviously the most difficult to get, and government is clearly the most realistic source from which to expect to obtain it.

The major problem of finance leads also to a secondary issue. Part of our difficulty in garnering more sympathy and more financing arises from the lack of influence on those in positions to help us. There is no professional organization in Canada concerned with Islam and the Middle East that may speak for the interests of the group as a whole. When the Learned Societies met in Montreal several years back, an ad hoc meeting of interested people was called to discuss the organization of a body to represent Islamic scholarship, and in the months following some considerable effort was expended by our colleague Lorne Kenny to survey all of those individuals with appropriate connections and interest whose names he could uncover. Sadly enough, the effort came to naught. It foundered apparently on the twin rocks of resentment of the "imperialism" of Toronto and McGill, as though the existence of those two centres somehow deprived the rest of the country of possibilities in Islamics, and of outright indifference on the part of many of those contacted. To the extent that the indifference is real, we students of Islamics in Canada perhaps deserve the minor role that we exercise in the country's academic life. I, like many of the rest of you, am not eager to assume responsibility for another organization nor to have another set of meetings to attend. Our maturation as a scholarly interest group, however, must eventually entail our ability to speak with a common and, therefore, more effective voice in the councils where our future is decided. At the same time, if and when we do establish a learned society for Islamicists and Middle Eastern specialists, we must not allow it to isolate us from the larger scholarly community of North America or the world. Our individual and collective participation in the Middle East Studies Association and the American Oriental Society, etc., will still be appropriate and, indeed, essential. An organization that cuts us off from these associations would do more harm than good.

There is another problem, at the moment relatively in the background, at least for most of us, but with the potential to cause great disquiet and disruption in our work. I refer to the relations between college-and university-based efforts in Islamic studies and the growing Muslim community of Canada. Muslims in this country, quite rightly, are concerned about the way in which their religious faith and elements of their cultural heritage are presented in courses of instruction and in the publications that Canadian-based scholars produce. In this respect Muslims are not unlike other religious groups or, for that matter, not unlike the various political, social, and ethnic entities that constitute the mosaic of Canadian society. All have the right to fairness in the academic forum, and to expect an unprejudiced and balanced treatment at the hands of scholars. Indeed, because religious commitments represent the most deeply held convictions and values of people, there is a moral responsibility that devolves upon the scholar whose work in some way touches upon religion to treat these commitments with the greatest respect possible. It is to be hoped that this responsibility will always be borne in mind and honored by students of Islam on the Canadian scene.

At the same time it must be remembered that the scholar is part of the academic community, which is committed to the life of the mind. His responsibility includes not only due respect towards his subject matter but also the obligation to be probing and critical, to follow where his inquiries may lead him. If the student of Islamics must answer in some sense to the Muslim community on the one hand, he must answer to his scholarly colleagues in the university as a whole on the other. The discharge of this latter responsibility may lead him to views and statements that are not palatable to some Muslims and, hence, to conflict with some members of the Muslim community. While the resulting tension may be unfortunate and result in bruised feelings and a sense of injustice among some Muslims, it is probably unavoidable, simply a part of the price that has to be paid for scholarship. Such tensions have always characterized the study of religion in the academic context, not only in regard to the relations of religious communities with outsiders but also to the internal dynamics of these communities as well. Most scholars see this disagreement as not only to be expected and endured, but also as a healthy stimulus to further inquiry and greater understanding.

There is a danger, however, arising from tensions between scholars and those outside the university, that they may result in assaults upon the right of scholars to pursue their inquiries or in attempts to control what scholars may or may not be allowed to teach or study. Unfortunately, such tendencies have manifested themselves among some elements of the North American Muslim community; a Canadian instance comes to mind in the case of the University of Toronto and the vendetta conducted against a prominent member of its staff. Another vivid example is the reaction of a Muslim group in the United States to the recent conference held at Arizona State University in Tempe. Not only was the report of the conference by an observer from the group false and misleading, perhaps even deliberately calculated to arouse resentment in Muslim readers, but it stated quite explicitly that non-Muslim scholars have no right to discuss matters essential to the Muslim faith. The papers at the conference were represented as a massive attack upon Islam, not by reason of their content, but on the ground that they were written by outsiders who ipso facto should be prevented from examining such subjects. The message of the reporter of the conference was an attack upon academic freedom and the intellectual life in uncompromisingly clear terms; this and any similar attacks must be resisted with equally uncompromising attitudes. They are no more tolerable than would be the use of academic privilege to launch a campaign against Islam and Muslims.

In the circumstances it is vital that professional students of Islam pursue their work with sensitivity and caution and that they keep their lines of communication with the Muslim community open. Exchange between scholars and the Muslim community is not only a matter of personal responsibility and social concern; it is also of vital academic interest. If those interchanges are held to be impossible in principle or always to be tainted with personal religious prejudice, it must follow that the search for inter-cultural and inter-religious understanding is hopeless and that the attempt to reach a broad intellectual grasp of the phenomenon of Islam in universally acceptable terms is vain.

Culture Conflict in the Classroom: An Edmonton Survey

Lila Fahlman

This paper presents a synopsis of a larger research project investigating the perceptions of Lebanese Muslim students and their teachers in two Edmonton high schools. The aim is to provide a descriptive record of the way the students and their teachers view themselves and each other in order to shed light on the structure behind their thoughts and actions. This should lead to a much needed understanding of the world of the Lebanese Muslim student who finds himself part of the Canadian school system and its socialization process.

The author, herself a Lebanese Muslim, has been part of the Canadian educational system as a student, teacher, and counsellor for over 50 years. In her experience, relationships between teachers on one hand, and parents and children of different ethnic backgrounds on the other, do not always foster an encouraging learning environment. The difficulties may be seen as a conflict between the value system of the home and that of the teacher or the school. The culture conflict within the school may deny the students the opportunity to develop integrity and self-esteem, and at the same time may destroy their sense of identity and their relationships within their families. Alienation, prejudice, and misunderstanding may cause these children to become dropouts and delinquents. Society may well lay the blame at the door of the school, but it is in fact symptomatic of a more fundamental socio-cultural problem.

Concern with this culture conflict as it affects Lebanese Muslim students led the author to undertake a preliminary study surveying the views of school held by a group of Lebanese Muslim mothers and their school-age children. The findings indicated a real lack of congruence between the home environment and the reality of the classroom, suggesting a need for better communication between the two worlds. It is to contribute toward such communication that the present study has been undertaken, following the premise that "education occurs in a social environment and one cannot separate active teaching from the environment if one is to understand what is occurring."

The research was conducted at two high schools in Edmonton to be identified here as schools A and B. Both are located in a part of the city where many Lebanese families live; A is vocational, B offers a standard composite program. Interviews with the teachers included eliciting their reactions to a brief summary of the students' views. The tape-recorded conversations were later transcribed for analysis. A total of 25 students were interviewed; eight at school A and seventeen at school B. Twelve teachers were interviewed; five from school A and seven from school B. What follows is a summary of the data received from students and teachers. Because of their overall similarity, the findings from the two schools are presented in combination, but differences are noted where relevant. The synopsis follows the topical sequence of the interviews, thus providing the reader with an outline of the data gathering procedure. Because of the focus of this volume, emphasis is on the presentation of students' views, while from the teachers' data only information directly related to Lebanese Muslim students is included.

Student Data

Lebanese Muslim students differ somewhat in their reasons for choosing to attend either school A or B. School A was generally chosen for a particular vocational program such as automotives. A suggestion by parents or previous attendance by older brothers or sisters were important reasons for enrolment at either school.

School B was favored because drugs and alcohol were less prevalent there, and the academic quality of the school was high. School B was referred to as a "clean" school with a better "reputation." Preference for school B is clearly expressed by the fact that the Lebanese Muslim population at school B was nearly quadruple that of school A. Students say that at school B the large number of Lebanese Muslims already attending served as an attraction for others to attend. Many feel that the school body knows that they are Muslim, that they speak Arabic, and shows an interest in them. On the other hand, school A was preferred because of its "lack of discipline" and the "grown-up feeling" it generated.

Attendance is not seen as a problem at either school by most students, though motivation varies. A majority of the students experienced language problems; many were put back a grade, and some still have problems understanding words. Among subjects, English presents a problem to most students at school A.

Alcohol and drugs present an issue of potential conflict at both schools. Lebanese Muslim students say they are not "into" drugs and alcohol, although their general use is prevalent, especially at school A. Some Lebanese Muslim students at A admitted they had tried them, but consequences to themselves and others had assisted them in discriminating between improper peer pressure and compromising situations and they had avoided a recurrence. Indeed, at school B many students say they did not attend school A because of the well-known heavy drug and alcohol use. B students add that they "hang around" with each other because they understand how each feels about drugs. They note that "other" students think they are "weird" or "square." Some of the Lebanese Muslim students speak openly with their "other" friends about abstaining from drugs and alcohol or deliberately say "it's against my religion."

At a more general level, some of the students feel that they are different, sometimes feel out of place, and cannot trust "anyone" except other Muslims. Some encounter discrimination at school from both students and teachers. They were referred to as "Arabs," "carpet riders," and "camel jockeys." Some of their peers made fun of their not eating pork. The recent conflicts in the Middle East and Iran have increased prejudices according to most of the students. But all of them stated unequivocally that it is in junior high school where most discrimination occurs. Since they had learned to handle prejudice and discrimination by the time they attended senior high school, it was not as traumatic an experience as at junior high.

The Student's View of Himself in his World

The students' view of the world indicates concerns about the future and about war, about man's material desires, about prejudice, and about the general lack of religious belief. They see this society as lacking in religion and the care of parents for children; some feel that drugs and liquor will ruin Western society. Unlike in Lebanon, in this society people do not "stand up for each other."

A strong family orientation was consistently expressed, with respect for parents and older persons generally approved. Students were cognizant of parental influence, a value they chose to project into their own future as elderly persons. At the same time they felt that their peers did not share their views, and criticized their non-Muslim friends for using expressions like "old man," "old lady," or "old bag," and "hag" when referring to parents or old people.

The students' attitudes toward teachers varied. They expressed preference for "a caring, strict teacher, who doesn't put you down but helps you." At school B some students perceived the teachers as holding grudges "because we are Lebanese," and "because so many of us go to this school." The teachers, they feel, "pick on us" and think "we're conceited, because we're Lebanese." More specifically, some say that the teachers "don't understand our religion" or "our values." This surfaced when two female students felt unable to participate in course activities requiring co-ed physical education and wearing shorts.

On the other hand, students recognized that, unlike in junior high school, Home Economics teachers provided alternatives to using pork once they were made aware of the Islamic prohibition. Overall, individual differences between teachers were widely recognized.

Lebanese Muslim students all say they are very close to their families. The values of the home, which are based upon the religion of Islam, are strong. While the family trusts the school, it opposes the values of the school when they conflict with the religious values of the home, especially where female students are concerned. Thus the wearing of shorts and co-ed physical education are forbidden by the parents. Parental discipline is reinforced by the extended family where older uncles, aunts, and cousins have a voice in the behavior of the younger generation. Most parents direct the aspirations of their children and regulate their dating practices. Besides trying to please their parents, they also say that they are expected to set an example for the younger members of the family. As for parental contact with the school, it is hindered by the fact that mothers often lack facility with English, and fathers work.

In relations with their peers, students at school B say they get along well, but they "stick with the Lebanese" and do not trust other peers "for anything important." At school A the few Lebanese Muslim students have most of their schooltime friends from outside their ethnic religious community, whereas outside of school the number of their Lebanese Muslim friends increases to about 50 percent. They view their Lebanese Muslim friends as "easier to talk to." Other peers, while they do not criticize, "just don't understand, because we are different and our values are different." Thus, where beliefs conflict, the students say "no" to their peers, and some say they are required to be more selective of their friends.

The students' personal perception is positive. They are concerned with completing their education and of making "the best of life God gave." In concrete terms, males have aspirations toward a trade, a profession, or a business. The females aspire towards social work, hairdressing, and teaching children, but they are concerned with the time required for training beyond high school. A number of students also feel "it depends upon your parents, what they want you to do."

Students' View of Value Conflict

The Lebanese Muslim students consider Islam as the source of their value system. They often refer to their religiosity with phrases such as "my religion is important to me," and "religion gives me values for living." On the other side, there were students in school A who said they were not religious; these lived away from the Muslim community and had fewer Muslim friends. Relating religious values to their living pattern, many say they "stick" by their parents' teaching and they have friends who are religious.

As for specific guidelines for behavior, the prohibition of the consumption of pork, alcohol, and drugs as well as restrictions on dating practices were mentioned as being adhered to as part of the value structure. Some see Islam as binding the family together; these students also said they attended to their prayers at the mosque or at home. Girls say that they are expected to marry a Muslim and that the discipline they receive from their parents in regard to dating is on account of that future marriage.

The Lebanese Muslim students' concept of success is strongly family-oriented: success means happiness, a home and a family, and education and a trade or business, "not money, but a good family and healthy kids."

Value conflicts are seen to arise in school both in and out of the classroom. For the students, their values conflict with the school and society at large. Drugs and alcohol are central: "fitting into the larger society is a battle because they drink." Some of their non-Muslim friends understand when the Muslim students tell them about their values and the discipline of their parents; some make snide remarks. When the male students go out with non-Muslim friends and drugs or drink are being consumed, they leave in order not to be involved with "that kind of thing." Others say it does not bother them when other students "do drugs" or drink; they do not do it themselves and stick to their values. Not eating pork also results in ridicule at times.

The female students find it difficult to explain to their peers why they cannot drink or "go out," so they tell only their "closest friends." The necessity to wear shorts, or participate in co-ed physical education causes some of the female students to skip physical education altogether. This, in turn, means a "clash with school requirements and results in a feeling on the part of students that teachers don't understand their values." This feeling is reinforced when teachers object to the Lebanese Muslim students speaking Arabic when they come together.

There are, on the other hand, some Lebanese Muslim students who see no conflict between their values and those of the school, and they have no difficulty being Muslims in this society.

Function of the School

Students in both schools express themselves strongly against assimilation, saying they are individuals as against conformists, and they want to retain their integrity. One male student sees the pressure of assimilation as having pushed him into "dope" like others, but "my parents and my religion brought me out of it." However, assimilation is also seen by one student as a means of getting along with others.

The school, according to common consensus, should not function as an agent of assimilation. Lebanese Muslim students say the teacher wants to make everybody alike, but "if a person is strong, the school can't change you." While many students prefer the public-type high school, most of them expressed a preference for their "own" (Lebanese Muslim) school at the elementary level, or even from kindergarten through grade twelve. Those who had language problems felt that such a school would have facilitated their entry into the public system. Also, students want to learn Arabic or maintain what they already know of it. Others feel that for Muslims, particularly those born in Canada, a separate school is necessary. One male student indicated he would build such a school if he were older and had money, because "I want to keep the Muslim kids Muslim."

Teacher Data

When confronted with the results from the student survey, teachers at both schools expressed surprise. They appreciated this information, which they felt would help them understand Lebanese Muslim students better. Evidently teachers were quite unaware of the particular identity problems of these students.

A probing of the teachers' views and experiences of Lebanese Muslim students revealed that many teachers were, in fact, unaware of this distinctive identity. Some teachers admitted to having to overcome an initially negative attitude toward Arabs. Several teachers cited language difficulties as a problem for this group of students.

On the question of discrimination, the general response was to play down the occurrence of friction, though some teachers noted the existence of some racist incidents. As to solving this and other student problems, the philosophy of the school was to hold students responsible without involving their parents. Teachers who had contacted Lebanese Muslim parents felt there was an indifferent attitude.

The teachers' view of the peer relationships of Muslim Lebanese students was mixed, but most felt that, as a group, they tended to stick together, while as individuals, they were "loners." The question of an underlying value conflict appeared remote to teachers. For one thing, they were unaware of the value system held by Lebanese Muslim students, and for another, they themselves had very mixed attitudes towards "values." Interestingly, on several specific issues, the teachers' views harmonized with those expressed by the Lebanese Muslim students. All teachers were highly critical of their own society's negative attitude toward the elderly, all were against drugs, and many against the the unqualified use of alchohol. Opinions on marriage and "women's lib" were often conservative.

As for their view of the Muslim Lebanese students, some teachers did not perceive them as different from the average student. Others noted particular traits such as their avoidance of pork. One teacher saw the group identity of the Lebanese Muslim students as a limiting factor, regimenting their thinking. Others said that the Lebanese Muslim students were interested in learning as a response to peer pressure, but had limited academic aspirations, especially the girls.

Finally, teachers, having been made aware of the divergence between their own perceptions and those of their Lebanese Muslim students, agreed that their professional education did not prepare them for dealing with such minority groups. They suggested that relevant training regarding minority values should be made available, for in the words of one teacher, "if I had such training, I would become more aware, would understand situations, become more tolerant, and even change some of my own attitudes and prejudices."

Summation

1. Teachers lack an awareness of the problems facing minority religious ethnic students.

2. Teachers take these students for granted and assume that they are no different from the majority of students.

3. Teachers perceive their role and the role of the school to be one of assimilating the minority religious ethnic students.

4. The teachers' view of man is reflected in their attitudes toward minority religious ethnic students and the classroom situation.

5. The teachers are unaware of the conflicts experienced by minority religious ethnic students, and fault the teacher education program for its inadequacy.

6. The Lebanese Muslim students do not want to assimilate but want to retain their sense of identity and integrity.

7. Some students experience a conflict between their value system, which is based upon Islam, and those values of the teacher and the school.

8. The students have a close relationship with their families, which are extended families and as such very supportive and influential.

9. The students feel discriminated against by teachers and fellow students, particularly at the junior high level, because of their ethnicity and their religion.

10. Students are concerned about the number of their peers who use drugs and/or alchohol. School B students chose school B over school A because school A has a reputation for drugs and alcohol. In both schools, teachers said they were unaware of the problem.

Recommendations

This study shows the need, as expressed by the teachers, for a change in the teacher education program. An intervention is required to increase the teacher sensitivity to and awareness of the problems encountered by minority religious ethnic students.

This may be accomplished by university courses designed to include a theoretical and practical program, which will attempt to increase the empathy, understanding, and awareness of teachers to a significant level. Making teachers aware of that which they take for granted, and by making the implicit explicit to teachers, will increase their level of awareness. Subsequently, their own critical reflection will result in a positive action toward their students and toward mankind in general.

Conclusion

The teachers display a range of awareness along the continuum from little to much awareness, depending upon the topic. Where the minority religious ethnic student is concerned the teachers display little awareness, if any. There is increasing awareness among teachers of the educational system, particularly the school board. Teacher education is the area where teachers have the most awareness. In other areas such as religion, social issues, social benefits, government control, and financial institutions, teachers are average, about the centre of a continuum. The teachers themselves have verified the need for education to teach minority religious/ethnic groups.

V

Indigenous Muslims

The American Muslim Mission in the Context of American Social History

C. Eric Lincoln

The United States of America began as a Protestant Christian establishment, and after 200 years was still close enough to her religious origins for a prominent theologian to aver with confidence that "to be a Protestant, a Catholic or a Jew are today the alternative ways of being an American."[1] Among the vast array of challenging implications to be drawn from Professor Will Herberg's famous aphorism are the following: religion in the United States is so closely identified with cultural or civil values as to take on the character of nationalism; and being "American" presupposes the Judeo-Christian heritage or experience. There is an inescapable irony in both propositions. In the first place, to the uncritical observer the most prominent feature of contemporary American life is its secularism, not its piety. In the second place, the founding fathers went to extraordinary lengths to insure the religious neutrality of the emergent nation by constitutional fiat. There could be no religious establishment, and there could be no religious test or requirement for equality of participation in the full range of common values incident to American citizenship. Nor may the national legislature make any laws to the contrary.[2] Nevertheless, a close examination of American secularism will reveal features that are startling in their religious tenor.

The principal elements of this "new" religion are derived principally from the Judeo-Christian tradition, and from the idealistic sentiments of what is commonly called "the American Dream." This is the religion I call "Americanity,"[3] and for all the prideful references to the separation of Church and State in the U.S., Americanity is the "established" faith, a fact of critical importance in understanding the implications of the Islamic presence in America.

However, despite a demonstrated sophistication in socio-political foresight, there is nothing to suggest that the founders of the United States of America had even a premonition of the eventual arrival of Islam upon these shores. While the first European settlers were themselves in search of religious freedom, their initial "errand into the wilderness" was to establish a Christian community — one which would become a beacon of perfection — a kind of religious demonstration project for all the world to see and emulate. But the "world" to which the notion of a "righteous empire"[4] was addressed was the turbulent, schismatic world of European Christianity. Islam, a "pagan" religion, was beyond consciousness and beyond contemplation. In the unfolding scenario of Western manifest destiny, the religions of the East, like the peoples of the East, belonged to an exotic history whose wheel had turned; in the peculiar balances of the historical order, the rise of the West meant the descent of the East. Eight hundred and eighty-eight years separate the Battle of Tours from the landing of the Mayflower at Plymouth Rock, and in that interim of nearly a full millenium Islam had long been displaced in the critical concerns of those who found, in the New World beyond the Atlantic Ocean, a world from which to mold a more perfect image of the Old World. Although Islam had lingered on in the Spanish Peninsula, and was spread among the American Indians by Blacks serving in the Spanish expeditions in the Americas in the 16th century,[5] it had never been an aspect of the English experience, and the American commonwealth was from the beginning a transplant of the Anglo-Saxon culture and expectations. That primary cultural impress has of course been modified by subsequent immigration, and by the development of an indigenous experience. But it has not been supplanted. Anglo-conformism remains the norm — indeed the *sine qua non* of American self-perception.

It is clear then that the religion of Islam is not in any substantial way a part of the critically valued American experience. It has no purchase in antecedent European-American traditions, and it played no part in the critical development of the indigenous American culture. Exclusionist immigration policies were aimed at reserving the country for Caucasian people in general and people of Western European descent in particular. In consequence, the development of the "Western Empire" proceeded in what must now be perceived as a deliberately created cultural vacuum, denying itself the wisdom and the culture of the East in the vain, short-sighted pursuit of a chauvinistic racial chimera.

While American immigration policies excluded both Asians and Africans, its commercial interests did not. Among the millions of Blacks who were made *involuntary* immigrants under the aegis of slavery, there were inevitably numbers of Muslims from the Islamic kingdoms of the West Coast of Africa. How many thousands (or perhaps tens of thousands) we shall never know, for the slavemasters had no interest in recording the cultural and spiritual achievements of their chattels. What is more, the slave trade required and maintained a determined myopia regarding the religious interests of its hapless human commodities: first to avoid the embarrassment of possibly selling an occasional Black Christian, but more often in support of the fiction that the very religious depravity of the Africans made them legitimate targets for spiritual rehabilitation through the dubious ministrations of chattel slavery. Under that convenient sanction, even recognizably Muslim Africans would fare no better than the rest, for Islam was considered the supreme cabal of infidels, when it was considered at all. In spite of all this, the evidence of a substantial Muslim presence among the American slave population is compelling, while in South America and the Caribbean that presence was common enough to be taken for granted and the cultural impress of Islam remains in high relief in those areas to this day.[6]

In sharp contrast to the prevailing practices in Roman Catholic Latin America, the Anglo-Saxon Protestant hegemony that defined the cultural and religious parameters of the slave-holding South (in what was to become the United States) considered it expedient to suppress *all* African religions of whatever kind. The fear of insurrection or revolt under cover of religion was deep and unremitting, and the common precaution was to disperse as widely as possible all those slaves known to have common tribal or language affiliations. This practice effectively precluded the cultic apparatus by means of which religions survive and propagate themselves. In spite of such discouragements, accounts persist of Muslim slaves who committed the entire Qur'ān to memory in an effort to keep the faith alive and to pass it on to others.[7] Inevitably, of course, such heroic efforts were unavailing, for the intransigence of the slave system, buttressed as it was by a formidable reticulation of customs and convention, could not and did not accommodate itself to the heroics of its victims. What the system did provide (after a hundred years of dereliction) was an alternative faith. As the generations succeeded each other, scarcely marked except by the momentary discontinuities of birth and death, into the vacuum left by the proscribed "native" religions of whatever sort of origin, Christianity, that is to say Protestant Christianity, eventually made its way. It took the better part of a century – from 1619 to sometime after the Society for the Propagation of the Gospel received permission to proselytize the slaves in 1701.[8]

It was not a permission easily obtained. At stake in sharing a religion with the Blacks was the spectre of sharing a community with them. The implications for economic prerogative, social status, political power, and even the transcendant bliss of the heavenly rest were unknown and troublesome in their anticipation. But the benefits, it was argued, would be many – not the least of which would be more tractable, more reliable, more loving, and more dedicated servants.[9] Was it worth the risk? Opinion was divided, and the compromise was a severely edited version of the faith dominated by careful selections of Pauline doctrine offered as Divine approval of the lowly condition of the slave. From the beginning of the Black experience in American Christianity, Black Christians were separated by race and by destiny. The churches were segregated and remain so to this day and sharing the faith has yet to accomplish the elementary principle of sharing the community. White churches and Black churches go their separate spiritual ways, while in the arena of social and political intercourse the mandates of the faith are still suspended in the interest of less respectable values.

Such is the backdrop against which Black Islam attempts resurgence. Why "Black" Islam? First, because it was the Black Muslims, that is, the "Moors" among the Spanish conquistadores, who first introduced Islam to the New World.[10] Second, because in the English colonies the only Muslim presence was among the slaves imported from Black Africa. Third, while there had been small enclaves of orthodox Muslims in America for many decades, their presence had been characterized by clannishness and quietism, not by proselytism or public identity and involvement.

The orthodox Muslims were more a spasm than an outpost of Islam, inundated by the floodtide of militant Christianity, the spirit and the symbol of Western ascendancy. In consequence, these "white Muslims" maintained a low profile. Perhaps subconsciously they considered themselves the logical targets for a Christian jihād, unaware, or more likely unconvinced, of the protections afforded all religions by the Constitution of the United States. In any case, they seemed content, or at least constrained, to keep Islam within the parameters of their ethnic associations. Certainly, the white Muslims provided no more opportunity and even less incentive for Black participation in the religion of Islam than the counterpart white church provided for a meaningful Black involvement in Christianity. And while their respective statuses within the American social structure were hardly analogous, their responses to the Black presence were not at all dissimilar.

Fortunately the African has a genius for religion that cannot be expunged. Blacks seldom wait to be won over by a religion. They take the initiative and whenever they adopt a faith they make it peculiarly their own. They had known Islam and Christianity in their homelands, a fact overlooked by their new masters. But in their new situation both were given new life and style; both became visible signs of a distinctive community.

The memory of Islam, however tenuous, was never completely lost to the slave experience. The major Black Christian denominations were formed long before the Civil War, and though routinely denigrated by the white church, were a recognized part of the Christian community. If they were considered exotic, it was because they were Black – not because they were alien – a problem Islam could not and did not escape.

There was no room and no occasion for a "new" religion in the post-Civil War United States. The Black church, split between Methodist and Baptist denominations, offered the newly emancipated Blacks the chance for self-respect in the form of religious self-determination, that is, the opportunity to *belong*—to be a part of an independent *Black* organization. Drawn by so heady and so novel an opportunity, and pushed by the white churches in which they had previously held a debased and segregated membership, the new Black Americans surged out of the white church and became proud members of "their own" Black churches—the African Methodist Episcopal Church, the Colored Methodist Episcopal Church, the National Baptist Convention, Inc., and so on. Through all this, there was a memory of Islam, but its time was not yet. It was to be another half-century before that memory would find vocal and physical expression among the hapless Blacks struggling for a negotiable identity and searching for their cultural roots.

In 1913, a Black "prophet" from North Carolina established a "Moorish Science Temple" in Newark, New Jersey.[11] Timothy Drew was not an educated man, but he had somehow learned enough about Islam to consider it the key to what would 50 years later be called "Black liberation." Islam was the religion of the Moors, the Black conquerors from Africa who once ruled much of Europe. How could anyone with such a heritage suffer the debasement which was the common lot of Blacks in America? Drew had no training in the social sciences, but he did have the perception to realize that there is a very definite relationship between what you are called and how you are perceived, and between how you are perceived and how you are treated. "It is in the name," he concluded; the Black man's problems began with accepting a pejorative nomenclature. Drew, who was born in 1866 and given the Christian name of Timothy, now proceeded to give himself a name indicative of his "Moorish" heritage—Noble Drew Ali. His followers were no longer to be known as "Negroes" or "Africans" but as "Moorish-Americans," thus preserving their newly won American citizenship, but making explicit their Islamic heritage. Each "Moor" was issued an appropriate name and an identity card making clear his religious and political status in a society where "Negroes," however pronounced their Christian pretensions, were not generally held in high esteem.

Drew's movement spread to Pittsburgh, Detroit, Chicago, and a number of cities in the South. Although it made use of what was known of the more romantic paraphernalia of Islam, including the Holy Qur'ān, the wearing of fezzes, Muslim names, and the repudiation of certain fundamental Christian beliefs, Noble Drew Ali's movement was essentially a mélange of Black nationalism and Christian revivalism with an awkward, confused admixture of the teachings of the Prophet Muḥammad. It was not Islam, but it was a significant recovery of the awareness of Islam.

After a violent eruption within the administration of his Moorish-Science Movement, Ali died of mysterious causes in 1929. Thereafter the movement languished, splintered, and was succeeded by a more vigorous, imaginative, and demanding version of Islam led by Elijah Muhammad.

Elijah Muhammad was born Elijah Poole in Sandersville, Georgia, on 7 October 1897.[12] One of 13 children born to an itinerant Baptist preacher, Poole was destined to become one of the most controversial leaders of his time. But controversy aside, in terms of the impress he made on the world he must be reckoned one of the most remarkable men of the 20th century. Among his more commonly recognized achievements were his enormous contributions to the dignity and self-esteem of the Black undercaste in America. Beyond that, and with perhaps infinitely more far-reaching implications, Elijah Muhammad must be credited with the serious re-introduction of Islam to the United States in modern times, giving it the peculiar mystique, the appeal, and the respect without which it could not have penetrated the American bastion of Judeo-Christian democracy. If now, as it appears, the religion of Islam has a solid foothold and an indeterminate future in North America, it is Elijah Muhammad and Elijah Muhammad alone to whom initial credit must be given. After more than a hundred years, "orthodox" Islam in America had not titilated the imagination of the masses, white or Black, and was scarcely known to exist before the "Black Muslims" – Elijah's Nation of Islam – proclaimed Elijah's "Message to the Black Man" in the name of Allah.

Elijah learned what he knew of Islam from a shadowy, mysterious evangelist who went by a variety of aliases, but who was most popularly known as Wali Farrad, or Wallace Fard. Fard claimed to have come from the Holy City of Mecca on a mission of redemption and restoration of the Black undercaste. He taught that the Black African Diaspora were all of Muslim heritage, "lost-found members of the tribe of Shabazz." The essence of his message was that Black debasement had occurred over the centuries because Blacks were separated from the knowledge of Allah and the knowledge of self. They were estranged from the one true God to whom they owed allegiance, and ignorant of their own history and their previous high status in the hierarchy of human valuation. The problem was to restore to the Lost-found Nation the truth, the only truth that could make them free. This was the formidable task bequeathed to Elijah Muhammad, when after three years of instruction, Fard ostensibly returned to Mecca after designating Elijah, "Messenger of Allah."

In his own words, Elijah set out to "cut the cloak to fit the cloth." The complexity of his task was beyond imagination, for as Messenger of Allah he had committed himself to nothing less than the restoration of the most despised and brutalized segment of American Christianity to a level of dignity and self-appreciation from which informed choices about religion could be made. His methods were sometimes ad hoc, and usually controversial, but they were always addressed to the realities of the situation rather than to an abstract theory whose relevance to his peculiar task had nowhere been demonstrated. Against him was a formidable array of forces, not the least of which were 350 years of solid Christian tradition in an avowedly, consciously, Christian society. His initial "parish" was the slums and the Black ghettos of the industrial cities, and his potential converts were the slum-created outcasts of a developing technocratic society. His "people" were those who were most battered by racism and stifled by convention, and whose experience of the white man's "invincibility" made the acceptance of Black inferiority seem as reasonable as it was pervasive. The Black intellectuals would scorn him, and white-appointed Black leaders would denounce him; the Christian Church would oppose him, and the local enclaves of orthodox Islam would repudiate him. But Elijah Muhammad was a man for the times. He was as dedicated as he was fearless; he was as imaginative as he was charismatic. He persisted in challenging the formidable phalanx of forces confronting him, and ultimately he prevailed. In the midst of his harassment by federal agents, local police, and others determined to silence him, he declared with characteristic boldness:[13]

I am not trembling. I am the man. I am the Messenger . . . I am guided by God. I am in communication with God . . . If God is not with me . . . protecting me, how can I come and say things no other man has said?

Muhammad drew freely upon the Bible, upon religious and secular mythology, and upon his own unique pedagogical constructs fashioned from experience. He met his converts where they were, ministering as far as he could to a spectrum of needs which transcended the spiritual to find their cruelest expression in more immediate exigencies, which were psychological, economic, social, and political. His "book" was the Qurʾān, but that was not the only book he found useful. His "law" was the law of Islam, but he created his own supplement to fit the limited understanding of his followers. His "God" was Allah, but how does one portray the reality of Allah to a people whose total experience is washed in the pus of racial oppression? He cut his cloak from the cloth available. Elijah Muhammad did not achieve orthodoxy for the Nation of Islam, but orthodoxy was not his goal. What he did achieve was a pronounced American awareness of Islam, its power and its potential. Because of him, there was a temple or mosque in a hundred cities where no mosques had existed before. There was a visible religious presence in the form of a hundred thousand Black Muslims – conspicuous in their frequent rallies and turnouts, and in their little groceries and restaurants and bakeries and other small businesses. The clean-shaven young Muslims hawking their newspapers on the streets, celebrating their rituals in the prisons, debating their beliefs in the media gave to the religion of Islam a projection and a prominence undreamed of in North America. Suddenly, the prison warden, and the social workers, and the people who depended on Black labor were saying that the Nation of Islam had done a better job of rehabilitating the Black *déclassé* than all of the official agencies addressed to that task. And there was a general, if grudging, awareness in the Black community that the Black Muslims had done more to exemplify Black pride and Black dignity, and to foster group unity among the Black masses than any of the more reputable, integration-oriented civil rights organizations.

By the close of Elijah's seigniory, the Nation of Islam was no longer exclusively a community of the poor, the fallen and the déclassé. With Malcom X as its chief public representative, the Nation of Islam had attracted a good number of college students and a showcase element of intellectuals and professionals, including doctors, college professors, and former Christian ministers. An increasing number of celebrities in the world of sports and entertainment, clearly influenced by the Nation, became Muslims. However, most of them joined more "orthodox" branches of Islam to avoid the stigma of belonging to an exclusively Black communion. A notable exception was Cassius Clay, who, after becoming the World Champion of heavyweight boxing, adopted the Islamic name of Muhammad Ali.

Under Elijah Muhammad, the Nation of Islam became the prevailing Islamic presence in America. It was not *orthodox Islam,* but it was by all reasonable judgements, *proto-Islam;* and therein lies a religious significance that may well change the course of history in the West.

After shaping and guiding the Nation of Islam for more than 40 years, the Honorable Elijah Muhammad died on 25 February 1975. Shortly thereafter, the mantle of leadership devolved on Wallace Deen Muhammad, Elijah's fifth son. It was a progression rather than a succession of leadership, for Wallace Muhammad was destined to walk in his own way rather than in the tracks of his father. While he himself had no illusion and no anxieties about orthodoxy, Elijah Muhammad had promised his people that the day would come when they would fully understand their religion and its book, the Holy Qur'ān, and when they would be universally recognized as full members of the world-wide Muslim community. The choice of Wallace Deen (later to be known as Warith Deen Muhammad), to head the Nation after Elijah's death seems intended to implement that promise.

Immediately following his election as Chief Minister of the Nation of Islam, Wallace began the decultification of the following he had inherited from Elijah. His procedures were bold and forthright, but they were fraught with dangers of many kinds. A distinctive feature of the cult phenomenon is that the allegiance of the followers is in a large part a response to the personal charisma of the leader, and the charisma does not lend itself to transfer or succession. This does not mean that a new leader may not have charisma of his own, but it does mean that Wallace did not necessarily inherit his father's ability to obtain obedience and respect. That is why the characteristic cult seldom survives the death of its founder. In the cult phenomenon, few "successors" are able to hold intact the disparate forces controlled by a charismatic founder. Wallace was no exception. The transfer of power was neither complete nor intact, and while the widely predicted catostrophic implosion did not occur, there was dissatisfaction, disillusionment, and an inevitable erosion of membership. An undetermined segment of the Nation either drifted free from involvement, or elected to follow the independent movement of Minister Louis Farrakhan, who remains the most prominent exponent of the original teachings of Elijah Muhammad. For the millions of Blacks whose lot has not been measurably improved by almost three decades of America's "new" racial policies, the romance of Elijah Muhammad's Nation of Islam still represents challenge and identity; and above all, it is a visible expression of the rage and hostility that still pervades the Black undercaste. To them, it is quite clear that the denied and the disinherited are still Black; the deniers and the disinheritors are still white; and Armageddon[14] remains inevitable. They see no compelling reason now to doubt Elijah, or to re-interpret his teachings.

Wallace's task as chief imām is ultimately ordered by the magnitude of his own ambitions. Now that he is confirmed in his leadership role, it is conceivable that he could, if he chose, fashion for himself a comfortable spiritual suzerainty that would demand little more of him than the normative political housekeeping needed to keep him in power. The models for such are many and familiar, and whatever its directions, the Nation of Islam *was* a going institution when Wallace Muhammad took it over. However, Wallace has made it clear that his first priority of office is to eradicate completely the Black nationalist image of the erstwhile Nation by a dramatic reconstruction of its social and political understanding. The sweeping changes implied in this effort alone are enough to give pause to someone less determined, but for Wallace, social reconstruction is only an obvious and necessary prelude to a much larger and even more formidable task. His ultimate goal is, of course, complete orthodoxy for the cult Elijah fathered and made internationally famous as the Nation of Islam.

Wallace Deen Muhammad is a dreamer, but he is a dreamer-cum-realist, and gentle, sensitive, and self-effacing. History may yet prove him to be one of the most astute religious leaders of this age, regardless of communion. A lifelong student of Islam, fluent in Arabic, and well conversant with the nuances of Qur'ānic ideology and its institutionalized projections, Wallace is no less a keen and perceptive observer of the American scene. Therein lies his potential for achievement and service to Islam. If he can bring the erstwhile Nation of Islam into fully recognized communion with orthodox Islam, he will have accomplished more for the propagation of that faith than any *Mujaddid* in modern times. The implications of such a feat are enormous, for they transcend at the outset the mere matter of a ready-made corps of new adherents, although a hundred thousand or so new additions to any religion is in itself a signal achievement. But beyond mere statistics, the presence of a prominently visible, orthodox Muslim community in the United States would have political, social, and economic implications, which might, in time, reverberate far beyond the realm of the spirit.

Ironically, perhaps the most imponderable obstacle between orthodoxy and the Nation of Islam is not the opposition of the purist keepers-of-the-gate inside Islam, but the far more elusive and impalpable body of tradition that defines Black religion in general. Black religion derives, in the first instance, from that aspect of the Black experience that made it difficult to resolve the apparent incongruities between Christianity and Black slavery. It was not only a repudiation of the concept that slavery was acceptable to God, but has always been a critical medium through which the Black community has institutionalized its efforts to effect Black liberation. Inevitably, this has meant a certain estrangement of the Black church from Christian "orthodoxy" as understood and practised by the white church. Hence, the salient tradition of Black religion has always been the sufficiency of its own insight.

Since practically all members of the Nation of Islam trace their religious origins to the Black Christian Church, there is little reason to believe that the notion of "orthodoxy" holds for them any values of overwhelming significance. Further, since Islam is no stranger to the enslavement of Blacks, even in contemporary times, many of those who came to the faith via the Nation of Islam, may well view Islamic orthodoxy as the Islamic counterpart of white Christianity – a possibility probably not overlooked in the careful strategies of Elijah Muhammad. Since Blacks have had more than sufficient reason to question "orthodox" interpretations of any faith in the long travail that is the Black experience, they have learned to rely on feeling – the *direct* experience of the Divine – rather than on the official formulas and prescriptions of the experts. Indeed, the traditional Black answer to questions of orthodoxy has always been:

> If we ain't got it right
> Ain't it a mighty wonder
> De Spirit's over here
> Instead of over yonder?
> If this ain't true religion
> How come I got the feelin'
> My soul done caught on fire
> And left this world a'reelin'?

Certainly there is impressive evidence that Wallace Deen Muhammad has given such problems the most painstaking scrutiny before determining his own strategy for making Islam, in a relatively short period of time, the major religion in America after Christianity.[15] The catalogue of changes Wallace has accomplished in only five years of leadership tenure is already long and detailed. There have been changes of doctrine, changes of structure and administration, changes of name, style, role, and office. There were changes of official attitude about race, political involvement, and military service. High-ranking members of the ruling hierarchy were demoted or reassigned; financing of the movement's superstructure was redesigned and a strict accounting system introduced. The Fruit of Islam was disbanded. Key elements underpinning Elijah Muhammad's mythological doctrines were either allegorized, reinterpreted, or quietly abandoned altogether, and the "blue-eyed arch-enemy," that is, the "white devils," were rehabilitated and welcomed into the movement as brothers. The American flag is now displayed in every Muslim school, and the Pledge of Allegiance is made before morning prayers are offered. Still, the chief imām confesses with the candor of new revelation:[16]

> The former leader, the Honorable Elijah Muhammad, taught something that was un-American and un-Islamic. Now that I am

leading the Community, following the Sunni (the way) of Prophet Muḥammad, I find it now more difficult because it seems that many Americans liked it better when we were isolated – separated from the American people. Many that I thought would congratulate me, have not.

In opting for corporate legitimacy for his Nation rather than for the personal emoluments traditionally available to such offices as his, Wallace was never far from the risk of losing everything. That risk was defused to some degree by the nature of his investiture. Although his name was presented for consideration by the surviving members of Elijah Muhammad's family, his appointment to office as Chief Minister of the Nation of Islam was given unanimous ratification by 20,000 members of the Muslim Nation (assembled in Chicago) on 26 February 1975. Once he assumed office, the chief imām immediately moved to dissociate himself and his office from the commercial interests so long a feature of the Nation of Islam. This strategy not only removed his office from the possibility of a conflict of interest, but it freed the new leader for the implementation of the grand vision that he had held since the days he headed the temple in Philadelphia in the late 1950s.

The "Islamization" of the Nation of Islam reached deeper and deeper. Ministers of Islam became "imāms"; temples of Islam became "mosques," and later, "masjids." Black people, believers and non-believers alike, were redesignated "Bilalians" in remembrance of Bilal Ibn Rabah, friend and confidant of the Prophet Muḥammad. The fast of Ramaḍān, traditionally celebrated in December under Elijah Muhammad, was rescheduled to coincide with the lunar calendar used by other Muslims throughout the world; and the Nation's official newspaper, *Muhammad Speaks*, was re-named *The Bilalian News*. The roles of women were upgraded, military service was no longer forbidden, and believers were urged to take an active part in the civil process. Malcolm X was rehabilitated and the Harlem mosque was renamed in his honor. In October 1976, the Nation itself changed names, becoming thereafter "The World Community of Al-Islam in the West" (WCI). Four years later the name would change again to The American Muslim Mission, "which," the imām explained, "speaks more to our aspirations and thrust."[17] During the same period the imām changed his own name from Wallace to "Warith" Deen Muhammad. He explained that this change was necessary because the man for whom he was named, Wallace Fard, had invested the name Wallace "with symbolism and mysticism," and that it had "an un-Islamic meaning."[18]

Finally, Imām Warith Deen Muhammad[19] made it clear that while most of the Mission's commercial holdings had been sold or placed in the hands of individual businessmen, the interest in the provision of economic opportunities for all who needed them was undiminished. This interest was made tangible in a dramatic development, which also exemplified the movement's new understanding of its civil responsibilities and opportunities. In February of 1979 the World Community of Islam signed a $22 million contract with the U.S. Department of Defence. The Muslims are teamed with Allen A. Cheng and Associates, a Chinese-American entrepreneur, and doing business as the American Pouch Food Company. They will manufacture an updated version of the C-rations previously used by the military. The marketing potential of the new industry is estimated at more than $60 million annually.[20]

Although the leadership of Warith Deen Muhammad has been aggressive and far-reaching, it has also been low-key. The Muslims are no longer "news" in the sense they were when Elijah Muhammad and Malxom X were the regular sources of newspaper headlines or television commentaries. This may well be a blessing in disguise. The energy crisis and America's chief political crises are all centred in areas of the world where Islam holds sway, and a more pronounced visibility of the growing Muslim presence in America might well drench the efforts of Warith Muhammad in a backwash of anti-Islamic sentiment. No one is more aware of this possibility than is the imām himself, and while he has not retreated from the principles of his faith, he has been diligent in showing himself and his movement to consist of reliable and responsible Americans, open and receptive to dialogue and co-operation with all who are receptive to them. In a book called *As the Light Shineth From the East*,[21] the imām attempts to spell out his position on the more controversial issues that nag at his leadership philosophy, or which otherwise threaten the rapprochement he wants between the American Muslim Mission and the diverse publics it wants to impress. Where Elijah advocated a separate Black nation, for example, Imām Warith declares: "I am a patriot of . . . the true blood of the Constitution of the United States";[22] "Now we are balancing [Elijah Muhammad's teachings] so we can develop an awareness in the children [of Islam] that they are not only members of a race but they are citizens – members of a nation – we want to grow in the full dimension of our country";[23] "My greatest desire for our community AMM is to . . . one day hear that a Muslim, a real Muslim, a genuine Muslim from our Community has become a governor, or senator, or head of some big American corporation."[24] The imām is a vocal supporter of the Equal Rights Amendment, and his work with prisoners and ex-convicts earned him an invitation to address the American Congress of Corrections composed of prison administrators from all over the United States and Mexico.

Obviously, the old Nation of Islam has come a long way under Warith D. Muhammad, but exactly how far is a very critical question yet to be determined. It is probable that those reforms designed to bring the movement into closer alignment with today's version of the American Dream will eventually be accorded the recognition and applause the imām has thus far found elusive. (He has already been honored with the Walter Reuther Humanities Award, and he shares the Four Freedoms Award with such laureates as Eleanor Roosevelt and John F. Kennedy.) Nevertheless, considering the increasing polarities between East and West, there is no guarantee that the same reforms will not militate against the prize the imām wants most – unqualified recognition for the American Muslim Mission (AMM) as a legitimate segment of world Islam.

The signals from the East appear to be encouraging. Warith Muhammad enjoyed cordial relations with former Egyptian president Anwar Sadat (as did Elijah Muhammad with Sadat's predecessor, General Nasser). A more weighty significance however, may be suggested by the fact that Warith was the only American observer invited to the Tenth Annual Islamic Conference of Ministers of Foreign Affairs (which met in Fez, Morocco); or in Warith's new role as a conduit for Islam's varied missionary enterprises in America. In 1978, a number of the oil-rich Persian Gulf states, including Saudi Arabia, Abu Dhabi, and Qatar named the American imām "sole consultant and trustee" for the recommendation and distribution of funds to all Muslim organizations engaged in the propagation of the faith in the United States.[25] A mosque estimated at $14–16 million is on the drawing board for the south side of Chicago, to be financed by contributions from the international community of Islam. About two million dollars have already been donated by just two donors, with an additional quarter-million given to the imām by one of them to be used directly for his educational budget.[26] Such largess is not without its hazards. Some established Muslim groups in the United States are unhappy about the attention the American Muslim Mission has received since Warith Deen assumed leadership, and in their pique they are quick to dismiss him as a propagator of (Elijah Muhammad's) "lies," and "no Muslim." Also, the risk that the American Muslim Mission will be seen to be manipulated by international politics is inescapable. Certainly, there is no lack of potential manipulators, as Imām Muhammad must readily admit; but the potential for manipulation is the critical test of both the man and the movement. If either should falter, Islam will be the loser in America, once again.

Notes

1. *See* Will Herberg, *Protestant-Catholic-Jew* (New York: Doubleday, 1955), p. 274.

2. *See The Constitution of the United States of America.*

3. *Cf.* C. Eric Lincoln, "Americanity, the Third Force in American Pluralism," *Religious Education,* vol. 70, no. 5 (1975): 485.

4. *Cf.* Martin Marty, *Righteous Empire: The Protestant Experience in America* (New York: Dial Press, 1970).

5. For a discussion of Spanish (Roman Catholic) precautions against the threat of the spread of Islam among the American Indians through Black proselytization and intermarriage with Blacks, *see* Clyde-Ahmad Winters, "Afro-American Muslims from Slavery to Freedom," *Islamic Studies* vol. 17, no.4 (1978): 187–90.

6. Ibid., pp. 190–205.

7. Such a man was Ayuba Suleiman Abrahima Diallo of Annapolis, Maryland. Diallo, also known as Job ben Solomon, eventually gained his freedom after 1731 through British interests impressed by his knowledge

and his strict observance of the Qur'ān. Winters, "Afro-American Muslims," p. 191. *Cf.* Kunte Kinte, Muslim protagonist in Alex Haley's celebrated *Roots* (New York: Doubleday, 1978).

8. The Society for the Propagation of the Gospel in Foreign Parts was the missionary arm of the Church of England. Originally organized in the interest of converting the Indians, the society turned its attention to the Blacks after the Indians repeatedly rejected the "white man's religion."

9. *Cf.* Cotton Mather, *The Negro Christianized, An Essay to Excite and Assist the Good Work, The Institution of Negro Servants in Christianity* (Boston: B. Green, 1706). Mather catalogues a long list of benefits, including Divine approval, to be gained by bringing the Blacks to Christ, while refuting the popular arguments for excluding them from Christendom.

10. Betty Patchin Green, "The Alcades of California," *Aramco World Magazine* (November-December 1976): 26–29.

11. For an account of the Moorish-Science Movement, *see* the following: Arthur H. Fausett, *Black Gods of the Metropolis* (Philadelphia: University of Pennsylvania Press, 1944); Arna Bontemps and Jack Conroy, *They Seek a City* (Garden City, New York: Doubleday, Doran, 1945). *See also* C. Eric Lincoln, *The Black Muslims in America*, 1st ed. (Boston: Beacon Press, 1961), pp. 51–55.

12. *See* C. Eric Lincoln, *The Black Muslims in America*, 1973 rev. ed. (Boston: Beacon Press, 1973) for a definitive study of the development of the Nation of Islam under the leadership of Elijah Muhammad, and of the impact of the movement on American racial and religious practices.

13. *Mr. Muhammad Speaks,* May 1960.

14. Elijah Muhammad taught that "the Armageddon," a final clash between the forces of good (i.e. Blacks) and the forces of evil (i.e. Whites), must take place "in the wilderness of North America" before the Black Nation could be fully restored. *See* Lincoln, *Black Muslims in America.*

15. Such a projection assumes that since Judaism has only about six million adherents in the U.S., it could be numerically eclipsed by a crusading Islam in relatively short order.

16. From an interview with Dirk Sager, correspondent for Station ZDF, German television; "Communicating for Survival," World Community of Islam (WCI) news release, 27 December 1979.

17. WCI News Release, 30 April 1980.

18. WCI News Release, 2 April 1980.

19. His official title was changed later to Leader and President of the World Council of Islam in the West.

20. *The Bilalian News,* 16 February 1979.

21. Warith D. Muhammad, *As the Light Shineth From the East* (Chicago: WDM Publishing Co., 1980).

22. "Communicating for Survival," 27 December 1979.

23. Ibid., 28 September 1979.

24. From a personal interview with Warith Deen Muhammad, 9 April 1980.

25. "Communicating for Survival," "Imam Warith Deen Muhammad, a Biographical Sketch," n.d.

26. From a personal interview with Warith Deen Muhammad, 9 April 1980.

Minister Louis Farrakhan and the Final Call: Schism in the Muslim Movement

Lawrence H. Mamiya

In the last chapter, Dr. Lincoln has described the changes that have occurred in the move towards Sunni Islam with the accession of Wallace (Warith) Deen Muhammad to his father's mantle of leadership. The focus of this chapter is on the schismatic counter-movement led by Minister Louis Farrakhan that is currently gaining influence in the Black community. Several articles on Wallace, including a *Playboy* interview, have completely missed this dissident group, partly, perhaps, because of Farrakhan's policy of not giving interviews.[1] But it is only a matter of time before the significance of the counter-movement becomes public.

Before examining Minister Farrakhan's position and programs in more detail, it is helpful to use Malcolm X's life and career to interpret and reflect upon the conflicting directions of the two groups. A simple typology might be composed of the "Old Malcolm" and the "New Malcolm": the Old Malcolm as Malxolm X under the leadership of the Honorable Elijah Muhammad and the New Malcolm as "El-Hajj Malik El-Shabazz," the Sunni Muslim convert after his pilgrimage to Mecca in 1964.

At the Edge of the Grave: Malcolm, Louis, and Wallace

Malcolm X's life and martyrdom have become a watershed event in the history of the Nation of Islam and in Black American history. Only Dr. Martin Luther King, Jr., could match the shadow of influence cast by him in the last 20 years. The directions and evolution of Malcolm's life show the paths that have been taken by Louis's Nation of Islam and Wallace's American Muslim Mission, formerly the World Community of Islam in the West.

Malcolm had a close personal relationship with both Louis and Wallace. He was influential in converting Louis in Boston and setting him on his path as a minister of the Nation. Wallace had taught Malcolm about the Qur'ān and some Arabic. In his autobiography, Malcolm said, "I felt that Wallace was Mr. Muhammad's most strongly spiritual son, the son with the most objective outlook. Always, Wallace and I had shared an exceptional closeness and trust."[2]

The three men became key participants in the "Elijah affair," an internal scandal that rocked the Nation and led to the silencing of Malcolm and eventually his final split from the Nation. Some would conjecture that it also led to his death. The affair referred to Elijah's consorting with his secretaries and fathering a number of children. When Malcolm learned about it through the Muslim grapevine, the stories were confirmed by Wallace. For his part in providing the confirmation, Wallace was ousted from the Nation by his father for a period of time, the first of three expulsions for disobedience. Malcolm himself was personally shocked and sought to prepare his followers and leaders on the East Coast: John Ali, National Secretary; Captain Joseph, who commanded the Fruit of Islam in Malcolm's Temple No. 7; and Minister Louis X of Boston. It was Minister Louis X and Captain Joseph who sent in the report that Malcolm was spreading false rumors. Malcolm believed that this report, and not his public comments about "chickens coming home to roost" after John F. Kennedy's assassination, led to his downfall. Malcolm felt betrayed by his old comrades. In fact, after Malcolm left the Nation, it was Minister Louis X who led the public attack in a series of scathing articles in *Muhammad Speaks* in 1965, denouncing his new position and calling him an "international hobo." Some passages read like a veiled death warrant although Louis eventually leaves vengeance to Allah:[3]

> Only those who wish to be led to hell, or to their doom, will follow Malcolm. The die is set, and Malcolm shall not escape, especially after such evil, foolish talk about his benefactor. . . . Such a man as Malcolm is worthy of death, and would have met with death if it had not been for Muḥammad's confidence in Allah for victory over his enemies.

I have elaborated on the "Elijah affair" only because the incident is still simmering in both groups. Wallace has used the event to begin to demythologize the semi-divine status his father had acquired in the Nation. He wanted his followers to see that the Honorable Elijah Muhammad was only a man, susceptible to human weaknesses. The gradual evolution to Sunni orthodoxy could only occur if Elijah Muhammad is viewed as a great teacher, and not as the Apostle of Allah he is believed to be by the Black Muslim community. In a speech in Detroit, "Warning to the Hypocrites," delivered on 2 December 1979, Minister Louis Farrakhan used the Elijah affair to criticize hypocrites (Wallace's group) who attempt to take advantage of such domestic events. He drew upon Biblical and Qurʾānic passages and stories (e.g. Noah lying naked before his sons, Absalom and David, and Lot and his wife at Sodom and Gomorrah) to warn against the fate of sons who betray their fathers.

In comparing Wallace and Malcolm, the New Malcolm is most appropriate. Malik Shabazz after Mecca began to de-emphasize the racial doctrines of the Nation. He began to differentiate between levels of people. He no longer saw all whites as devils, although to him many whites still acted like devils. However, he no longer held to a metaphysical view of whites as intrinsically evil. This is the path that Wallace has taken. However, while he was still alive, the New Malcolm did not go as far as Wallace has. He did not allow whites to join his newly formed organizations – the Muslim Mosque Inc. or the Organization for Afro-American Unity. He saw the possibilities of working with whites on selected issues but not as members. Malcolm's overwhelming concern was for the Black masses, and he believed white membership would lead to an erosion of Black independence.

If anyone in the Muslim movement closely resembles Malcolm X in career and style it is Minister Louis Farrakhan. Although he is shorter than Malcolm in physical appearance, he is also as fair-skinned as Malcolm was. Born in the Bronx, New York, but raised in Boston, Minister Farrakhan's career path has been almost exactly the same as Malcolm's. Malcolm was influential in Farrakhan's conversion from professional violinist and calypso singer to minister in the Nation. Minister Louis X took over the Boston mosque that Malcolm founded and later, after the split, he was awarded Malcolm's Temple No. 7 in Harlem, the most important pastorate in the Nation after the Chicago headquarters. He was also appointed National Spokesman or National Representative after Malcolm's demise and began to introduce the Hon. Elijah Muhammad at Savior Day rallies, a task which once belonged to Malcolm. Like his predecessor, Farrakhan is a dynamic and charismatic leader and a powerful speaker with the ability to appeal to the masses of Black people. Both men also started newspapers for the Nation. Malcolm X founded *Muhammad Speaks* (now called *Bilalian News*) in the basement of his home. In 1979 Louis Farrakhan began printing editions of *The Final Call,* a name which he resurrected from early copies of a newspaper that Elijah Muhammad put out in Chicago in 1934. The "final call" was a call to Black people to return to Allah as incarnated in Master Farad and his Apostle Elijah Muhammad. For Farrakhan the final call has an eschatological dimension; it is the last call, the last chance for Black people to achieve their liberation.

The major difference between them is that while Malcolm X was evolving, changing his views from the Old Malcolm to the New, Louis Farrakhan has remained consistently the same. In 1965 Minister Louis X sharply criticized Malcolm's defection from the Nation, for turning his back on Elijah Muhammad, the man who was responsible for changing Malcolm from a hoodlum and pimp to one of the most feared and articulate voices of the 1960s. In a speech in Harlem on 18 May 1980, Minister Farrakhan said:[4]

Yes, I even stand on Malcolm X. If Malcolm had not made the *turn* that he did, I would not have a guide to keep me from making the same mistake. He was an example for me instead of me being an example for him. He knew one day that I would be the National Representative. Because he died I have a chance to live.

This new Malcolm, then, still remains as a negative example for Louis Farrakhan.

Where Malcolm's religious experience at the ḥajj in Mecca and his world travels in Muslim countries and in Africa had deepened and broadened his views of humanity, drawing him closer to Sunni orthodoxy and the Muslim brotherhood, Farrakhan's world travels have led him to examine the hypocrisies of classical Islam, especially in regard to race. In his autobiography, Malcolm wrote:[5]

> America needs to understand Islam, because this is the one religion that erases from its society the race problem. Throughout my travels in the Muslim world, I have met, talked to, and even eaten with people who in America would have been considered "white" – but the "white" attitude was removed from their minds by the religion of Islam. I have never before seen *sincere* and *true* brotherhood practiced by all colors together, irrespective of their color.

In a contrary view Minister Farrakhan said in his Harlem speech:[6]

> I am here as a servant of Allah and black people (not Mecca). I see Muslims taking advantage of Blacks in Arabia and Africa. I will not jump over one black Christian to find brotherhood with a Muslim. . . . If you [orthodox Muslims] are so interested in the Black Man in America, why don't you clean up the ghettoes in Mecca. . . . The ghettoes in the Holy City where the Sudanese and other black African Muslims live are some of the worst I've seen anywhere. . . . I see racism in the Muslim world, clean it up!

Scholars like Bernard Lewis, Chancellor Williams, John Henrick Clarke, and Allan and Humphrey Fisher have provided ample documentation of the problems of racism within Islam.[7] Afro-American intellectuals and the Black Muslims have often characterized Christianity as the "slave religion." That label is correct for the slave trade on the west coast of Africa. But it also applies to Islam and Muslim activity in the east coast slave trade. Nevertheless, Farrakhan's challenge is for Muslims to live up to their professed ideals.

During the years 1975 to 1978 when Chief Imām Wallace D. Muhammad began introducing sweeping changes in the Nation, Minister Farrakhan traveled widely abroad, pondering the consequences of those changes. In an interview he said:[8]

I have visited Christian, Muslim, Socialist, Capitalist and Communist countries. Wherever I found a plurality of races, I consistently found the Black Man on the bottom. This deepened my realization of a necessity for a specific message to Black people to remedy the many ills we suffer.

After a period of silence for several years following the Hon. Elijah Muhammad's death, Louis Farrakhan has begun to publicly challenge Wallace's group, the American Muslim Mission, and to rebuild the Nation of Islam by returning to Elijah Muhammad's message and program.

Black Particularism: The Message, Program, and Organization of the Nation of Islam under Minister Louis Farrakhan

In spite of the turgidness of his writing and his grandiose sociological schemes, Professor Talcott Parson's conception of "pattern variables" may be helpful in establishing a framework for analyzing the Black Muslim-Bilalian movement in the United States. According to Parsons, "pattern variables" are a series of polar opposites held in dialectical tension in any social situation.[9] They are descriptive of the general directions or options available to any social group. The pattern variables of "universalism vs. particularism" are most helpful in interpreting what has happened to the movement in the last five years. "Universalism" tends to move in the direction of a larger, more inclusive sense of human life and society, toward openendedness, a constant breaking of barriers and boundaries. "Particularism" moves in the opposite direction, towards exclusion, rigidly holding to boundaries, a particular sense of peoplehood. Universalism vs. particularism underlies my use of the interpretive devices of the "Old Malcolm" and the "New Malcolm." The attempt of the Prophet Muḥammad to break the boundaries of tribalism in 7th-century Arabian society by introducing Islamic universalism is another example of this phenomenon. Yet, the dialectical tension still exists in all religious groups. In spite of the constant warnings against tribalism in the Qur'ān, tribalism still persists in 20th-century Saudi Arabian society. The Black Muslim-Bilalian movement, too, exhibits similar tensions.

It must be stated at the outset that Black particularism or Black nationalism is a reaction to centuries of racial oppression in the United States of America. The defenders of black nationalism state that it is a reaction to white supremacy by the victims of oppression. Black nationalism, black solidarity, they assert, is a step toward liberation.

Black nationalism exhibits itself in the following ways in the Nation of Islam:

1. The opening creed or the "Shahadah" of the Black Muslims says, "In the name of Allah who came in the person of Master Farad Muhammad, the Beneficient, the Merciful, the One God to whom all things is due, the Lord of the Worlds and his Apostle, the Honourable Elijah Muhammad, the last of the Messengers of Allah." Allah is identified as the incarnation of a Black person; God is Black and the place of the Prophet is usurped by the Hon. Elijah Muhammad. He is given the place of honor because, it is said, he saw and knew Allah (Master Farad) personally, which of course is doubly heretical in orthodox Islam (to identify a human being as God, and to say that one saw God).

2. Black Muslims believe in the metaphysical view that identifies whiteness with evil and white people with the devil. The long-standing Western tradition of identifying blackness and darkness with evil is thus dramatically reversed. In the story or myth of Yakub, which contains this metaphysical perspective, Black Muslims are taught that Mr. Yakub, a Black mad scientist in rebellion against Allah, created the white race, a weak hybrid race devoid of any humanity. The white race would rule for 6,000 years through trickery and deviousness, causing chaos and destruction; at the end of their time white rule would end in a cosmic apocalyptic battle with the Black Man, the Original Man, who would emerge as the victor. This central myth of Yakub functions as a theodicy, as an explanation and rationalization for the pain and suffering inflicted upon Black people in America. For example, when a cellmate in a Massachusetts state prison whispered to him, "The white man is the devil," Malcolm Little described the statement as having the powerful, jarring impact of a revelation of religious truth upon him. The "revelation" made sense of his experience; the chaos of the world behind prison bars became a cosmos, an ordered reality. It explain-

ed his father's early death at the hands of the whites and the hunger pangs that came when boiled dandelion greens did not suffice for nine children and a widow. It explained why he dropped out of school at the eighth grade when a white teacher told him he ought to be realistic and think of becoming a carpenter instead of a lawyer even though he was at the head of his class. Finally, it explained all the years of hustling and pimping on the streets of Roxbury and Harlem as "Detroit Red," a "bad dude," and his arrest and incarceration for armed robbery. That was the beginning of Malcolm X and his story has been repeated many thousand times over in the 44-year history of the Nation under Elijah Muhammad's guidance.

Minister Farrakhan has described his conversion from a so-called professional musician, a violinist and singer, to minister in the Nation. He gave up his musical career twice, he said, once outside the Nation and a second time within it because the Messenger asked him to. He wrote and performed the only song and music ever recorded and officially approved by the Nation, "A White Man's Heaven is a Black Man's Hell." He also wrote the only play performed in the Nation concerning the trial of a white man by Blacks called "Orgena" or "A Negro" spelled backwards.

After his father's death in February 1975, Imām Wallace Muhammad attempted to move the Nation in the direction of Islamic universalism by reinterpreting the basic racial doctrine in a symbolic manner. Following Malcolm X's lead, he put emphasis upon attitudes, values, and behavior, upon "mindedness," how a person thought. Malcolm said,[10]

> We were truly all the same (brothers) – because their belief in one God had removed the "white" from their minds, the "white" from their behavior, and the "white" from their attitude.

For Wallace the devil is a "mind," an attitude. A person who is born white is not *ipso facto* evil or the devil. Whiteness is a symbol for evil only when it is linked to the attitudes and values that characterize white supremacy and racism. Blackness, on the other hand, is a symbol for goodness and humaneness. Just as it is possible to have a black person with a white mind, that is, one who acts and thinks white – the proverbial "Oreo" or "Uncle Tom," it is also possible to have a white person who thinks black – a "reverse Oreo."

Minister Farrakhan has argued that these symbolic reinterpretations of doctrine do a great injustice to Elijah Muhammad's teaching. When the Messenger said that the white man is the Devil, he really meant it, physically and metaphysically. In a similar vein, when Elijah claimed that God is a Man (Master Farad), he meant it as literal fact and not as allegory. Farrakhan feels deeply that Wallace has betrayed his father's teaching. "Even though Imam Wallace D. Muhammad," he said in Detroit, "disagrees with his father, he would be nothing by himself without that father."[11]

Farrakhan's position is that the little man from Sandersville, Georgia, with only a third-grade education, Elijah Muhammad, has unlocked both the Bible and Qur'ān for Black people with a message of liberation. He feels that Elijah's uniqueness was his ability to use *both* sacred scriptures to deliver his message, recognizing the predominance of Christianity in the Black community. At the City College of New York he said,[12]

> Send the Arabs in with all their oil money and their Qur'āns and let them try to convert the people in Harlem to Islam. See what will happen? They can't do it. They can't begin to talk to the guys in the street. Send Mao Tse-Tung in. He was able to organize 700 million Chinese in China. Do you think he can organize Harlem? No! Black people need a special and unique message. This was the Hon. Elijah Muhammad's contribution. He understood the psyche and condition of the Black Man in America.

According to this view, the message of the Nation is intended to unlock the self-knowledge of the Black masses. Its principle is found in all liberation movements, namely, an oppressed people can only be freed by themselves.

3. The program of the Black Muslims under Farrakhan's leadership remains the same as demanded by the Hon. Elijah Muhammad. The 10 points of the program listed in every issue of *Muhammad Speaks* constitute the demands of social and economic justice for all Black people – equality of employment and education, the freeing of Black prisoners, who constitute 75 percent of the national prison population, a denigration of all attempts to integrate with whites, and Black control of Black institutions. The most distinctive point of the program is the demand for a separate land or territory, fertile

and rich in minerals, for Black people. Although the Muslims under Farrakhan have continued to remain vague about the exact location of this territory (in the U.S. or abroad), it is the demand that has received strong emphasis. Part of the reason for this emphasis is that in a time when Black nationalism has waned and assimilation into the American mainstream has continued apace with a tenfold increase in the Black college student population, the demand for a separate land underlines in the strongest way possible the continued alienation of the members of the Nation of Islam from American society and the rejection of the American way of life.

In a personal interview I asked Minister Farrakhan how realistic was it to continue pressing for a separate territory. He replied, "Anything is possible. Blacks are owed this land as reparations for centuries of slave labor. Besides, whoever thought that the Vietnamese would win against the United States? Yet they defeated the mightiest world power. Anything is possible in this world. Inshallah."[13]

As one of his first acts of reorganizing the Muslim Movement and bringing about the major changes he wanted, Mujaddid Warith Muhammad completely dismantled the Fruit of Islam. Trained in karate and sometimes in the use of firearms, the Fruit was created by Master Farad to act as the "moral right arm" of Black Islam. Its members provided security, searched everyone who entered a mosque or major meeting, acted as ushers, and sometimes as enforcers of the strict code of discipline. The Fruit of Islam had become an "élite organization" within an organization, as Dr. Lincoln pointed out in his study.[14] Raymond Sharieff, Elijah Muhammad's brother-in-law, was the Supreme Captain of the national organization. Wallace claimed that this group had become a "political order," a "hooligan outfit, a hoodlum outfit." Men were "viciously beaten," he said in an interview with a reporter, "simply for asserting their rights or for failing to sell their quota of newspapers." He was shocked to learn upon assuming leadership that more than 10 believers were killed, "for no other reason than that they didn't want the FOI completely dominating their lives."[15] If any group within the internal structure of the Nation would provide organized opposition to Wallace's ideas it was the Fruit; this must also have played a part in his decision to dissolve them.

In his attempt to rebuild the Nation of Islam upon the foundation of the Hon. Elijah Muhammad's message and program, Minister Louis Farrakhan has resurrected the Fruit of Islam and its female counterpart, the Muslim Girls Training or MGT. These two groups form the basis of the new Nation. Many of those who left Wallace's group, disillusioned at the changes he instituted, were key members of the Fruit. Now in rallies and meetings across the country, Farrakhan makes a special effort to point to the new Fruit of Islam, the guards standing tall and erect with short hair, bow ties, and suits, all spit and polish. He chides the audience, "You left the Nation and its discipline. You have gone back to drinking alchohol, smoking reefers, eating pork, and boogie-ing. All the progress we made has been lost. The brothers are back on the street shooting dope and dying. The sisters are on the street corners hookin' for the white man." Turning to the MGT members, women in Muslim dress with long gowns and headdresses, "Black families are breaking up at an unprecedented rate," continues the National Spokesman, "and Black women and children are left unprotected because there is no man around."[16] The silence in the audience is deafening as people nod assent.

It is difficult to estimate how many people left the Nation as a result of the changes introduced by Wallace. Both the old Nation and the new American Muslim Mission have been reticent on the question of membership. Wallace himself told Dr. Lincoln if there has been a decline it has not been noticeable. However, the young Imām Sabir Alaji of Poughkeepsie told me that there were about 1,200 members in the early 1970s at its peak in Temple No. 7 in Harlem (now the Malcolm Shabazz masjid) when he was a member under Minister Farrakhan's leadership. Now there are about 400 members. If the Nation's second-largest mosque is an example, there has been some decline in membership, although Minister Farrakhan's popularity may have been responsible for the two-thirds drop in Harlem when he left. At a "Welcome Home Brother Farrakhan" rally in Harlem on 18 May 1980, which was not widely publicized, an enthusiastic, cheering crowd of 10,000 to 12,000 people attended.

The strategy of the leaders of the resurrected Nation of Islam is to continue holding large rallies and meetings, relying primarily upon

the charisma of Minister Farrakhan. These meetings are also fund-
raising events and places of recruiting new members. When a siz-
able financial base is established, the Nation will begin setting up
mosques or temples and stores for economic activity. When Imâm
Wallace took over he inherited an empire with an estimated value of
between $60 to 80 million. Minister Karriem Abdel Azziz, Farra-
khan's chief of staff, said to me, "It was like a coup. We [the Nation]
lost all the resources that the Hon. Elijah Muhammad had built
up." [17]

Socio-Economic Conditions and the Changes in Black Islam

In attempting to explain why the changes in the Nation have been
on the whole successfully implemented, most analysts have emphasized only the change in leadership when Wallace Muhammad replaced his father. [18] While the factor of leadership is very important
in any analysis, it does not completely explain the changes. It is my
hypothesis that the internal socio-economic conditions of the Nation
have also contributed to the shift in ideology and are now affecting
both groups. A quasi-Weberian analysis of the changes in the Black
movement will illustrate this thesis. I refer to Max Weber's *The Protestant Ethic and the Spirit of Capitalism,* where he posited a dialectical relationship between religious ideas and socio-economic conditions. He argues that religious ideas can have "unintentional" economic consequences by affecting the "spirit," that is the attitude and
mentality of believers. [19] Weber did not argue that Calvinistic Protestantism created capitalism, but rather that it created the "spirit" or
the motivational attitudes which affected the lifestyle of its believers. Another theoretical idea I will use in this analysis is Weber's
concept of "elective affinity." Elective affinity refers to a believer's
selection or election of which religious ideas he or she will follow. [20]
The resonance between the social location or class conditions of the
believer and the religious idea are crucial. In spite of what religious
élites say, the mass of believers decide for themselves what is most
important in the message. Briefly, my hypothesis is that the Nation
of Islam, which began as a lower-class movement, has become increasingly middle-class and that this phenomenon has affected both

groups. Wallace's American Muslim Mission has retained a largely middle-class membership, while Farrakhan's resurrected Nation is seeking to find its mass base again in its lower-class origins.

There is no direct evidence, no hard data or statistics, that anyone can give for the subtle class shift which has been occurring in the Nation of Islam ever since its founding in the Detroit ghetto called Paradise Valley in 1930 by Master Farad. Concerning any vital information on membership or finances in the Nation, a common phrase is often repeated, "Those who know don't say and those who say don't know." Nevertheless, there is indirect evidence for changes in socio-economic conditions in the Nation from recent interviews, historical sources, and from the resonance of the leaders' messages and actions with the lifestyle and morality of their members.

Ever since Elijah Muhammad took over the mantle of leadership of the Nation, when Master Farad mysteriously disappeared in 1934, his message of Black nationalism tinged with a strong dose of economic uplift: "do for yourself," was directed at the Black masses. Like all Black mass movements the Black Muslims attempted to "capitalize on the lower-class Black Man's despair and reservations about the white man."[21] Elijah Muhammad spent much time visiting and corresponding with the Black outcasts of society, particularly those in prison. When Malcolm X and his followers went "fishing" in Harlem – expeditions to proselytize for the Nation – they quickly learned to stop going to Black main line denominations where they were often snubbed. Instead they waited in front of the numerous small storefront churches where curious members would often stop, ask questions, and talk.

Almost all of the recruiting techniques and messages of the Nation were designed to appeal to the Black lower class. There is an interesting illustration of this phenomenon in the Fisk University oral history tapes of Miss Sharon Scott, who recounts her experience in the Black Muslim movement. After her freshman year at Fisk, Miss Scott, the daughter of a Black physician from the Midwest, dropped out to join the Muslims in Nashville in 1970. This was at the height of campus turmoil across the country, and in her personal search for identity she felt that the Muslims were a radical Black group with a sense of direction about itself. Like all new recruits she was given a letter, about one paragraph long, which she had to copy in her own handwriting and submit to the head minister for approval. Unless the letter were copied perfectly with no mistakes, it had to be re-copied again, sometimes a dozen times. Miss Scott viewed this exercise as "ridiculous" and her response was, "Why don't they Xerox it?"[22]

What Miss Scott failed to realize is that this exercise is a commitment mechanism for the Nation. When a poor, uneducated, often illiterate person who can barely write an X for his name, takes the time to copy a letter over and over again until it is perfect, that person is well on his way toward membership in the Nation. The commitment mechanism is a simple test of patience, obedience, and discipline; it is in Muslim terms a test of "submission" – "As-lama" to Allah and the Nation. Yet, Miss Scott's response, "Why don't they Xerox it?" points to fundamental problems and dilemmas for the Nation of Islam. How does a basically lower-class movement accommodate itself to the middle class?. Further, what happens when a lower-class movement itself unintentionally becomes middle-class?

The program of the Hon. Elijah Muhammad strongly emphasized developing an independent Black economy from farms to retail outlets and the rigorous Muslim code of morality emphasized economic activity. Their ascetic lifestyle encouraged thrift and savings, not buying on credit, nor spending money on foolish pleasures like dancing or sporting events, and not wasting it on frivolous things like cars, clothes, and records. It was a rigorous ethic without much humor. Black Muslims became well known for their honesty and hard work so that they were often able to obtain jobs more easily than other Blacks. In his study, Lincoln correctly called them "Black Puritans."[23] Weber argued that it was the internalization of the "Puritan ethic" in the lifestyle of its believers that unintentionally created the conditions for the breakthrough to a capitalistic economy from a feudal one. In the case of the Muslims, the internalization of a Black Puritan ethic created the conditions that would favor major changes in Black Muslim ideology.

It is my opinion, and the opinion of several others within the Muslim movement, that the program of the Hon. Elijah Muhammad over the past 44 years had succeeded to a large extent. I offer two illustrations of this position. Imām Sabir Alaji and his wife taught in a Muslim school in the Bronx for a number of years. Their desire was to start their own Muslim school in the Mid-Hudson. After saving and scrimping they recently bought a large house and began renovating it for their own school. When asked for his opinion of a class shift in the movement, Alaji replied, "But I'm not rich, I'm poor." However, by all standards of socio-economic status (education and income) this young imām, who was a struggling college student five years ago, had become middle-class.[24]

In another personal interview the head secretary of the Oakland, California, masjid, Sister Evelyn Akbar, said:[25]

> Everybody who has been in the movement for 10 years or more has moved upward. You can't help it because the Hon. Elijah Muhammad's message was strongly economic. If Elijah Muhammad was about anything, he was about uplifting people's education and economics.

She also gave examples of a number of young Black lawyers and doctors she knew who kept tapes of Elijah Muhammad for their own security and inspiration, to help them overcome obstacles and make it through difficult years of law school and medical school. "Some have become Muslims and some are not," she said, "but the message reached them."

What happens, then, when a movement's religious morality and lifestyle have produced the unintended consequences of changing its class conditions? What kinds of changes are needed for accommodation?

Prior to Elijah Muhammad's death, the Nation of Islam began to make appeals and overtures to the Black middle class. Its acquisition of a Black bank in Chicago, its future plans for a Muslim hospital, and an accredited university-level educational system called for the kinds of skills and knowledge that only the Black middle class possessed. In the issues of *Muhammad Speaks* prior to the change in leadership, there was a noticeable toning down of the racial doctrine, less use of the term "white Devil," for instance. The reason for this, in Lincoln's perception, is that members of the Black middle class who have been the victims of racism are chary of being called racists themselves.[26] Also, Black nationalism has found fertile soil in the Black lower class because that class has less to lose economically and materially than the middle class. It can risk more in being alienated from white society.

A few months after Elijah's death, Wallace Muhammad declared, on 18 June 1975 at McCormick Palace in Chicago, "There will be no such category as a white Muslim or a black Muslim. All will be Muslims. All children of God."[27] When the shock waves settled some members left the Nation, but those who stayed rationalized the changes in the manner of Ms. Akbar: "The message of Elijah Muhammad did not fit the times. Times have changed and people have changed."[28] Imām Ali Rasheed, head of the Malcolm Shabazz Masjid in Harlem, said in an interview:[29]

> Those who were indoctrinated by racism were disappointed because the race game had ended. But the majority of the people were open to social change and social revolution. We lost people who lacked the understanding, who couldn't make the transition, but we have gained others as a result of the change.

Discipline was the watchword for the Nation under Elijah. Discipline was particularly appealing to those who lived in grinding poverty and whose lives lacked structure. The efficient, military bearing of the Fruit of Islam guards attracted the young men who hung out on the streets, while the women found the Muslim stress on family structure and discipline within the family appealing. At times the discipline became very stringent and overbearing. In her oral history tape, Sharon Scott said, "The men in particular have it hard, they are under a lot of strain.... You could see it in their eyes."[30]

When Wallace Muhammad announced the relaxation in the disciplinary system and dress code, it was favorably accepted by the members. Men were no longer compelled to sell their quota of newspapers and women were allowed to go out alone at night. Sports are now encouraged for youngsters and masjids even sponsor baseball teams. Music, too, is not frowned upon. In her own statement Ms. Akbar welcomes the change:[31]

> I was searching for spirituality and morals when I joined the Muslims [over five years ago]. I was looking for a strong family

life. . . . Basically, I'm in my early 30s with a college education. People my age—we felt we needed the stability, morality and sense of some type of justice and belief in God. Our secular education had left God out. The transition to the Qur'ān and the Prophet Muḥammad under Wallace was a relief. Elijah Muhammad gave us discipline. . . . But I feel I don't need the security of a uniform anymore. The relaxation of the discipline has made things easier with my parents. They couldn't understand all the things I could or couldn't do before. You know there was not that much flexibility. I couldn't go to take night classes. Under Wallace I could and I finished my education. Or even sports, except for Muhammad Ali, sports were not encouraged. Tonight I'm going to see the Oakland A's play.

The barriers of racial doctrine and the restrictions of a strict disciplinary system have been removed by the American Muslim Mission. The way is now open for recruiting the Black middle class more actively. The Mission has also moved toward major accommodations with the mainstream of American life. Political participation and voting are now encouraged. Muslims can be drafted. The red and white crescent and star flag of the Nation of Islam has been replaced by the American flag in all masjids. Wallace endorsed Jimmy Carter for President. He has also enjoyed the kind of respectability among Black civil rights leaders that his father and Malcolm X never had.

The Nation of Islam as resurrected under Farrakhan's leadership has continued the policy of being separated and alienated from American society. Where Wallace has downplayed the racial factor, Farrakhan has made it a major theme in his critical speeches. More importantly, the Black Muslims are now returning to "fish" again from the fertile ground of the Black masses or the Black underclass. As Eddie X, a recent convert to the Nation in Greenville, Mississippi, said to me, "What attracted me to Farrakhan was his deep concern for the despised and rejected of American society. I don't see Wallace's group as being concerned with the outcasts. They seem to me to be Arabicized intellectuals, spouting Arabic phrases at you."[32]

My hypothesis of a growing class split between the two factions of the Muslim-Bilalian movement is not meant to be deterministic or one-sided. Obviously, there are middle-class symphathizers in Farrakhan's Nation, and Wallace's American Muslim Mission does have programs for the black lower-class, like their prison program. These are general tendencies within each group; the social location of the believers often affects which leader they will follow and which part of the message they will internalize in their lives.

Conclusion: The Future

Schisms are not new in the life of the Nation of Islam and this latest one does not apear to be fatal to the movement. In the 1960s Hamaas Abdul Khaalis led a secessionist communion of orthodox Hanafi Muslims out of the Nation. They are the Washington, D.C., group with which the basketball star Kareem Abdul Jabbar is associated. When Master Farad mysteriously disappeared in 1934, a struggle for leadership broke out in Detroit, and his chief spokesman "Minister of Islam" Elijah Muhammad had to flee with his faction to the Chicago's south Side to establish Mosque No. 2. Minister Farrakhan said to me, "If you want to understand what is happening in the Nation now, go back to the history of the early years in Detroit."[33] Obviously he was identifying himself with Elijah Muhammad. But he was also also obliquely referring to another splinter group led by Abdul Muhammad, who rejected Master Farad's teaching that Black Muslims were not Americans and owed no allegiance to the American flag. Abdul Muhammad's group was instead based upon loyalty to the American Constitution and the American flag.[34] This splinter group, which did not survive, was meant to refer to Wallace's American Muslim Mission.

There have been rumors of jihād between both the Wallace and Farrakhan factions. Violence is always a possibility since it has occurred in other splinter Muslim movements before (Malcolm X's assassination and the murders of seven members of Khaalis's family in January 1973 in Washington D.C.). Many male Muslims have had self-defence training in the Fruit of Islam, and the prison background of some members may influence their response to a volatile situation. Wallace Muhammad has explicity instructed his followers to ignore the Farrakhan faction, to pay them no attention in the hope that they will go away. Farrakhan's position is that "We will not be the aggressors. But if they attack, the Holy Qur'ān instructs us to fight back. An eye for an eye." Thus far, the situation has remained at the level of rumor but both leaders travel with many body guards.

What does the future hold for both groups? Wallace's adoption of Islamic universalism and his inheritance of the resources of his father's empire place him in a very strong position. His leadership also coincides with an Islamic ferment and renaissance that the world has been witnessing for several decades, ever since the discovery of black gold in the deserts of Saudi Arabia in 1938. World Muslim leaders have always been interested in establishing an indigenous Muslim outpost in America. Wallace's accession to leadership of the Nation of Islam gave them an unprecedented opportunity for establishing a permanent American Muslim movement. He has been given the title of Mujaddin (reviver of religion) and the rights of certifying who makes the ḥajj to Mecca from the United States. Besides attracting the Black middle-class, Wallace's position of universalism has opened the possibility of recruiting interested white converts. It has also opened direct lines of communication to African Muslims, who are often found worshipping in the Mission's masjids. With its move to Sunni orthodoxy, the American Muslim Mission will be less subject to the conflicts between charismatic personalities. A more routinized, institutionalized charisma, the "charisma of office" to use Weber's term, will help thwart some of the conflicts that have plagued the Muslims in the past. As Ms. Akbar said, "Consistently as a community we have been followers of personality rather than knowledge. Now we have knowledge." The Mission's schools are the only ones in the U.S. that offer training in Arabic from elementary grades upwards. Because of the long years involved in using the language properly, one can predict that future American Islamic scholars will come from Wallace's group.

Minister Farrakhan's Nation of Islam is heavily dependent upon his own charismatic energy and upon the vicissitudes of a particularistic position, namely the ebb and flow of Black nationalism. For example, we saw the rise of Black nationalism in the 1960s and witnessed its relative decline in popularity in the 1970s. However, for the decade of the 1980s the prospects for the continued growth of Farrakhan's Black Muslim movement look very good only because the economic and racial conditions in America are very bad. Deep racial hostility and economic insecurity are heightened among the members of the Black underclass that has been the major carrier of Black nationalist ideology. Predictions of a recession in the American economy in the 1980s will take the form of a major depression in the Black community like that of 1974–75.[35] With the Black unemployment rate more than double that of whites, and the unemployment rate of Black teenagers at 42 percent nationwide (close to 80 percent in sections of Brooklyn and Harlem) and the gains of the 1960s slipping away, Minister Farrakhan is finding large responsive audiences for Muslim soldiers in the Final Call to Black Islam. The racial rebellions in Miami, Orlando, Chattanooga, etc., are only a harbinger of things to come. Malcolm X's words in the early 1960s are still applicable today only because America has not yet learned from the past: "Black social dynamite is in Cleveland, Philadelphia, San Francisco, Los Angeles . . . the black man's anger is there fermenting."[36] It is this anger and resentment that will give birth to a new generation of Black Muslims in America.

Notes

1. Bruce Michael Gans and Walter L. Lowe, "The Islam Connection," *Playboy Magazine* (May 1980);Yvonne Haddad, "Islam and American Blacks," *The Link* vol. 2, no. 4 (September-October 1979): 6–7; and Peter Goldman, "Afterthoughts: 1979," in *The Death and Life of Malcolm X*, 2nd ed. (Urbana, Illinois: University of Illinois Press, 1979).

2. Malcolm X and Alex Haley, *The Autobiography of Malcolm X* (N.Y.: Grove Press, Inc., 1964), p. 297.

3. Farrakhan is quoted in Goldman, *Death and Life*, p. 248.

4. Minister Louis Farrakhan, speech at "Welcome Home Brother Farrakhan" rally at the Nat Holman Gymnasium, City College of New York, Harlem, New York, 18 May, 1980. Hereafter referred to as Harlem speech.

5. Malcom X, *Autobiography*, p. 340.

6. Farrakhan, Harlem speech.

7. For Islam's problem with race see the following: Bernard Lewis, *Race and Color in Islam*, (New York: Harper Torchbooks, 1971). Allan G.B. Fisher and Humphrey J. Fisher, *Slavery and Muslim Society in Africa*, (New York: Anchor Books, 1972); and Chancellor Williams, *The Destruction of Black Africa*. (Chicago: Third World Press, 1976). Williams pre-

sents a strong critique of Islam's role in the destruction of the classical African kingdoms of Mali, Songhay, Ghana, and Timbuktu. *See also* John Henrik Clarke, author of chapter 9, "Time of Troubles (1492–1828)" in *Horizon History of Africa,* Alvin M. Josephy, Jr., ed., (New York: American Heritage Publishing Co., 1971).

8. Haki R. Madhubuti, ed. "Black Books Bulletin Interviews Minister Abdul Farrakhan," *Black Books Bulletin,* vol. 6, no. 1 (Chicago: Institute of Positive Education, Spring 1978).

9. Talcott Parsons and Edward Shils, *The General Theory of Action* (Cambridge: Harvard University Press, 1951).

10. Malcolm X, *Autobiography,* p. 349.

11. Farrakhan speech, "A Warning to the Hypocrites," 2 December 1979, Detroit, Michigan. Hereafter referred to as Detroit speech.

12. Farrakhan, Harlem speech.

13. Lawrence H. Mamiya, personal interview with Minister Louis Farrakhan, Harlem, New York, 18 May 1980.

14. Eric C. Lincoln, *The Black Muslims in America* (Boston: Beacon Press, 1963; 2d ed. 1973), p. 222.

15. Goldman, *Death and Life,* p. 433.

16. Farrakhan, Harlem speech.

17. Lawrence H. Mamiya, personal interview with Minister Karriem Abdel Azziz, Harlem, New York, 18 May 1980.

18. *See* Gans and Lowe, "Islam Connection"; Haddad, "Islam and American Blacks"; Goldman, *Death and Life.*

19. Max Weber, *The Protestant Ethic and the Spirit of Capitalism* (New York: Charles Scribner's Sons, 1958).

20. Hans Gerth and C. Wright Mills, eds. and trans., *From Max Weber: Essays in Sociology* (New York: Oxford University Press, 1946).

21. Lincoln, *Black Muslims,* p. 69.

22. Brenda Sloan, "Sharon Scott Interview" (Nashville, Tennessee: Fisk University Oral History Project, 10 December 1972).

23. Lincoln, *Black Muslims,* pp. 83–98.

24. Lawrence H. Mamiya, personal interview with Imam Sabir Alaji, Poughkeepsie Masjid, 31 January 1980, Poughkeepsie, N.Y.

25. Lawrence H. Mamiya, personal interview with Sister Evelyn Akbar, Oakland Masjid, 30 April 1980, Oakland, California; hereafter referred to as Akbar interview.

26. Lincoln, *Black Muslims,* p. 171.

27. *Nashville Tennessean*, "Rule Switch Allows Whites As Muslims," 19 June 1975.

28. Akbar interview.

29. Lawrence H. Mamiya, personal interview with Imām Ali Rasheed, Malcolm Shabazz Masjid, April 22, 1980, Harlem New York.

30. Brenda Sloan, "Sharon Scott Interview."

31. Akbar interview.

32. Lawrence H. Mamiya, personal interview with Eddie X at Office of the Delta Ministry, 7 February 1980, Greenville, Mississippi.

33. Mamiya, Farrakhan interview.

34. Lincoln, *Black Muslims*, pp. 17–18.

35. Robert B. Hill, *Black Families in the 1974–75 Depression* (Washington, D.C.: National Urban League Research Department, 1976).

36. Malcolm X, *Autobiography*, p. 312.

VI

Statements from within the Tradition

Islamic Ideals in North America

Ismʿail R. Al-Faruqi

Some contemporary historians have speculated that Muslim sailors were the first to cross the Atlantic and arrive on the shores of the New World. Others have speculated that Christopher Columbus was guided to these shores by Andalusian or Moroccan Muslim navigators and assistants whose services he had hired. The spectacular nature of these speculations led not to renewed scholarly examinations of the claims, but to widespread propagation and expansion of them. The Muslims of the world were anxious to rediscover their legacy of past accomplishments, and the Muslims of North America were anxious to discover their roots in history. The greater and more daring the accomplishments, and the farther back the roots of American Muslims could be projected/discovered, the greater the psychic satisfaction. It was therefore natural for them to be delighted by such claims, and to repeat, expand, and spread them with relish.

If the origin of the Islamic presence in North America is still a subject of speculation, the settlement of African Muslims in North America in the 16th to 18th centuries is certain. The fall of al Andalus to European power was a cataclysm for millions of Muslims. It is indeed probable that some of them who had fallen captive to Spanish power might have constituted the first human cargoes shipped to America. It is equally probable that those who were unable to cope with the cataclysm might have volunteered to travel to the un-known. Of such events we have no record. Later, as sugar planta-tions in the Caribbean Islands demanded more and more hands to work them, the Spaniards, the Dutch, the French, the English, and finally the Americans began a systematic raiding of the coasts of Africa south of the Sahara to hunt and seize humans for sale in the slave markets of the New World. There can be little doubt that some of these unfortunates were Muslims, for we know that by 1600 a large proportion of the populations of what are now Mauretania, Senegal, Gambia, and Guinea were Muslim.

The climate of slavery was not one in which Muslims could per-petuate their religion or culture. Slave masters gave the slaves their own names, forced them into their own faith, and rejoiced in seeing in them the reflection of themselves. Little did it matter whether the slave was replica or caricature. It was sufficient that his old identity was obliterated. If the slave failed to realize the new identity, the master saw the failure as natural, because the slave was an *unter-mensch.* Unfortunately, nothing is known about these early Mus-lims in America. Some of their practices may have survived in Afro-American traditions; or, having affected those traditions, the heri-tage may still be deducible from them. To my knowledge, no such study has yet been made. I have heard arguments pointing to the ex-istence of village or town names, of words in the Afro-American vocabulary, and of oral traditions still being passed on. But a schol-arly study of the matter is badly needed and most eagerly awaited.

Muslims from the Near East and other parts of the Muslim world began to emigrate to North America in the last quarter of the pre-vious century. Their purpose was similar to that of other immigrants to North America, namely, to escape from undesirable conditions in the old country and search for fortune in the new. Among the oldest immigrants who lived as a group and succeeded in preserving their identity are the Muslim communities of Cedar Rapids (Iowa), De-troit (Michigan), Edmonton (Alberta), and London (Ontario). The Balkans, where the Ottoman Empire was receding; Aden, which British rule had made an open roadstop for the ships of the world; and Syria-Lebanon, where political unrest and administrative in-stability were at their highest, were the sources from which the immigrants came. The period between the two world wars saw a large number of immigrants from Syria-Lebanon, the Balkans, South Russia, Caucasia, and Turkey, where postwar conditions left much to be desired. There was an influx into Canada, of Muslims from the British Commonwealth countries to which Muslims had first emigrated in pursuit of service with British forces. Very few Muslims came to study since domination of their homelands by Britain, France, and Italy made it imperative for them to study in the colonizing countries.

After World War II Muslim immigrants began to arrive in North America in significant numbers. Independence from European colonialism and the ascendency of the United States on the world scene attracted Muslim students from everywhere. Their protracted stay and free mixture with fellow students and local communities, and the opportunities for study-*cum*-work programs, paved the way for them to change status or to return as immigrants if conditions at home proved to be less than expected. The failure of their home governments to provide opportunities for employment and/or advancement, to solve chronic problems whether economic or political, and their oppressive – even tyrannical – police regimes provided further impetus to professionals and to the educated to emigrate. The desire to improve the quality of life and the promise of good fortune in North America certainly played an important role. More important, however, was the near total bankruptcy of their home political regimes. That bankruptcy was evident on the moral, spiritual, educational, economic, social, and political levels. It is not surprising that all post-independence regimes were caricatures of Western models, whether democratic or dictatorial, or that their social, political, and economic ideals were caricatures of democracy, national integration, and social justice. One and all, these regimes were proper instruments of neo-colonialism, whether deliberately or otherwise. In Muslim countries, an essential failure was their separation from Islam, the only ideal capable of moving and inspiring the masses. Nationalism, secularism, democracy, socialism, and communism are all impotent, as they provide no "cause" that can appeal to idealism. They are unable to command the loyalty of Muslims, and can furnish no internal energy to push the Muslim to self-exertion, or to hold him back from temptation. Such would have been provided by Islam and the imām-quality it develops and requires as base and criterion. But Islam was deliberately neglected – indeed combatted.

Muslims saw evidence of this bankruptcy in the dissolution of the Syrian-Egyptian union in 1961, the Pakistani-Indian War of 1965, and the Arab-Israeli War of 1967. The despair into which these debacles plunged the Muslim world vented itself in massive emigration to North America and other Western countries. In 1968, the government of Egypt declared emigration legal and free. Hundreds of thousands of Muslim professionals and other middle- and upper-class persons arrived in North America after these dates, constituting a real Muslim brain drain.

Today, immigrant Muslims in North America number about two million. One-fifth of them are here temporarily as students and visitors; the remainder are permanent residents.

There had been conversions to Islam among Americans prior to the 1930s when Elijah Muhammad launched his movement. Their numbers, however, were small, and their effect upon the Islamic presence in North America was limited. The first American-born individual to significantly change that presence was Elijah Muhammad. He began in the thirties to call the Afro-Americans to abandon the identity imposed upon them as slaves and to return to their original Muslim African identity. His call spread rapidly among them and assumed visible proportions in the big cities after World War II. The movement spread vigorously in the ghettos of American cities. The headquarters in Chicago became a hive of administrators, public relations officers, business entrepreneurs, and preachers. The appearance of Malcolm X on the scene, his rebellion against Elijah Muhammad following his conversion to Sunni Islam in Mecca, and his assassination all helped the Islamic movement to grow. The demise of Elijah Muhammad and the Sunni reforms of his son Warith Muhammad have relaxed the discipline and done away with the paramilitary youth organization, Fruit of Islam. The vigor and enthusiasm are still the same, proportionate to Muslims' capacities, and to the challenges. If anything, the movement is growing, in number, in consciousness, in understanding of, and attachment to, the genuine ideals of Islam.

Although no adequate statistics are available, American-born Muslims number about two million. One-and-a-half million belong to the World Community of Islam in the West (recently renamed The American Muslim Mission). About half a million Afro-Americans are Muslim and belong to various other organizations, mostly Sunni. About 5,000 white Americans have joined the ranks of Islam.

The Afro-Americans who responded favorably to Elijah Muhammad's call did not do so because of their ancient attachment to a Muslim African identity. The memory of that identity had been lost in the intervening centuries. The motivation for their re-entry into Islam came directly from the appeal of Islam, and from the malaise of their social, cultural, and spiritual existence. The ideals of Islam provided the external objective stimulus. An analysis of them will provide an understanding of their movement. The same ideals also attracted other Afro-Americans, as well as white Americans who were introduced to Islam by Muslim students, immigrants, or visitors.

To begin with, Hellenized Christianity, the religion of the culture in which they were immersed, could have no hold on the Afro-American mind. Whether because of their Islamic tradition, or that of African archaic religions, the Afro-American could hardly understand, and much less digest, the myths of Hellenized Christianity. The transcendence and incarnation of God, monotheism, and the trinity, salvation as fait accompli and yet-to-be-accomplished, the Kingdom of God as here and not-here, God's death and resurrection, vicarious guilt, suffering and merit, original sin and fallenness, the church as body of God – all these have remained utterly opaque and incomprehensible to him. His subscription to them hardly ever went beyond lip service. His innate innocence, his simple common sense, his awareness of being imposed upon and pushed from all directions by his masters, his will to life and happiness, and his sense of justice were all contradicted and violated by a religion that seemed to deny them theoretically while its adherents denied them in practice. Nothing in his background could serve as a base for the myths of Christianity; nothing in his veins and muscles could welcome its values; and nothing in his experience could warrant acceptance of its paradoxes. Asceticism and monkery, world- and life-denial, individualism, and personalism, ran against the grain. That is why Christianity had a different meaning for Afro-Americans than for white Anglo-Saxons. That is why it gave rise among the former to a great variety of evangelistic churches whose range extends all the way to heterodoxy. That is why for the most part, Christianity for the Afro-American was little more than an exercise in self-excitement, a subjective attempt at self-transport, where the tribal dance was replaced with singing. That is why the inner quietude of Western Christianity gave way to orgiastic celebration; and its disciplined resoluteness and patient resistance, to surrender and acquiescence.

Christianity's apparent collusion with misery, its blessing and recommendation of poverty, agreed with the slave master's design to exploit the Afro-Americans and keep them in poverty. Its rejection of culture and emphasis on simple faith agreed with the design to keep them ignorant. Its denigration of the body, of the flesh, and of the world agreed with that of keeping them in abject conditions. Finally, its doctrine of original sin implanted in them a complex of inferiority, impotence, and submission, and its eschatology implanted a renunciation of any will to improve their conditions in this world. Their adherence to Christianity, of whatever sect, was an ideal case for the Nietzschean analysis of slave-morality, for the Marxist theory of religion as opium.

The irrelevance of social justice to Christianity enabled white racism to make the Afro-American a pariah in the land of his birth, even after his emancipation from slavery. He is a de facto second-class citizen, even when his acculturation has reached very high degree. His color is a pollutant always to be kept at a distance. Indeed, the gap between the races is widening, not contracting, despite the gains on the legal front. Official pronouncements on the part of government and public bodies run far ahead of implementation, and real gains may or may never follow upon them. The ideal of equal opportunity remains empty without the prerequisites of equal preparation of Afro-Americans and equal disposition towards them by the whites. Like so many whites in all classes of society, Afro-Americans turned their backs on Christianity as time proved its incapacity to deal with social problems. True, the modern library is full of books and essays that seek to present Christianity as religion of social concern. Their logic is unconvincing because none dares to address itself to the world- and life-denial endemic to Christianity, or to the paradoxes at the core of its creed. The result is that these attempts of the theologians hardly ever go beyond the classroom. Outside, in the high-rise office building where decisions are made, Christian concern is hardly ever a motive or factor in politics, education, government, or business.

Islam, on the other hand, offered a more attractive creed. In contrast to the Christian view of the fallenness of man and creation, Islam teaches that man is created innocent. Adam's disobedience was Adam's, not humanity's. Moreover, it was repented by Adam and forgiven by God. Man is placed on earth as God's viceregent, to fulfil the will of God and to prove himself morally worthy in the process. Indeed, Islam teaches that God created man perfect, in the best of forms, and equipped him with all that is necessary for fulfilment of his raison d'être. Hence, man is responsible and God will reckon with him. This world is the only world. *Al Akhira,* or the other world, is judgement and consummation of reward and punishment, not another world projected as an alternative to this world. Nor is it postulated out of a condemnation of this world and the need to make man accept his misery in the here and now. Islam finds the meaning of human life in man's cosmic function as the sole bridge through whose free action the higher part of God's will (namely, the moral) becomes fulfilled in history. Islamic humanism does not deify man. Nor does it make him the measure of all things. It regards him as the crown and ultimate purpose of creation, but under God Whose servant he is.

Islam teaches that poverty is the promise of Satan, that the good things of life belong to Muslims to enjoy, that Muslims ought to be healthy, clean, strong, and productive. It holds men responsible for their own misery, and urges them to rise, to strike out in the wide world and seek God's bounty. It regards productive work, bringing welfare to oneself, to one's dependents and neighbors, and to mankind, as worship. Even the rituals of worship Islam regards as possessing dimensions of worldly welfare whose non-realization vitiates the rituals themselves. God's viceregency on earth consists of *tamkīn fi-al-ʿard* (seizing the earth with strength), *iṣtiʿmar* (reconstruction of the earth), and doing good deeds for the sake of and in obedience to God. God has made the world beautiful: He ornamented the firmament and created beautiful and goodly objects for man to use and enjoy. He has made the whole creation subservient to man to the end of proving himself morally worthy. Islam teaches that the realization of the absolute in this world is indeed possible, that it is precisely man's obligation to pursue and actualize it. Hence, Islam impinges upon history and seeks to move it toward fulfilment of the divine patterns. For Islam, history is of crucial significance.

Islam teaches an ethic of action. In its purview, personal intention, good will, and purity are indeed values. But if the moral agent does not go beyond them to enter space and time, and there so interfere in the events as to deflect their courses towards the good, their value becomes very small. That is why Islam had to develop the law, to institute the umma with political, judicial, economic, administrative, and social organs to implement it. The unity of God, Islam interprets as transcendence before which all humans are equal in creatureliness, and hence as equally subject to the law of God whether as agents or subjects of moral action. That is why the umma is necessarily universal, intended to cover humanity. Islam countenances no color, no race, no chosen people complex, no nationalism, no relativism in anything that matters. Political action is viewed by Islam, to use the expression of Muhammad Iqbal, as the expression of its spirituality. Every individual, it holds, is a shepherd responsible for his circle; and the umma is responsible for mankind. The highest standard is justice. The Muslim is obliged to realize it in his person, his family, his country, the world, or on the other side of the moon. Likewise, he is obliged to redress the balance of justice whenever and wherever it is upset by anyone, be he commoner or king.

The evil of social injustice in North America is sufficient to pull its victim away from the status quo and urge him to seek a change. If he happens to be Afro-American, the dominant ideology or religion which had never penetrated his mind has less attraction and less power to keep him from preparing for conversion to another faith. The inherent merits of Islam, its values, its capacity to correct the evils of racism and injustice, and to inspire men to assume the burdens of self-salvation by their own effort, do the rest. Hence, Islam has spread through da'wa, the clear call of men and women to specific duties and rights presented as God's commandments and perceived as sure solutions to the problems facing them.

Islam confers upon the Afro-American, or the victim of injustice, a new identity as well as a new dignity. It teaches him that his misery is not imposed by God, but by His enemies; that its removal is both possible and obligatory. And it promises him success here as well as in the hereafter if he succeeds in getting rid of injustice. In fact, it teaches him that with Islam, he cannot lose. Islam convinces him that he has right of usufruct in the world under God. It sobers him up with a feeling of responsibility, with the demand that his burden is worldwide in scope and comprehensive in coverage. Islam balances this universal responsibility with ummatic mutuality, reassuring every member that the whole umma is responsible for him. Upon conversion to Islam, the forsaken, downtrodden victims of injustice, and the racially discriminated Afro-Americans, acquire as their own the world community of Islam with its billion souls.

Muslim immigrants have come to these shores to study or to seek livelihood and opportunity for professional advancement. In most cases, they are beggars at the Western altar of knowledge; or receivers of Western affluence and economic development. This is the way Muslim immigrants see themselves.

The "immigrant" mentality stands on two necessary assumptions: a home country and culture perceived as bankrupt, despised, hated, forsaken, left behind; and a new country and culture seen as alien, awesome, superior, admired, and desired but not yet appropriated or mastered.

However, many Muslim immigrants, who may have come in search of Western knowledge, professional advancement, or wellbeing, have awakened in this process to a fuller recognition of Islam, their religion and their cultural tradition. It is immaterial that their awakening has come late in life, or that it has come only at the challenge of the new culture. It takes a rubbing stone to prove the gold present in a piece of ore; but that does not change its golden nature. Once the Islamic vision is recaptured, a radically new outlook on life, emigration, on the new world and one's role in it, is obtained. How does Islamic consciousness achieve this?

First, the Islamic vision removes all consciousness of guilt which the immigrant may feel at having emigrated and, as it were, forsaken the country of his birth. In this view he is personally responsible for the unfavorable temporal circumstances which led to his decision to emigrate, and would have been to blame had he suffered their continuation. Allah – May He be glorified – incited him to take his fate into his own hand and alter it radically by emigration, if the road to a radical transformation of the home country and its circumstances is blocked (Qur'ān 4 : 97–98).

Second, the Islamic vision removes all consciousness of guilt that the immigrant may feel at his success in the new station. Many successful immigrants are overwhelmed by feelings of gratitude to their adoptive country, which they seek to express by extraordinary acts of charity and thanksgiving. Noble as these sentiments may be, they mask a guilt complex which is appeased by the said acts of generous giving. Far more serious is the realization, implied in such guilt feeling, of the absolute goodness and superiority of the new location. The Islamic vision wipes out this feeling by convincing the immigrant that the success is not his, but God's; that it is God Who so oriented and manipulated his life and his new circumstances as to bring about success. Being God's grant to him, his success is innocent and free, perfect ḥalāl which he may appropriate, possess, and enjoy in good conscience (Qur'ān 48 : 18–20). Indeed, the Islamic vision opens the immigrant's mind to a new vista of opportunities for greater success by its teaching that the whole world is the Muslim's to develop in fulfilment not only of his basic needs, but also of his need for comfort, pleasure, joy, and even luxury (Qur'ān 67 : 15; 8 : 26).

Third, the Islamic vision lays before the eyes of the immigrant a new challenge and a new promise, by imposing upon him the duty to call all non-Muslims to Islam, and reminding him that in word as well as in deed he is obliged to be the witness of God on earth, His viceregent who establishes the institutions of Islam and makes God's word and judgement supreme. In North America, and the West generally, there is so much atheism, so much abnegation of religious truth, so much rejection of the most fundamental tenets of Judaism and Christianity, so much skepticism, as to arouse and shake the least sensitive religious conscience. The person endowed with the vision of Islam cannot witness the scene with indifference.

Sooner or later, he must come to the realization that his emigration from his land of birth, permitted and arranged by God, and made by Him successful through re-establishment in the new land, were links in a nexus of purposes leading to his new assignment as "caller to God." His is a new task whose fulfilment awaits him as a new glory, a completion of his faith, a discharge of the most sacred duty, a testament unto history. Hasn't God sent him to his new *Medina* that he may freely call the people to the truth? that he may by his eloquence, his "bon example" and his "greater jihād" convince mankind of the truth that God is God, ultimate Cause and ultimate End, sole Creator and Master, Whose commandments are before all humans to be obeyed?

Fourth, the Islamic vision provides the immigrant with the criterion with which to understand, judge, and seek to transform the unfortunate realities of North America. Here is a whole continent giving itself to alcohol and drugs, to sexual promiscuity and exploitation, to family destruction and individualism, to cynicism and pessimism, to racism and discrimination, to the pursuit of Mammon at the cost of morality and justice, to the rape of Mother Nature, to political and economic imperialism against the rest of humanity. Certainly, the continent is groaning with pain, and it is crying out for help which only the person with the vision of Islam can give. For such a one is the only person professing as well as living a categorical NO! to all these evils at once, the only one whose "No" is backed up by the strongest arguments, the longest history, and the greatest achievements of success at implementation.

Fifth, the Islamic vision provides the immigrant with the deepest love, attachment, and aspiration for a North America reformed and returned to God, to carry forth His message and Law unto mankind, in this and all other spaces. Nothing could be greater than this youthful, vigorous, and rich continent turning away from its past evil and marching forward under the banner of Allahu Akbar! And none could be more motivated to bring it about, to serve it with all his energies and to lay down his life for its cause, than the person with the vision of Islam. Above all, the Islamic vision provides the orientation necessary for the health and sanity of this continent, namely, the subjection of the life of its peoples to the moral law; of their corporate and political conduct to peace and justice, to international assistance and co-operation with the victims of injustice and poverty everywhere. The Islamic vision enables North America to increase its mastery and use of nature, but disciplines it with responsibility to the generations of the future and to God for His gift of nature and his other creatures who are no less our equals. The Islamic vision endows North America with a new destiny worthy of it. For this renovation of itself, of its spirit, for its rediscovery of a God-given mission and self-dedication to its pursuit, the continent cannot but be grateful to the immigrant with Islamic vision. It cannot but interpret his advent on its shores except as a God-sent gift, a timely divine favor and mercy. It will not fail to recognize in the person with Islamic vision a true son, though born overseas, whose spirit is nearly identical with that of the early founders of the New World, who ran away from oppression and tyranny seeking a haven where they would remold their lives under God, seek His bounty, and raise high His banner.

Sixth, the Islamic vision provides immigrants, as well as native-born converts, with a sense of mission. A new calling stirs them from their complacency and spiritual lethargy. Their life is infused with a new meaning, a new significance whose dimensions are cosmic. In short, whereas before the vision of Islam has taken possession of them they were matériel and instruments for processes of history which they did not understand, let alone control, now they are subjects of these processes, orienting them towards greater goals. They are people with a cause, with the noblest cause! As such, they are entitled to respect above all by themselves, and certainly by their hosts whom they can now define better than the latter can, and whose goals in history and ultimate destiny they can better articulate.

The Future of the Islamic Tradition in North America

Muhammad Abdul-Rauf

The hospitable American melting pot, which had been largely dominated by the Judeo-Christian tradition, has had added to it in recent decades the distinctive traditions of Islam. Driven by political and economic pressures at home, or lured by better educational opportunities and the prospect of success to those who struggle hard, large numbers from various Muslim lands chose to seek better fortunes in the free American climate. This is particularly true since the 1960s, although the trickle of immigrants from Islam has been increasing since the late decades of the 19th century.

The presence of Islam on the American horizon, and the increase in intimate contacts between America and the Muslim world, has resulted in the conversion of many American citizens to Islam, particularly from amongst the Afro-Americans. Impressed by the simplicity of its tenets and its emphasis on equality and the fundamental dignity due to the human person, Americans of African origin feel that in embracing Islam they not only gain a new respectable identity but also are restored to the faith of their ancestors.

Eighty years of Islamic presence has spawned numerous Muslim organizations both at the local and national levels. Many mosques have been built and others are in the process of construction or in the planning stage. They serve as rallying points and places of worship and communal activities. There are also Muslim organizations inside prisons across the United States; some with rooms assigned for prayers and Qur'ānic study sessions. Other religious needs of the Muslim inmates, such as a pork-free diet, providing time for the Friday noon congregation, and adjusting meal timetables during Ramaḍān, are now usually met by the authorities of these institutions.

In recent years, the question of Islamic adaptability to the modern age of technology has engaged the attention of social scientists and scholars of comparative religion. In this context, the case of the American Muslims striving to survive in an alien culture is of special interest. Can Islam, said to be a total way of life, survive at this time of rapid jolting changes? How can American Muslims, one may wonder, cope with the demands of this dynamic and highly technological environment while still clinging to traditions whose roots were laid down in a desert town 14 centuries ago?

In my opinion, based on personal experience and direct observation, and also inspired by the outlook of Islam itself, one can safely assert that Islam and its basic values have every chance not only to survive intact in America but also to flourish in honor and dignity. Islam has a long history of expansion outside its original territory, always surviving as a religion, under all geographic and climatic conditions. It has also been invaded by powerful cultural influences, but has remarkably resisted all attempts at changes and modification, co-existing with, and even absorbing, cultural patterns not in conflict with its religious framework.

Islam is at once a religion and a culture. As a religion, it covers three areas; doctrines, rituals, and non-ritual human activities. As a culture, it includes patterns of living its people may forge and assume in their efforts to meet the challenges of life within the framework of the religious teachings. Its religious features are perpetual, but its people's cultural patterns may adjust to the changing needs of time and place.

The Islamic teachings pertaining to the belief in the monotheistic attributes of God, in his Angels, in the Sacred Books, in his Messengers, and in the Day of Judgement, as well as those pertaining to the ritual duties – namely the declaration of the faith (shahāda), keeping up the five daily prayers (ṣalāt), payment of alms (zakāt), fasting during Ramaḍān (*ṣiyām*), and pilgrimage to Mecca once in a lifetime by those who can afford it physically and financially (ḥajj) – aim at the spiritual elevation of the individual, although they also inspire a sense of unity among the members of the community. On the other hand, Islamic teachings pertaining to the vast area of all types of human interactions and non-ritual activities aim at guiding the individual and society in the struggle to survive and to achieve the optimum degree of satisfaction and happiness on earth consistent with the overall objective of salvation in the Hereafter. This third category may be subdivided into two divisions. There are specific tenets in the form of commandments or prohibitions, such as the commandments to tell the truth, honor parents, deal honestly, show charity to the poor, be neighborly, respect human life and show kindness to elderly people, and the prohibitions of the vices of lying, mistreating parents, stealing, cheating, fornication, murder, drinking alcohol, consuming pork, usury and hoarding. Besides, there are general injunctions, such as the commandment to consume good things and to act righteously, and the prohibition against consuming harmful things or seeking to hurt oneself or wrong any other in any way.

Two observations are relevant here. Whereas the Islamic teachings pertaining to monotheistic theology, tawḥīd, and those pertaining to ritual practices, *ʿibādāt*, are fundamentally spiritual tenets, they also, as we have seen, have their social and disciplinary values. And whereas the third category of Islamic teachings that guide the individual and society in searching to fulfil their needs on earth seem to be first and foremost concerned with what we may describe as secular, materialistic, and organizational matters, they certainly also have their ultimate spiritual value. Observing them is intimately related to salvation in the Hereafter, the ultimate aim of a Muslim. On the other hand, and this is our second observation, the first two categories, as they are so fundamentally spiritual, constitute the core of the Islamic doctrine. They have to be upheld and practised as given: not to be subjected to modification or intellectual reinterpretation, ijtihād. The third area of Islamic teachings, which aims at reducing tension, promoting progress, fostering domestic stability, and political justice, and a successful economy, leaves room for ijtihād and manoeuvrability. A Muslim society may choose alternatives within these injunctions – for example, any nourishing diet, any decent dress, and any type of architecture for their houses and mosques. They are free to choose productive professions and develop their arts, music, and recreational activities. The total sum of these cultural patterns that may be developed or assumed by a given Muslim society may be called "Islamic culture."

The elements of an Islamic culture, therefore, may not be inherent in Islam. They are patterns of culture or a mode of life developed or adopted by a Muslim community. Therefore, when a Muslim moves into an alien culture, carrying with him his cultural heritage, he is at liberty to adjust to the host culture so long as he maintains the core of his religion, including all the specific Islamic tenets in all areas. And this is true in the case of the Muslim community in America.

It should be apparent, then, that there is no sharp line of distinction between secularism and spiritualism in Islam. Muslims strive to strike a balance between the needs of the body and those of the soul. So long as such a balance is maintained, it makes no difference whether a Muslim community pursues a simple camel ecology or a complex jet economy. In other words, there is no inherent conflict between the demands of the advanced American technology and the spirit-elevating teachings of Islam.

In the democratic American climate, Muslims are not hindered from practising their religious ideals, nor are they denied earning full rewards for their labor. They can, and do, build their own mosques, own special burial grounds, develop their cultural institutions, incorporate their Muslim societies, and hold large meetings. During the opening ceremony of the Islamic Center, Washington, D.C., in June 1957, President Eisenhower declared, "We shall fight with all our might to defend your right to worship according to your conscience." Like anyone else, Muslims are guaranteed freedom of worship, freedom of expression, and freedom to gather together. Any prejudice they may suffer because of their faith can be investigated and justice be restored by accessible agencies who are ready to welcome such complaints.

Like all American citizens, Muslims can invest their resources without any limitations; they can climb all ladders of success; can own personal real estate property; can earn, through the legal process, a permanent resident status and naturalization; and they get paid equal rewards for their services. American Muslims partake of the blessings of the most advanced technology; and some of them have been able to effectively contribute to this technological advancement, including medical technology and the conquest of space. In recent years, the visibility of Islam in the United States has attracted the attention of the Christian leadership. Islam is praised by Catholic bishops in their inaugural sermons, and Islam has been granted an Observer Status at the meetings of the Governing Board of the National Council of Churches (NCC). Moreover, the NCC has established a Task Force on Christian-Islamic Relations. The Director of that office, with headquarters at the Hartford Seminary Foundation, Hartford, Connecticut, has been seeking to build bridges of mutual understanding and goodwill.

There can be no special hardship in practising the Islamic religious teachings in America, whether it is the recitation of shahāda or payment of alms or fasting during the month of Ramaḍān. Muslims can, and they do, take leave to make pilgrimages to Mecca; and even when the time of making prayer falls within the working hours, this duty can be performed during the break periods such as the lunch hour.

On the other hand, the dynamism of the Islamic teachings pertaining to human activities outside the ritual domain, which have to be translated into cultural patterns, can fairly easily be adjusted to the American context. In fact, Muslims sometimes bring along with them some pleasant varieties of diet, fine dresses, and beautiful art, which add to the diversity of American culture.

The difficult question of interest that can be earned on bank saving accounts is not peculiar to American Muslims. The problem, however, has become easier with the creation of interest-free Islamic banking systems, in which American Muslims may also invest their surplus funds. They exist in some Muslim countries and in Europe. Moreover there are now in all large cities stores which distribute ḥalāl meat, from animals slaughtered by Muslims according to the prescribed manner. Lastly, criticism of the status of women in the Muslim world, which we do not fully endorse, cannot be extended to America. The American Muslim girl is as literate and as educated as her brother. Her problem is scarcity of competent male

Muslim spouses. Frequent vacations in Muslim countries is, therefore, recommended, not only for this reason but also in order to maintain closer contacts with the Muslim fatherland. Polygamy, illegal in America, is not a recommended Islamic practice. And the pattern of conjugal relationships in which authority and the burden of domestic responsibilities fall on the shoulders of the male partner, constitutes no real problem in America. In our view it is healthier and more compatible with human nature; and it eliminates a great deal of causes of domestic friction. In this regard, we recommend close contacts and frequent visits between Muslim families to counteract the effect of alienation which seems to be inherent in the modern economic structures. Moreover, the modest dress recommended for a female Muslim, which allows only the face and hands to be exposed, should be no source of embarrassment. If fancy dresses of all kinds are tolerated in America, wearing a decent dress by female Muslims should provoke no repulsive feeling. Prejudices suffered at work by newly converted American girls who adopt such a dress on conversion have been duly redressed by competent government agencies. In the mid-1970's, the Equal Employment Opportunity Commission sent me a report on such a case in which Merrill Lynch in New York were obliged to restore a Muslim girl to her position with payment of all salaries and promotions she would have earned since the date of her dismissal.

Strict prohibition in Islam of such evil practices as drinking alcohol, taking harmful drugs, dating, and indulging in pre-marital relations, enhances the success and welfare of the observing Muslim and protects him/her from the undesirable consequences of these vices.

American mothers of non-Islamic background go out of their way in gratefully praising Islam, which has protected their own Muslim children from falling victim to drug addiction and from the influence of their peers. Instead, their youngsters get busily interested in the work of their Islamic institutions and in giving talks to classes and various groups on the merits of their faith of which they are proud. Prohibition of pork, which is a significant element in the American diet, causes no hardship. Muslims can find full satisfaction in the multiple bounties available in the American market. Even in an airplane, a Muslim passenger can be provided with a special pork-free meal if he should intimate his desire at the time of making a reservation.

The American Muslim community, however, is too young, too small, and still insufficiently united as to be politically effective. There is no Muslim lobby or a Muslim Senator or a Muslim Congressman; and Muslims have no influence whatsoever in the news media. Forces unfriendly to Islam take advantage of the situation. Islam is often demeaned and insulted openly and subtly by the media; and there is no adequate effort to remedy these injustices. Middle East studies departments are dominated by scholars who have little regard for Islam. These damaging factors can be counter-productive, especially at a time of general awareness and the need to foster better international relations. However, these prejudices have not been without some advantage. The painful injustices are provoking deeper awareness, especially among the rising generations, of the merits of their religion and greater pride in their traditions. They are seeking to equip themselves with better education, diversifying their interest in order to assert their rights and defend the honor of their heritage in the American environment. In this way, they will contribute more greatly to the glory of the country of their choice and also will be able to build better bridges of understanding and co-operation between the United States and the Islamic fatherland, creating relationships of justice and equality. On the other hand, wealthy Muslim nations ought to help the American Muslim community sincerely and effectively, not only in their efforts to raise mosques, but also to build schools and effective cultural institutions that can spread the noble virtues of Islam.

In conclusion, the adjectival term, "Islamic," in such a phrase as "Islamic culture," need not be treated as an official trademark. Any system that upholds the Islamic ideals of liberty, equality, and human dignity, although it may not carry that label, need not necessarily be considered un-Islamic or anti-Islamic. Since any system, political, economic, or otherwise, that does not violate the Islamic religious and moral precepts can be incorporated into an "Islamic" structure, and since the American constitution guarantees religious freedom, the American Muslims have great latitude in selecting features of the general American life to forge and nurture a viable American Muslim community. Admittedly, there are indeed some deep-seated misunderstandings about Islam, but it is up to the Muslims to work for the eradication of these misconceptions and to set up models of the righteous teachings of their faith. This writer optimistically envisages the growth of such a community as developing into an organic element of the multi-cultural American social fabric, dovetailing the major values expressed in the American constitution and the Declaration of Independence with our fundamental Islamic values to contribute toward a viable 21st-century American society that can truly live under the divine protection of the One Mighty God, Allah, in Whom we trust.

VII

Appendices

Appendix I

Directory of Muslim Associations in Canada*

Newfoundland

St. John's Muslim Association
c/o Dr. Muhammad Irfan
2 Edmonton Place
St. John's
AIA 2N7

Prince Edward Island

P.E.I. Muslim Group
c/o Dr. Awni Raad
12 Poplar Avenue
Charlottetown
CIA 6S7

Nova Scotia

Islamic Association of Maritime
P.O. Box 116
Dartmouth
B2Y 3Y2

New Brunswick

Muslim Association of N.B.
P.O. Box 611
Rothesay Avenue
Saint John
E2L 4A5

Quebec

Association des Etudiants
    Musulman
Laval University
Quebec City

Islamic School of South Shore
2860 Mannille
Brossard
J4Y 1P5

Muslim Community of Quebec
P.O. Box 925, Stn. B
Montreal
H3C 3K5

Muslim Students' Association
McDonald College
P.O. Box 334,
Ste. Anne de Bellevue
H9X 1C0

Ontario

Association of Islamic
    Community Gazi Husrev-Beg
15 Lockton Crescent
Willowdale
M2K 1J6

Brantford Muslim Association
P.O. Box 174
Brantford
N3T 5M8

---

* In alphabetical order within each province, from east to west.

Cambridge Muslim Association
P.O. Box 2022
Hespler
N3C 2V6

Croatian Islamic Association
P.O. Box 244, Stn. N
Toronto
M8V 3T2

Islamic Association of Sudbury
P.O. Box 1148, Stn. B
Sudbury
P3E 4S6

Islamic Center of Toronto
56 Boustead Avenue
Toronto
M6R 1Z5

Islamic Foundation of Toronto
182 Rhodes Avenue
Toronto
M4L 3A1

Islamic School of Ottawa
P.O. Box 2364, Stn. D
Ottawa
K1P 5W5

Islamic Society of Canada
384 Driftwood Avenue, U-12
Downsview
M3J 1P3

Islamic Society in Niagara
    Peninsula
7071 Oakwood Drive
Niagara
L2E 6S5

Islamic Society of Peel
P.O. Box 513
Brampton
L6V 2L4

Islamic Shia Ithna Ashri Union
    of Toronto
7340 Bayview Avenue
Thornhill
L3T 2R7

Kingston Islamic Society
P.O. Box 876
Kingston
K7L 4X8

Millat Community Association
203 Bayview Fairways Drive
Thornhill
L3T 2Z1

Muslim Association of Hamilton
P.O. Box 4484, Stn. D
Hamilton
L8V 4S7

Muslim Society of Waterloo &
    Wellington Countries
P.O. Box 2726, Stn. B
Kitchener
N2H 6N3

Muslim Student Federation
c/o CYSF, York University
Ross Bldg., Room S 156
Downsview
M3J 1P3

Noor-E-Islam Society of Canada
P.O. Box 272, Stn. L
Toronto
M6E 4C2

North Bay Muslim Association
c/o Sabih Uddin
Dean's Pharmacy
North Bay
P1B 4Y3

N.W. Ontario Muslim Association
624 Strand Avenue
Thunder Bay
P7B 5B3

Ontario Muslim Association
73 Patricia Avenue
Willowdale
M2M 1J1

Ottawa Muslim Association
P.O. Box 2952, Stn. D
Ottawa
K1P 5W9

Sarnia Muslim Association
281 Cobden Street
Sarnia
N7T 4A2

Talim-Ul-Islam
7 Four Winds Drive
T H 8 Downsview
M3G 1K7

Toronto & Region Islamic
  Congregation (TARIC)
P.O. Box 66, Stn U
Toronto
M8Z 1TO

Windsor Islamic Association
1320 Northwood Street
Windsor
N9E 1A4

Manitoba

Manitoba Islamic Association
247 Hazelwood Avenue
Winnipeg
R2M 4W1

Muslim Students Association
University of Manitoba
Winnipeg
R3T 2N2

Saskatchewan

Islamic Association of
  Saskatchewan
P.O. Box 3572
Regina
S4P 3L7

Islamic Association of
  Saskatchewan
Sub P.O. 6, Box 330
Saskatoon
S7N 0W0

Alberta

Calgary Muslim Association
P.O. Box 1602
Calgary
T2P 2L7

Canadian Islamic Cultural &
  Educational Foundation
9014–90 Street
Edmonton
T6C 3L9

Lac La Biche Muslim
  Association
P.O. Box 641
Lac La Biche
T0A 2C0

British Columbia

B.C. Muslim Association
P.O. Box 34395, Stn. D
Vancouver
V6J 4P3

Appendix II

Directory of Muslim Associations in the United States*

Arkansas

Crescent Club
Student Program Office, Union
University of Arkansas
Fayetteville, AR 72701

California

American Turko-Tatar Assoc.
P.O. Box 1215
Burlingame, CA 94010

Black Student Union
Cal State-Long Beach
6101 E. 7th Ave.
Long Beach, CA 90801

Institute of Islamic Studies
3435 Overland Ave.
Los Angeles, CA 90034

Islamic League of America
P.O. Box 391
Palo Alto, CA 94302

Islamic Center of S. California
434 S. Vermont
Los Angeles, CA 90005

Islamic News & Dawa Service
429 E. Cypress
Los Angeles, CA 90037

Islamic Society
2530 Thayer Street
Riverside, CA 92570

Islamic Society of Orange County
437 E. Commonwealth Ave.
Fullerton, CA 92715

Islamic Society of Riverside
407 Campus Drive
Riverside, CA 92507

Islamic Soc. of San Diego
4935 Curry Drive
San Diego, CA 92115

Muslim Assoc. of Los Angeles
8844 Orion Ave.
Supelveda, CA 91343

Muslim Brothers of America
974 Southwest Drive
Hollywood, CA 90043

Muslim Brothers of America
128 S. Wheatherly Drive,
Beverly Hills, CA 90211

Southern Calif. Islamic Soc.
P.O. Box 854
Downey, CA 90241

Stanford Islamic Society
Box 2067
Stanford, CA 94305

* In alphabetical order by state and by name; courtesy the Islamic Center, Washington, D.C.

Colorado

Colorado Muslim Society
1401 Ash Street
Denver CO 80201

Connecticut

Albanian Muslim Community
21 Lonsmeadow Drive
Wolcott, CT 06716

Islamic Community of Fairfield
   County
93 Greenleaf Drive
Stanford, CT 06902

Delaware

Islamic Society of Delaware
109 Dutton Drive
New Castle, DE 19720

District of Columbia

Committee for Islamic Culture
Suite 43
1789 Lanier Pla., N.W.
Washington, D.C. 20009

Islamic Society of Washington,
   D.C.
P.O. Box 23318
Washington D.C. 20010

Florida

Al-Akhban Institute of Science &
   Technology
P.O. Box 1810
Fort Walton, FL 32548

Islamic Society of Central Florida
P.O. Box 1164
Winter Park, FL 32790

Islamic Society of Tampa
P.O. Box 1330
Brandon, FL 33511

Georgia

Islamic Society of Augusta
3008 Silverwood Drive
Martinez, GA 30907

Islamic Society of Georgia
172 Vine St., S.W., #7
Atlanta, GA 30314

Illinois

Chicago Insitute of Islamic Culture
P.O. Box 100
Chicago, IL 60690

American Muslim Mission
7351 So. Stoney Island Ave.
Chicago, IL 60649

Islamic Society of NIU
Holmes Student Center
Northern Illinois University
Dekalb, IL 60115

Islamic Society of Springfield
247 Saxon Drive
Springfield, IL 62704

Muslim Religious Cultural Home
1800 North Halsted Street
Chicago, IL 60614

Indiana

Assn. of Muslim Sci. & Engineers
P.O. Box 27344
Indianapolis, IN 46227

The Assn. of Muslim Social Sci.
2020 E. South Country Line Rd.
Indianapolis, IN 46227

Indianapolis Muslim Assn
P.O. Box 21050
Indianapolis, IN 46168

Islamic Students' Association
International House
215 North College Ave.
Muncie, IN 47306

Iowa

Islamic Assn of Cedar Rapids
2999 First Ave., S.W.
Cedar Rapids, IA 52404

Kansas

Islamic Association
Activity Center at Union
Kansas State University
Manhattan, KS 66606

Muslim Society
1428 Tennessee
Lawrence, KS 66044

Kentucky

Islamic Cultural Assn. of Louisville
914 S. 34th Street
Louisville, KY 40211

Louisiana

Muslim Assn. of New Orleans, Inc.
6244 Waldo Drive
New Orleans, LA 70122

Maryland

Islamic Society of Baltimore
P.O. Box 7647
Baltimore, MD 21207

Muslim Community Center of MD
9229 E. Parkhill Drive
Bethesda, MD 20014

Massachusetts

Harvard Islamic Society
Phillips Brooks House
Harvard University
Cambridge, MA 02138

Islamic Council of New England
P.O. Box 69
Roxbury Post Office
Roxbury, MA 02119

Society for Islamic Brotherhood
724 Shamur Ave.
Roxbury, MA 02119

Michigan

American Islamic Institute
17514 Woodward Ave.
Detroit, MI 48203

American Muslim Society of
  Dearborn
17514 Woodward
Detroit, MI 48203

Federation of Islamic Associations
25351 Five Mile Road
Redford Twp, MI 48239

International Muslim House
407 N. Ingalls
Ann Arbor, MI 48104

Islamic Youth Assn.
232 Ferris Ave.
Highland Park, MI 48203

Minnesota

Pakistan International Students Assoc.
229 Coffman Union
University of Minnesota
Minneapolis, MN 55455

Mississippi

Islamic Association of Mississippi
  State University
P.O. Box 2880
Mississippi State, MS 39762

Missouri

Muslim Students Organization
210 Waters Hall
University of Missouri-Col.
Columbia, MO 62011

New Jersey

Committee for Unified Newark
502 High Street
Newark, NJ 07102

Garden State Islamic Cultural
    Foundation
424 Mt Prospect Ave.
Newark, NJ 07104

Garden State Islamic Cultural
    Foundation
P.O. Box 412
South Orange, NJ 07070

Islamic Coordination Council of
    North America
99 Woodview Drive
Old Bridge, NJ 08857

Islamic Service Organization
99 Woodview Drive
Old Bridge, NJ 08857

Islamic Society and Friends
50 Hastings Road
Old Bridge, NJ 08857

Islamic Soc. of Central Jersey
P.O. Box 8261
Trenton, NJ 08650

Jehada Islamic School, Inc.
220 Parker Rd., #103
Elizabeth, NJ 07208

Mosque Foundation of New Jersey
80 Grandview Ave.
N. Caldwell, NJ 07647

New Mexico

Islamic Society of University of
    New Mexico
1500 Calle del Ranchero, N.E.
Albuquerque, NM 87106

New York

ACA of Islam International
111 West 118 Street
New York, NY 10026

Albanian American Islamic
    Community
1325 Albermarle Road
Brooklyn, NY 11226

Ansar of Islam, Inc.
676 St. Marks Ave.
Brooklyn, NY 11216

Association of Muslim Students in
    Northern New York State
P.O. Box 634
Potsdam, NY 13676

Coordinating Council of Islamic
    Affairs
4950 W. Brook Hills Drive
Syracuse, NY 13215

Council of Islamic Organizations of
    America
5825 Kings Highway
Brooklyn, NY 10123

Elmhurst Muslim Society
Elmhurst Hospital Center
79-01 Broadway
Elmhurst, NY 11373

Four-State Islamic Coalition
107 Joralemon Street
Brooklyn Heights, NY 11210

International Islamic Community
Room No. 3351A
United Nations Secretariat
New York, NY 10017

International Muslim Society
303 West 125th Street
New York, NY 10014

International Muslim Society, Inc.
P.O. Box 37
Manhattanville Station J
New York, NY 10027

Islamic Assn. of Long Island
P.O. Box 1225
Lake Grove, NY 11755

Islamic Community, Inc.
5110 19th Ave., #19-A
Brooklyn, NY 11204

Islamic Congress, Inc.
21-28 33rd Street
Long Island, NY 11105

Islamic Mission of America
143 State Street
Brooklyn, NY 11216

Islamic Progressive Community, Inc.
595 Crown Street
Brooklyn, NY 11213

Mid Hudson Islamic Assn
P.O. Box 27
Amenia, NY 12501

Muslim Education Cultural Assn
Cornell University
Ithaca, NY 14853

Muslim World League
P.O. Box 4174
Grand Central Station
New York, NY 10017

Persian Muslim Community of NY
53 A Van Corlandt Ave.
Ossining, NY 10562

Shia Muslim Assn of North
    America
108 53–63 62nd Drive
Forest Hills, NY 11375

Turkish North America
500 Fifth Avenue
New York, NY 10036

Ohio

Ahmadiyya Movement in Islam
637 Randolph Street
Dayton, OH 45408

Islamic Assn of Cincinnati
2515 Fairview Ave.
Cincinnati, OH 45219

Islamic Foundation
P.O. Box 3055
University Station
Columbus, OH 43210

Islamic Revivalist
P.O. Box 91192
Cleveland, OH 44101

Miami Valley Islamic Assn
135 S. Burnett Rd.
Springfield, OH 45505

Muslim Brotherhood of
    Youngstown, OH
851 Fairfax Ave.
Columbus, OH 43202

Muslim House
13 Stewart Street
Athens, OH 45701

Pennsylvania

Albanian American Muslim Soc.
157 W. Girard Ave.
Philadelphia, PA 19123

Assn. of Muslim Social Sci.
323 Bent Rd.
Wyncote, PA 19095

International Muslim
    Brotherhood
4637 Lancaster Ave.
Philadelphia, PA 19121

Islamic Medical Association
P.O. Box 9024
Pittsburgh, PA 15524

The Islamic Party
P.O. Box 56835
Pittsburgh, PA 15208

Islamic Society of Greater
    Harrisburgh
223 W. Jackson St.
York, PA 17403

Koba Islamic School
4637 Lancaster Ave.
Philadelphia, PA 19121

Muslim Assn of Pittsburgh
P.O. Box 7504
Pittsburgh, PA 15213

United Brotherhood of Islam
2005 Buffalo Rd.
Erie, PA 16510

Islamic League of America
1818 North 34th St.
Texas City, TX 77590

Texas

Islamic Soc. of Greater Houston
P.O. Box 17174
Houston, TX 77031

Islamic Assn of North Texas
609 Baghdad Street, North
Grand Prairies, TX 75050

Islamic Assn of Tarrant County
P.O. Box 17184
Fort Worth, TX 76107

Virginia

Muslim Development Corp.
5115 Franconia Rd., Suite G
Alexandria, VA 22310

West Virginia

Islamic Assn of West Virginia
P.O. Box 8215
Nitro, WV 25143

Muslim Student Associations (MSA)

Alabama

MSA-U. of Alabama
840 E. Beacon Park, #D
Birmingham, AL 35209

Arizona

MSA-Arizona State U.
P.O. Box 1313
Tempe, AZ 85281

MSA of Tucson
P.O. Box 10900, Student Union
University of Arizona
Tucson, AZ 85720

California

MSA-UC-Berkeley
300 Eshlam Hall
University of California
Berkeley, CA 94720

MSA-Cal Poly, Pomona
P.O. Box 2335
Montclair, CA 91763

MSA-Cal Poly SLO
Box 106 A.S.I.
San Louis Obispo, CA 93401

MSA-Cal State U.
2279 Alderbrook Way, #D
Sacramento, CA 95825

MSA-Fresno
2067 E. Shaw Ave., #C
Fresno, CA 93740

MSA-Greater Los Angeles
P.O. Box 77084
Los Angeles, CA 90007

MSA-Santa Barbara
P.O. Box 13825
Santa Barbara, CA 93107

MSA-UCLA
c/o Yahya Azab
Dept. of Biology, UCLA
Los Angeles, CA 90024

MSA-USC
Box 77004
University of Southern Calif.
Los Angeles, CA 90007

Colorado

MSA-Colorado State U.
Box 703, Student Center
Fort Collins, CO 80521

MSA-Denver
P.O. Box 10233
Denver, CO 80210

Florida

Muslim Students Association
P.O. Box 13051
University Station
Gainesville, FL 32604

MSA of Greater Miami
295 Northwest Drive
Miami, FL 33126

Georgia

MSA of Atlanta
P.O. Box 95145
Atlanta, GA 30314

Hawaii

MSA-University of Hawaii
EWC Box 2028
1177 East West Road
Honolulu, HI 96848

Idaho

Muslim Students Association
P.O. Box 3034
Moscow, ID 83843

Illinois

MSA
1721 S. 9th St.
Charleston, IL 61920

MSA of Greater Chicago
2718 W. Lawrence Ave.
Chicago, IL 60625

MSA-Monmouth College
Box 752 Gibson Hall
Monmouth, IL 60115

Indiana

Muslim Students Assn
P.O. Box 38
Plainfield, IN 46168

MSA-Indiana State U.
20 Farrington St., #403
Terre Haute, IN 47807

Muslim Students Assn
216 Nimitz Drive
West Lafayette, IN 47906

Iowa

MSA-Iowa State U.
164 University Village, #C
Ames, IA 50010

Kansas

MSA-U. of Kansas
P.O. Box 11, Kansas Union
Lawrence, KS 66044

Muslim Students Assn
907 W. 19th Street
Topeka, KS 66604

Maine

MSA-U. of Lowell
P.O. Box 1137
Lowell, MA 01854

Maryland

MSA-Greater Washington, DC
6467 Sligo Mill Road
Takoma Park, MD 20012

Michigan

MSA-Western Michigan U.
Box 326 Student Services Bldg
Western Michigan University
Kalamazoo, MI 49008

Minnesota

Muslim Students Assn
P.O. Box 14204
Minneapolis, MN 55414

Missouri

Muslim Students Assn
477 Graywood Drive
Ballwin, MO 63011

Nebraska

MSA-U. of Nebraska
115 Ferguson Hall
University of Nebraska
Lincoln, NB 68588

Nevada

MSA-UNLV
Consolidated Student Union
4505 Maryland Park
Las Vegas, NV 89154

New Mexico

MSA-NMSU
Box 3602
University Park
Las Cruces, NM 88003

New York

MSA-Columbia U
106 Earl Hall
Broadway at 117th Street
New York, NY 10027

MSA-Stony Brook
c/o M. Kutkut
Dept. of Mathematics
SUNY-Stony Brook
Stony Brook, NY 11794

North Carolina

MSA-U North Carolina
Box 33, Student Union
Chapel Hill, NC 27514

MSA-Southwestern Carolina
6110 Mosswood Court, #C
Charlette, NC 28213

MSA-NCSU
Box 5217, NCSU
Raleigh, NC 27607

North Dakota

MSA-ND State University
c/o Dept. of Plant Pathology
Fargo, ND 85102

MSA-UND
c/o Kouroush Taj Bakhsh
University of North Dakota
Grand Forks, ND 58202

Oklahoma

MSA-Oklahoma State U.
Student Union #368
Stillwater, OK 74074

Oregon

MSA-Oregon State University
P.O. Box 35
Corvallis, OR 97330

MSA-U of Oregon
P.O. Box 3587
Eugene, OR 97403

MSA-Portland State U.
2805 Southeast Francis
Portland, OR 97202

Pennsylvania

MSA-Cheyney State College
6530 N. Smedley St.
Philadelphia, PA 19126

MSA of Pittsburgh
c/o Dept of Mathematics
University of Pittsburgh
Pittsburgh, PA 15260

MSA-Temple University
Foreign Students Advisor
Mitten Hall
1300 W. Columbia
Philadelphia, PA 19122

MSA Women's Committee-Phila.
P.O. Box 5237
Philadelphia, PA 19126

Tennessee

MSA-Knoxville
Box 7818, University Station
Knoxville, TN 37916

MSA-Nashville and Vanderbilt
Box 6045, Station B
Nashville, TN 37235

Texas

MSA-UT, Austin
P.O. Box 7679
Austin, TX 78712

MSA-UT Arlington
Box 19762, UTA Station
Arlington, TX 76010

MSA-Southern Methodist U.
Box 1701, SMU
Dallas, TX 75275

MSA-North Texas State U.
Box 9407
Denton, TX 76203

MSA-University of Houston
Box 320, University Center
Houston, TX 77004

Muslim Students Association
P.O. Box 2067, Station 1
Kingsville, TX 78363

Utah

MSA of Logan
1342 Utah State University
Logan, UT 84322

Virginia

MSA-Virginia Polytechnic Inst.
903 University City Blvd, #H94
Blacksburgh, VA 24060

MSA
127 Burnham Place
Newport News, VA 23606

Washington

MSA-U. of Washington
P.O. Box 137, HUB
Pullman, WA 99163

West Virginia

MSA of Morgantown
P.O. Box 114
Morgantown, WV 26505

Wisconsin

Muslim Students Association
4513 Martin Drive
Milwaukee, WI 53208

MSA of North Western Wisconsin
900 W. Clairemont
Eau Claire, WI 54701

Mosques

Alabama

The Islamic Center
P.O. Box 3332
Birmingham, AL 35205

Masjid Al-Amin
117 North 19th Street
Birmingham, AL 35209

Arizona

Islamic Center of Arizona
6215 E. Shea Blvd.
Scottsdale, AZ 85254

Islamic Center of Tempe
616 S. Forest
Tempe, AZ 85281

Islamic Center of Tucson
P.O.Box 4172
Tucson, AZ 85717

California

Fiji Jamaatul Islam of America
373 Alta Vista Drive
San Francisco, CA 94080

Islamic Center of San Francisco
400 Crescent Street
San Francisco, CA 94110

Islamic Center of Southern
   California
845 South St. Andrews Place
Los Angeles, CA 90005

Islamic Center of So. California
434 S. Vermont
Los Angeles, CA 90005

Islamic Cultural Centre
847 Chamberlain Ct.
Mill Valley, CA 94941

Islamic Masjid
P.O. Box 1088
San Jose, CA 95108

Jamaate Musjidul Islam Center
820 Java Street
Inglewood, CA 90302

Masjid Al-Momin
4321 South Broadway
Los Angeles, CA 90037

Masjid An-Noor Al-Ummah
384 W. Acacia
Altadena, CA 91001

Masjid An-Nur
764 N. Mount Vernon
San Bernardino, CA 92410

The Mosque
781 Bolinas Ave.
Fairfax, CA 94930

Muslim Mosque
P.O. Box 22085
Sacramento, CA 95822

3 new mosques without addresses:

Chico Mosque
Chico, CA

Lodi Muslim Mosque
Lodi, CA

Stockton Islamic Center
Stockton, CA

Connecticut

Islamic Center of Connecticut
P.O. Box 34
Weatoque, CT 06089

District of Columbia

Community Mosque
770 Park Road, N.W.
Washington, D.C. 20010

Fazl Mosque
2141 Leroy Place, N.W.
Washington, D.C. 20008

Hanafi Madhab Center
7700 16th Street
Washington, D.C. 20011

The Islamic Center
2551 Massachusetts Ave., N.W.
Washington, D.C. 20008

Masjid Baitullah
238 Kenyon Street, N.W.
Washington, D.C. 20010

Masjidul Muqarrabeen
1616 F. Street, N.E.
Washington, D.C. 20019

Mosque Tempe #4
1519 4th Street, N.W.
Washington, D.C. 20001

Florida

Mosque Al-Mujahideen
P.O. Box 136
Flowersview, FL 32567

Georgia

Islamic Center of Atlanta
60 Ashby Street, S.W.
Atlanta, GA 30314

Illinois

Albanian Islamic Center
44010 S. Harlem
Chicago, IL 60600

Al-Shaheed Mosque
1400 South Union
Chicago, IL 60607

As-Salam Mosque
4819 S. Ashland Ave.
Chicago, IL 60609

Islamic Center of Greater Chicago
1810 Pfingsten Road
Northbrook, IL 60062

Islamic Center of Greater Peoria
1501 Spring Bay Road
East Peoria, IL 61611

Islamic Community Center
345 Heine Street
Elgin, IL 60120

Jama'at Al-Muslimin
10050 S. Halsted
Chicago, IL 60643

Masjid Dawah
4109 W. Madison Street
Chicago, IL 60624

Masjid Ul-Sabequeen
2057 East 75th Street
Chicago, IL 60614

Mosque Foundation
P.O. Box 9100
Chicago, IL 60629

Mosque of Omar, Inc.
11365 Forest Ave.
Chicago, IL 60627

Muslim Community Center
1651 N. Kedzie Ave.
Chicago, IL 60647

Muslim Community Center,
   Inc.
149 Vernon Drive
Bolingbrook, IL 60439

Indiana

Al-Amin Mosque (MSA
   Headquarters)
2501 Director's Row
Indianapolis, IN 46241

Islamic Center
809 East 8th Street
Bloomington, IN 47401

Islamic Center of Michigan City
P.O. Box 110, Brown Road
Michigan City, IN 46360

Islamic Teaching Center
2020 E. South Country Line Rd.
Indianapolis, IN 46227

Masjid Fajr
309 East 25th Street
Indianapolis, IN 46205

Iowa

Islamic Center of Iowa
P.O. Box 213
Cedar Rapids, IA 52406

Cedar Rapids Islamic Center
1335 9th Street, N.W.
Cedar Rapids, IA 52405

Islamic Center of Des Moines
1021 27th Street
Des Moines, IA 50311

Islamic Center of Des Moines
308 Second
West Des Moines, IA 50265

Kansas

Islamic Center of Greater Kansas
P.O. Box 891
Kansas City, KS 66103

Masjid Al-Malik
1325 East 10th Street
Wichita, KS 67214

Kentucky

Jama'at Al-Mumineen
P.O. Box 11443
Louisville, KY 40211

Louisiana

Baton Rouge Islamic Center
P.O. Box 17443
Baton Rouge, LA 70893

Maine

Islamic Center
57 Chaplin Terrace
Springfield, MA 01107

Islamic Center of New England
470 South Street
Quincy, MA 02169

Masjid Al-Arkam
14 Duxbury Rd.
Worcester, MA 01605

Maryland

Masjid Saffat
1335 N. Myrtle Ave.
Baltimore, MD 21217

Michigan

Albanian Islamic Center
20426 Country Club Rd.
Harper Woods, MI 48236

Al-Mominin Mosque
1554 Virginia Place
Detroit, MI 48209

Dearborn Islamic Mosque
9945 West Vernor Highway
Dearborn, MI 48120

The Islamic Center
15571 Joy Road at Greenfield
Detroit, MI 48238

Islamic Center
110 International Center
Michigan State University
East Lansing, MI 48824

Masjid Al-Rahman
1106 South Burdick St.
Kalamazoo, MI 49001

Minnesota

Islamic Center of Minnesota
1128 Sixth St., S.E.
Minneapolis, MN 55414

Islamic Center of Minnesota
P.O. Box 567
Minneapolis, MN 55440

Missouri

Islamic Center of Greater Kansas
  City
P.O. Box 891
Kansas City, MO 64141

Islamic Center of St. Louis
3834 Westpine
St. Louis, MO 63108

New Jersey

Beit Al-Quraish
476 18th Avenue
Newark, NJ 07108

Circassian Community Center of
    America
P.O. Box 8304
Haledon, NJ 07508

Denullah Mosque, Inc.
69 Van Ness Place
Newark, NJ 07108

Islamic Center of Jersey City
17 Park Street
Jersey City, NJ 07304

Jamaat Ibad-er-Rahman
26 Gifford Ave.
Jersey City, NJ 07304

Masjid Al-Muhaajireen, Inc.
Ezaldeen Village, Dar Ave., Elm.
Hammonton, NJ 08037

Masjid Baitul Khaliq, Inc.
49 Prince Street
Newark, NJ 07103

The Muslim Mosque, Inc.
32 Chestnut St.
Paterson, NJ 07051

United Islamic Center of Paterson
P.O. Box 3032
Paterson, NJ 07059

New York

Albanian Mosque
111 Venduzer Street
Staten Island, NY 10301

Dar-ul-Islam Masjid-ul-Salat
Elmira Correctional Facility
Box 500
Elmira, NY 14902

Islamic Center of New York
1 Riverside Dr.
New York, NY 10023

Islamic Center of Niagara Frontier
40 Parker Street
Buffalo, NY 14241

Islamic Center of Rochester
P.O. Box 255
Rochester, NY 14624

Islamic Center of South Tier
370 Main Street
Johnson City, NY 13790

Islamic Masjid of Staten Island
117 Venduzer Street
Staten Island, NY 10301

Lackawana Islamic Mosque
154 Wilkesbarre Ave.
Lackawana, NY 14218

Masjidul Muslimin
335 Atlantic Avenue
Brooklyn, NY 11201

Muslim Center of New York
144–77 41st Avenue
Flushing, NY 11355

Staten Island Masjid
230 Benzigen Ave.
Staten Island, NY 10301

Yasim Mosque
52 Herkimer Place
Brooklyn, NY 11216

Ohio

Alfalaq Mosque
651 Edgewood – Third Floor
Akron, OH 44307

First Cleveland Mosque
13405 Union Ave.
Cleveland, OH 44120

Islamic Center
478 W. Thornton St.
Akron, OH 44307

Islamic Center of Central Ohio
1428 East Broad St.
Columbus, OH 43205

Islamic Center of Cleveland
9400 Detroit Ave.
Cleveland, OH 44120

Islamic Center of Toledo
722 East Bancroft St.
Toledo, OH 43608

Mosque Al-Mumin
P.O. Box 91192
Cleveland, OH 44120

Oklahoma

Masjid Al-Salaam
2604 E. 6th St.
Tulsa, OK 74104

Masjid An-Nur
420 E. Lindsey St.
Normam, OK 73069

Pennsylvania

Al-Mujahidden Mosque
1732–34 N. 19th St.
Philadelphia, PA 19121

First Masjid of Islam
1831 Wylie Ave.
Pittsburgh, PA 15219

The Islamic Center
1740 N. 19th St.
Philadelphia, PA 19121

Islamic Center of Homewood
553 N. Homewood Ave.
Pittsburgh, PA 15208

Islamic Center of Philadelphia
325 N. Broad St.
Philadelphia, PA

Islamic Center of Pittsburgh
549 N. Neville St.
Pittsburgh, PA 15213

Mosque Foundation of
  Pennsylvania
2732 North Marvin St.
Philadelphia, PA 19122

Rhode Island

Islamic Center
582 Oranston St.
Providence, RI 02914

South Carolina

Masjid Jihadul Islam
Dar-ul-Islam
625 Manning Ave.
Sumter, SC 29150

Texas

Austin Mosque
1906 Nueces Street
Austin, TX 78700

Virginia

Islamic Community Center of
  Northern Virginia
6010 Columbia Pike
Falls Church, VA 22041

Washington

Islamic Center of Seattle
3040 South 150th St.
Seattle, WA 98100

Wisconsin

Islamic Center of Madison
116 North Orchard
Madison, WI 53715

Islamic Center of Milwaukee
1513 E. Hartford Ave.
Eau Claire, WI 54701

Masjid Muhammads

There is a Masjid Muhammad at each of the addresses below. In a few, the name of the mosque is given with the address. Listings are alphabetized by state. This list has been adapted from the one published in *Bilalian News* (24 October 1980) p. 30.

Alabama

3424 26th Street North
Birmingham, AL 35207

1559 Duval St.
Mobile, AL 36605

P.O. Box 10217
Prichard, AL 36610

1309 27th Ave.
Tuscaloosa, AL 35401

Arizona

1046 W. Buckeye Rd.
Phoenix, AZ 85001

1830 Park Ave.
Tucson, AZ 85719

Arkansas

1717 Wright Ave.
Little Rock, AR 72202

California

1001 8th St.
Bakersfield, CA 90090

1300 East Palmer
Compton, CA 90221

1329 B. Street
Fresno, CA 93706

2104 Orange Ave.
Long Beach, CA 90806

4016 S. Central Ave.
Los Angeles, CA 90011

1882 S. California Ave.
Monrovia, CA 91016

779 Evelyn Ave., No. G
Mountain View, CA 94043

1652 47th Ave.
Oakland, CA 94601

1307 Van Nuys Blvd.
Pacoima, CA 91331

861 N. Fair Oaks Ave.
Pasadena, CA 91103

P.O. Box 727
Pittsburgh, CA 94555

521 South 10th St.
Richmond, CA 94804

4104 Park Ave.
Riverside, CA 92507

2952 35th St.
Sacramento, CA 95817

2575 Imperial Highway
San Diego, CA 92102

1805 Geary Ave.
San Francisco, CA 94115

841 E. Main St.
Stockton, CA 95202

Colorado

3104½ Downing St.
Denver, CO 80205

2815 Fairfax St.
Denver, CO 80207

Connecticut

670 State St.
Bridgeport, CT

3284 Main St.
Hartford, CT 06120

361 Mill Rock Rd.
New Haven, CT 06514

97 Main St.
Stamford, CT 06908

Delaware

301 W. 6th St.
Wilmington, DE 19601

District of Columbia

1519 14th St., N.W.
Washington, D.C. 20011

Florida

2942 Commonwealth Ave.
Jacksonville, FL 32209
Masjid El Ansar
5245 N.W. 7th Ave.
Miami, FL 33127
P.O. Box 2271
Pensacola, FL 32503
509 E. Magnolia Dr., Suite 228
Tallahassee, FL 32301
1515 E. 7th Ave.
Tampa, FL 33605

Georgia

1225 Bankhead Way
Atlanta, GA 30318
735 Fayetteville Rd., S.E.
Atlanta, GA 30316
2742 Spenola St.
Columbus, GA
117 E. 34th
Savannah, GA

Illinois

Masjid Elijah Muhammad
7351 S. Stony Island
Chicago, IL 60649
Decatur, IL
485 N. Indiana Ave.
Kankakee, IL 60901

302 Berry Ave.
Lockport, IL 60441
1717 St. Charles Rd.
Maywood, IL 60153
210 Morgan St.
Rockford, IL
723 E. Chicago Ave.
East Chicago, IN 46312
1226 Sheridan Rd.
North Chicago, IL 60064

Indiana

641 Sycamore St.
Evansville, IN 47718
1004 E. Pontiac St.
Fort Wayne, IN 46806
1473 W. 15th Ave.
Gary, IN 46407
2405 N. College Ave.
Indianapolis, IN 46205
302 E. 10th St.
Michigan City, IN 46360
Masjid Mujaheeduun
431 S. Dundee
South Bend, IN 46119

Iowa

1430 University
•Des Moines, IA 50314

Kansas

1240 Clay Ave.
Topeka, KS
1007 N. Cleveland
Wichita, KS

Kentucky

572 Georgetown St.
Lexington, KY 40508
2129 Grand Ave.
Louisville, KY 40211

Louisiana

1801 Texas St.
Baton Rouge, LA

2626−32 Magnolia St.
New Orleans, LA 70113

P.O. Box 9202
Shreveport, LA 71109

135 E. Brown Village Rd., Rte 5
Slidell, LA 70458

Maine

35 Intervale St.
Boston, MA

495 Union St.
Springfield, MA

Maryland

900 Pine St.
Baltimore, MD 21207

514 Wilson St.
Baltimore, MD

Rte 1, Box 30B
Hurlock, MD 21643

Michigan

Masjid Wali Muhammad
11529 Linwood
Detroit, MI 48206

402 E. Gillespie
Flint, MI

814 S. Division Ave.
Grand Rapids, MI 49507

13759 Hamilton Ave.
Highland Park, MI 48203

1009 N. Westhedge Ave.
Kalamazoo, MI 49007

235 Lahomia
Lansing, MI

2444 Park Ave.
Muskegon Heights, MI 49444

114 N. 4th St.
Saginaw, MI 48601

Minnesota

3759 4th Ave. South
Minneapolis, MN 55409

Mississippi

307 E. Division St.
Biloxi, MS

1208 Jones Ave.
Jackson, MS 39204

Missouri

2715 Swope Parkway
Kansas City, MO 64130

1434 N. Grand Blvd.
St. Louis, MO 63106

Nebraska

1438 N. 27th St.
Lincoln, NB

2440 Templeton St.
Omaha, NB 68111

Nevada

615 S. Van Buren
Las Vegas, NV

New Jersey

2018 Atlantic Ave.
Atlantic City, NJ 08540

107 N. Centre St.
Atlantic City, NJ 08401

910 Broadway
Camden, NJ 08103

143 Catherine St.
Elizabeth, NJ 07201

295 Jackson St.
Jersey City, NJ 07205

257 S. Orange Ave.
Newark, NJ 07103

245 Broadway
Paterson, NJ 07501

321 Grant Ave.
Plainfield, NJ

1001 E. State St.
Trenton, NJ 08609

New Mexico

8005 Central, N.E.
Albuquerque, NM

New York

936 Woodycrest Ave.
Bronx, NY 10452

120 Madison St.
Brooklyn, NY

615 Michigan Ave.
Buffalo, NY

89–25 Merrick Blvd.
Jamaica Queens, NY

Masjid Malcolm Shabazz
102 West 116th St.
New York, NY

370 North St.
Rochester, NY 14605

111 Kirk Ave.
Syracuse, NY 13205

200 Square St.
Utica, NY 13501

North Carolina

31 Eagle St.
Ashville, NC

1230 Beattlesford Rd.
Charlotte, NC 28126

1009 W. Chapel Hill St.
Dunham, NC

430 Gillespie St.
Fayetteville, NC 28301

508 S. Queen St.
Kinston, NC 28501

420 Hill St.
Raleigh, NC 27610

525 S. Center St.
Stateville, NC

711 S. 8th St.
Wilmington, NC 28401

1500 English St.
Winston-Salem, NC 27105

Ohio

875 Garth Ave.
Akron, OH 44320

1063 N. West Bend Rd.
Cincinnati, OH 45224

Masjid Willie Muhammad
2813 E. 92nd St.
Cleveland, OH 44104

1677 Oak St.
Columbus, OH 43205

627 Salem Ave.
P.O. Box 244;
Dayton, OH 45406

P.O. Box 2381
Sandusky, OH

743 W. Liberty St.
Springfield, OH 45506

P.O. Box 426
Toledo, OH 43601

2527 Niles Rd.
Warren, OH 44484

131 W. Woodland Ave.
Youngstown, OH 44501

Oklahoma

1322 E. 23rd St.
Oklahoma City, OK

538 E. Oklahoma St.
Tulsa, OK

Oregon

P.O. Box 11374
Portland, OR 97211

Pennsylvania

19 W. Third St.
Chester, PA 19013

1301 Parade St.
Erie, PA 16503

1725 Market St.
Harrisburg, PA 17103

1319 W. Susquehanna Ave.
Philadelphia, PA 19122

7222 Kelly St.
Pittsburgh, PA 15208

Rhode Island

232–34 Pavilion Ave.
Providence, RI 02905

South Carolina

808 Giesburg Drive
Anderson, SC 29622

1998 Hugo Ave.
Charleston, SC 19405

5119 Monticello Rd.
Columbia, SC 29203

410 N. Coit St.
Florence, SC 29501

110 Willard St.
Greenville, SC 29605

281 Russell St.
Orangeburg, SC 29115

Tennessee

504 Kilmer St.
Chattanooga, TN 37404

709 Coolege St.
Knoxville, TN 37921

4412 S. Third St.
Memphis, TN

3317 Torbett St.
Nashville, TN 37209

Texas

810 N.W. Second Ave.
Amarillo, TX

1035 Gladys St.
Beaumont, TX

725 Villa Dr., #33
Corpus Christi, TX 78408

2604 S. Harwood
Dallas, TX 75215

1201 E. Allen Ave.
Fort Worth, TX 76104

6641 Bellfort Ave.
Houston, TX 77459

1726 Oak St.
Midland, TX 79701

1720 Hayes
San Antonio, TX 78202

901 W. Morris
Tyler, TX 75702

Virginia

2202 Garfield Ave.
Lynchburg, VA

1011 W. Fayette St.
Martinsville, VA 24112

1145 Hampton Ave.
Newport News, VA 23607

714 Church St.
Norfolk, VA

115–121 Harrison St.
Petersburg, VA 23803

400 Chimborazo Blvd.
Richmond, VA 23260

822 Campbell Ave., S.W.
Roanoke, VA 24016

Washington

1325 E. Yesler
Seattle, WA 98144

1423 South "K" St.
Tacoma, WA 98405

Wisconsin

1200 Milwaukee Ave.
Racine, WI 53404

Masjid Sultan Muhammad
2507 N. Third St.
Milwaukee, WI 53212

Sources of Publications

Publications are available from a growing list of sources, of which the following are a few.

American Trust Publications
7216 S. Madison, #5
Indianapolis, IN 46227

The Islamic Center
2551 Massachusetts Ave., N.W.
Washington, DC 20008

Five-part Islamic School
  Curriculum, texts in English, by
  Dr. M. Abdul-Rauf:
vol. 1. *Biography of the Prophet;*
vol. 2. *Muslim Creed;*
vol. 3. *Islamic Mode of Worship;*
vol. 4. *Moral Islamic Guidance;*
vol. 5. *Interpretations of Selections
        from the Holy Qur'ān*

Islamic Center & Mosque
P.O. Box 213
Cedar Rapids, IA 52406
Has publications list

Islamic Center of Detroit
15571 Joy Road
Detroit, MI 48228

Islamic Productions
739 E. Sixth Street
Tucson, AZ 85719
Texts and Tapes
Free catalog on request

Islamic Service Organization
99 Woodview Drive
Old Bridge, NJ 08857

International Graphics
  Publishing
6467 Sligo Mill Rd.
Takoma Park, MD 20012

MSA Islamic Book Service
P.O. Box 264
Plainfield, IN 46168
Books, other literature, cards

Glossary

The Arabic terms in this book may be transliterated in various ways as represented by the bracketed words after some entries. We have tried to use the most common forms. [Eds.]

ʿAbbāsid A dynasty of Arabs, descendants of the paternal uncle of Muḥammad, who ruled from Baghdad (749–1258 A.D.).

ādāb Official culture including code of conduct in Islamic civilization; in modern Arabic, confined to literature.

ʿahd Agreement, covenant, treaty. Early seen as designating the relationship between God and man; in later times, commonly seen as a political treaty or agreement.

ʿahd Allah Covenant of God with mankind, implying binding commitments and responsibilities.

Ahmadiyya (Aḥmadīya) The name given to adherents of Mirza Ghulam Ahmad Kadiani, outstanding religious figure from the Punjab. Recognized by most as a separate Muslim sect.

al-Akhira The "other world" or "hereafter."

ʿālim (pl. ʿulamāʾ) A scholar or learned individual, especially in the legal or religious sciences.

Allahu Akbar A phrase of praise meaning "God is great."

apnā (Urdu) Adjective meaning that which belongs to one's own family or tradition, as opposed to that which is foreign or ghair.

aqiqa Legal requirement of Muslim law involving the shaving of the newborn child's hair after seven days and the sacrificing of a sheep.

ʿasabiya (ʿaṣaba) Legal term for male relation on father's side.

ashrāf An honorific term meaning noble, distinguished, implying relationship to early Muslim nobility.

Barmaki (al-Barāmika) A leading family in Iran, often political secretaries or state overseers (**wazirs**) of the early Abbasid Caliphate, Yahya having risen to unprecedented success under Harun al-Rashid.

Barmakids Collective designation for Barmakī **wazirs** who held great power from 786–803 A.D.

bayʿa (baiʿ) Agreement to acknowledge Muḥammad as sovereign or leader.

bint al-ʿamm Female cousin on the father's side; preferential marriage to father's brother's daughter (Arab tradition).

bismilla Literally, "in the name of God," a phrase used at the commencement of any activity; celebration of introducing child to Islamic teachings.

caliph A deputy, or vicegerent, and the title given to the successors of the Prophet.

daʿwa Literally, "a plea for the help of God," or call, in the religious sense, interpreted as a charge or responsibility placed upon believers.

dhikr Literally, "remembering," but commonly the religious ceremony of praise found in Sufi circles.

dhimmī A follower of a religion tolerated by Islam, i.e., Christianity and Judaism.

Eid (Eid al-Fitr) The festival celebrating the breaking of the fast month, Ramaḍān.

Eid prayers Prayers at the termination of the fast which incorporates prayers for remission of sins and divine assistance in misfortune.

faḍl Surplus, remnant, overflow, or of secondary importance.

fard (fard 'ayn) A religious duty enjoined on every Muslim, such as prayer, fasting, pilgrimage, etc.

fiqh In the first instance, jurisprudence, but may be regarded as the entire set of rules derived from the **shari'a.**

ghair (ghaira) Foreign, strange, not of Muslim culture.

ghar (Urdu) The immediate household.

hadith (pl. ahadith) Normally translated as "tradition," but in actuality a report of some activity or saying of the Prophet. Sometimes refers to the entire corpus of reports.

halal That which is lawful or acceptable.

hajj The pilgrimage to Mecca, one of the required duties of every Muslim, health permitting.

Hanafi fiqh A legal school of the Sunnis, deriving from Abū-Hanifah (699–767 A.D.).

hijra Immigration of the Prophet from Mecca to Medina in 622. This became the founding year of Islamic chronology.

'ibadat The ordinances of divine worship, such as prayer, fasting, etc. incumbant on all believers.

ifta' The act of delivering a formal legal opinion.

iftar Breaking of the fast.

ijma' The consensus of the community as the basis for a legal pronouncement, principally Sunni.

ijtihad Individual, (as opposed to divine) involvement in the determination of legal interpretation.

imam Among Sunnis, the leader of the congregation in prayer, and by extension of the Muslim community. Among Shī'is, the spiritual successors of Muhammad and the proper leaders of the umma.

Inshallah "If God wills," an invocation common to Muslims.

isra The journey undertaken by Muhammad from Mecca to Jerusalem subsequent to his ascension to God in the heavens.

istina' The relationship between two parties involving personal obligation, concern, and affection, usually with lifelong importance.

iṣtiʿmar Rebuilding and reconstruction of the community on earth.

jamat khana (jamaʿat khāna) Ismaili term designating religious community organization.

jihād War against all who are not Muslim; sometimes the battle against personal evils.

juma (jumʿa) Friday, day of corporate prayer.

Kaʿba (Kaaba) A simple square shrine, originally built by Abraham in Mecca, and the centre of Muslim religious activities.

kāfir (pl. kufr) Literally, "the one who covers up the truth," but generally the word for unbeliever.

kamadia Member of the Ismaili hierarchy of religious leaders.

khatīb The preacher officiating at the Friday prayer.

khums An Ismaili term meaning benevolence.

masjid Mosque, place for performing religious duties.

mawālī Converts to Islam who had no Arab ancestry.

Medina Literally, "The City," refering to Yathrib, which became the home of Muḥammad after his flight from Mecca.

Millet (millāt) A religious community or confessional group that became part of Ottoman governance.

miʿraj Ascension of Muḥammad to heaven where he met with God.

mīthāq A covenant or agreement, confirming a lifelong mutual bond.

moulid Birthday celebration of the Prophet or of famous Muslim saint.

muḍaraba Silent partnerships.

muezzin The mosque functionary who calls the faithful to prayer.

Mughal (Moghal, Mongol) Timurid dynasty from Afghan mountains who conquered North India. Mughal is the Indo-Persian form of "Mongol," which was applied to Northern Turks in India.

Muhammad (Mohammed, Muḥammad, Mahomet) Literally, "The Praised One"; the name of the Prophet as transliterated by contemporary scholars.

Muḥarram The Islamic month, the first ten days of which the Shī'īs lament the martyrdom of Husain, the grandson of the Prophet.

Mujaddid The renewer, or reformer. Based on Muslim eschatological hope that a renewer will appear every 100 years.

mukhi Ismaili leadership term, implying great purity and insight.

muṣtana' (pl. **muṣtana'un**) Protégé or devoted individual who accepts the leadership or superiority of an important man as his guide.

nasia (nasi'a) Credit, delay of payment.

Pathān Ethnic group whose origins are in the Pakistan-Afghanistan region; early Muslim dynasty in India.

purdah The system of seclusion in India, designed to screen women from male strangers, which includes using the veil.

qāḍi Judge, magistrate; in classical times, the head of the local court.

qiyās Deduction by analogy.

Qur'ān (Koran) The word of Allah, as received by the Prophet and embodied in the holy book of Islam.

Qur'ānkhwani Formal recitation of the Qur'ān in any context.

rak'a Ritual of bowing, which is part of Muslim prayer.

Rajputs Converts to Hinduism who became part of the Indian warrior class, who became part of the Muslim empire under Akbar and retained leadership positions within Indo-Muslim society.

Ramaḍān The ninth month of the Muslim calendar (December in the Christian calendar), during which no food nor drink may be consumed during daylight hours.

ribā Literally, "increase," but has come to mean interest or usury.

ṣadqa Literally, "alms," but has been used both as obligatory tax (zakāt) and as voluntary gift giving.

ṣalāt Liturgical form of prayer, recited five times per day.

ṣaniʿ (ṣaniʿā) Protégé, one protected by institution of iṣṭinaʿ.

shahādah The declaration, "There is no god but God and Muḥammad is His Prophet," the foundational belief of Muslim faith.

shaykh Honorific term applied to aged relatives or the patriarch of the tribe; also used to designate religious leaders or Sufi saints.

shariʿa The law or entire corpus of rules guiding Muslim life.

Shīʿa Shortened version of Shīʿat-ʿAlī, connoting those who see "true religious" leadership as belonging only to ʿAlī and his descendants. Shīʿi is the adjectival form, Shīʿites the common transcription for the collective noun. Represents a Muslim minority tradition.

shūrā Literally, "the consultation," deriving from the Qurʾānic commendation to believers to consult together; in modern parlance, a legislative assembly.

ṣiyām Fasting, spiritual discipline through deprivation, most specifically during **Ramaḍān.**

siwāk Arab toothbrush; instrument for cleaning teeth made from thorn-like plant.

Sufi (ṣūfī) The practitioner of the mystical tradition in Islam.

sunna The custom of the Prophet, incorporated into the ḥadith.

Sunni Majority division within Islam of those who accept the entire first generation of Muslim leaders as legitimate, in contrast with Shīʿis who accept only ʿAlī and his descendents.

sura A "chapter" in the Qurʾān.

syed (saiyid or sayyid) A lord in its original meaning, but used almost universally as a title of a descendent of the Prophet.

tamkīn fī-al-ʿard Triumphant possession of the earth as a gift from God.

taqiya (taqīya) Camouflaging principles when admitting them would invite persecution; especially utilized by the Shīʿites.

tariqa (ṭarīqa) Literally, "the way," but has become the word for primarily mystical religious orders.

tawḥid Literally, "making one," but theologically referring to the oneness of God or the oneness and single nature of all reality.

'ulama' *See* 'alim.

Umayyad The first Muslim dynasty, centred in Damascus, that ruled the Muslim empire from 661 to 750 A.D.

umma The community of believers, including all those who confess Islam.

Wahhabiyyah Reform movement begun by Ibn 'Abd-al-Wahhāb in the Najd in Arabia, which gained the support of the Sa'ūd family and eventually became the central ideology in the area. Generally held strict views drawn from conservative Ibn-Taimiyyah (d. 1328) who rejected much of Sufi Islam and became strongly intolerant of any form not built on the Qur'ān. Preached a new form of purification of Islam. Collectively known as **wahhabism.**

wali Roughly equivalent to "saint," implies special mystical knowledge and gifts. These figures became objects of cultic activity and honor.

waqf An endowment for religious purposes, or for the collective good, such as hospitals, libraries, etc.

zakāt A yearly "tax" paid by Muslims as a contribution to community welfare or as a charitable gift.

Selected Bibliography

Abu-Laban, Baha. "Middle East Groups." Ottawa: Department of the Secretary of State, 1973.

———. *An Olive Branch on the Family Tree: The Arabs in Canada.* Toronto: McClelland & Stewart, 1980.

Abu-Laban, Sharon McIrvin. "Stereotypes of Middle East Peoples: An Analysis of Church School Curricula" in *Arabs in America: Myths and Realities,* Baha Abu-Laban and Faith Zeadey, eds. Wilmette, Ill.: Medina University Press International, 1975, pp. 149–69.

———. "The Arab-Canadian Family" in *Arab Studies Quarterly* 1 (1979): 135–56.

Ahmad, Imtiaz, ed. *Family, Kinship and Marriage among Muslims in India.* New Delhi: Manohar, 1976.

Ahmad, Shaikh M. *Economics of Islam: A Comparative Study.* 2d ed. Lahore: S.H. Mohammad Aschraf, 1958.

Alami, A. "Misconception in the Treatment of the Arab World in Selected American Textbooks for Children." M.A. thesis: Kent State University, 1957.

Ali, S.A. *Economic Foundations of Islam.* Calcutta: Orient Longmans, 1964.

Allahdin, Abdulla: *Extracts from the Holy Quran and Authentic Traditions of the Holy Prophet Muhammed,* 11th ed. Secunderabad, India, n.d.

Al-Qazzaz, Ayad. "Images of the Arab in American Social Science Textbooks" in *Arabs in America: Myths and Realities,* Baha Abu-Laban and Faith Zeadey, eds. Wilmette, Ill. Medina University Press International, 1975, pp. 113–32.

———. *The Arab World: A Handbook for Teachers.* San Francisco: Tasco Press, 1978.

———. "Textbooks and Teachers: Conveyor of Knowledge and Agent of Socialization" in *The Middle East: The Image and Reality,* J. Freelander, ed. Los Angeles: U.C.L.A., 1980.

Amiji, H. "The Asian Communities" in *Islam in Africa,* J. Kritzcek, ed. New York: Van Nostrand & Reinhold, 1969.

Ansari, Ghaus. *Muslim Caste in Uttar Pradesh*. Lucknow, India: Ethnographic & Folk Culture Society, 1960.

Aoki, T. et al. *Canadian Ethnicity: The Politics of Meaning*. Vancouver: Center for the Study of Curriculum and Instruction, University of British Columbia, 1978.

Aossey, Yahya Jr. *Fifty Years of Islam in Iowa 1925-1975*. Cedar Rapids: Unity Publishing Company, n.d.

Aswad, Barbara C., ed. *Arabic Speaking Communities in American Cities*. New York: Center for Migration Studies of New York Inc., and Association of Arab-American University Graduates Inc., 1974.

Awan, Sadiq Noor Alam. *The People of Pakistani Origin in Canada: The First Quarter Century*. Ottawa: S.N.A. Awan (under the auspices of the Canada-Pakistan Association of Ottawa-Hull), 1976.

Barclay, Harold. "An Arab Community in the Canadian Northwest: A Preliminary Discussion of the Lebanese Community in Lac La Biche, Alberta" in *Anthropologica* N.S. 10 (1968) : 143–56.

————. "The Perpetuation of Muslim Tradition in the Canadian North" in *Muslim World* 59 (1969) : 64–73.

————. "A Lebanese Community in Lac La Biche, Alberta" in *Minority Canadians: Immigrant Groups*, Jean Leonard Elliott, ed. Scarborough, Ont.: Prentice-Hall of Canada, 1971, pp. 66–83.

————. "The Lebanese Muslim Family" in *The Canadian Family*, K. Ishwaran ed. Toronto: Holt, Rinehart and Winston, rev. ed., 1976, pp. 92–104.

————. "The Muslim Experience in Canada" in *Religion and Ethnicity*, Harold Coward and Leslie Kawamura, eds. Waterloo: Wilfrid Laurier University Press, 1978, pp. 101–13.

Bharati, A. *The Asians in East Africa*. Chicago: Nelson Hall, 1972.

Black, Hillel. *The American Schoolbook*. New York: William Morrow and Co. Inc., 1967.

Boyan, Douglas R., ed. *Open Doors: 1978-79*. New York: Institute of International Education, 1978.

Brockelmann, Carl. *History of the Islamic Peoples*, Joel Carmichael and Moshe Perlman, trans. New York: Capricorn Books, 1969.

Canada: Secretary of State. *The Canadian Family Tree: Canada's Peoples*. Don Mills, Ont.: Corpus, 1979.

Canadian Arab Friendship Association of Edmonton. *A Salute to the Pioneers of Northern Alberta*. Edmonton: Canadian Arab Friendship Association, 1973.

Canadian Society of Muslims. "Report: On the Image of Islam in School Textbooks in the Province of Ontario, Canada." Unpublished manuscript, n.d.

Choudhry, M.I. and Khan, M.A. *Pakistani Society, A Sociological Analysis.* Lahore, Pakistan: Noorsons, 1964.

Clarke, Peter. "The Ismaili Sect in London" in *Religion* 8, no. 1 (1978): 68–84.

Corbett, David C. *Canada's Immigration Policy: A Critique.* Toronto: University of Toronto Press, 1957.

Davidson, F.M. "Ability to Respect Persons Compared to Ethnic Prejudice in Children" in *Journal of Personality and Social Psychology* 34 (1976).

Davis, A.J. "Teachers, Kids and Conflicts: Ethnography of a Junior High School" in *The Cultural Experience: Ethnography in a Complex Society,* J.P. Spradley and D.W. McCurdy, eds. Chicago: Science Research Association Inc., 1972.

Delury, George E., ed. *World Almanac and Book of Facts.* New York: Newspaper Ent. Assn. Inc., 1980.

Eglar, Zekye. *A Panjabi Village in Pakistan.* New York: Columbia University Press, 1961.

Elkholy, Abdo A. *The Arab Moslems in the United States.* New Haven, Conn: College and University Press, 1966.

Esmail, A. "Satpanth Ismailism and Modern Changes Within It: With Special Reference to East Africa." Ph.D. diss., Edinburgh University, 1972.

Fahlman, Lila. "The Use of Student Perceptions to Plan and Improve Curriculum" Ed. CI 549. Unpublished paper, University of Alberta, 1979.

Fathi, Asghar. "Mass Media and a Muslim Immigrant Community in Canada" in *Anthropologica* N.S. 15, (1973): 201–30.

———. "The Arab Moslem Community in the Prairie City" in *Canadian Ethnic Studies* 5 (1976): 409–26.

Ganam, Saleem Ameen. *Islam: A Universal Religion.* Edmonton: Canadian Islam Research Bureau, 1976.

Gran, Peter. *Islamic Roots of Capitalism.* Austin: University of Texas Press, 1979.

Grisworld, William, et al. *The Image of the Middle East in Secondary Textbooks.* New York: MESA, 1975

Grunebaum, G.E. von. *Islam.* London: Routledge & Kegan Paul, 1955.

Haddad, Yvonne. "Muslims in Canada: A Preliminary Study" in *Religion and Ethnicity,* Harold Coward and Leslie Kawamura, eds. Waterloo: Wilfrid Laurier University Press, 1978, pp. 71–100.

———. "The Muslim Experience in the United States" in *The Link* 2 (September/October 1979): 1–14.

Hamdani, D.H. *Muslims in Canada: A Century of Settlement 1871–1976.* Ottawa: Council of Muslim Communities of Canada, 1978.

Hawkins, Freda. *Canada and Immigration: Public Policy and Public Concern.* Montreal: McGill-Queen's University Press, 1972.

Honigmann, John J. "Women in West Pakistan" in *Pakistan: Society and Culture,* Stanley Maron, ed. New Haven, Conn.: Human Relations Area Files, 1957. pp. 154–176.

Ibn Khaldun. The *Muqaddimah: An Introduction to History.* Franz Rosenthal, trans. 4 vols. New York: Pantheon, 1958.

Jarrar, Samir A. "Images of the Arabs in United States Secondary School Social Studies Textbooks: A Content Analysis and a Unit Development." Unpublished Ph.D. diss. Florida State University, 1975.

Kenny, L.M. "The Middle East in Canadian Social Science Textbooks" in *Arabs in America: Myths and Realities,* Baha Abu-Laban and Faith Zeadey, eds. Wilmette, Ill.: Medina University Press International, 1975, pp. 133–47.

Kettani, Ali M. *Al-Muslimūn fi Euroba wa Amrika,* vol. 2. Dar Idris, Iraq: 1976.

Khattab, Abdelmoneim M. "The Assimilation of Arab Muslims in Alberta." M.A. thesis, University of Alberta, 1969.

Korson, J. Henry. "Modernization, Social Change and the Family in Pakistan" in *Pakistan in Transition,* W.H. Wriggins, ed. Islamabad: University of Islamabad Press, 1975, pp. 15–59.

Levy, Reuben. *The Social Structure of Islam,* 2d ed. Cambridge: Cambridge University Press, 1962.

Lewis, Bernard. *The Arabs in History,* 3rd ed. London: Hutchinson University Library, 1964.

Lincoln, C. Eric. *The Black Muslims in America.* Boston: Beacon Press, 1961.

Lovell, Emily Kalled. "A Survey of the Arab-Muslims in the United States and Canada" in *Muslim World* 63 (1973): 139–54.

Madan, T.N., ed. *Muslim Communities of South Asia.* New Delhi: Vikas, 1976.

Makdisi, Nadim. "The Moslems in America" in *The Christian Century,* vol. LXXVI, no. 34 (26 August 1959): 969–71.

Malcolm X, with Alex Haley. *The Autobiography of Malcolm X.* New York: Ballantine, 1973.

Massoud, Muhammad Said. *I Fought as I Believed.* Montreal: by the author, 1976.

McDiarmid, Garnet and Pratt, David. *Teaching Prejudice.* Toronto: The Ontario Institute for Studies in Education, 1971.

Megaro, G. *Vittorio Alfieri: Forerunner of Italian Nationalism.* New York: Columbia University Press, 1930.

Merton, Robert. *Social Theory and Social Structure* Glencoe, Ill.: Glencoe Illinois Free Press, reprint ed., 1957.

Mujahir, Ali Musa Raza. *Islam in Practical Life.* Lahore, Pakistan: Shaykh Muhammad Ashraf, 1968.

Murphy, Robert and Kasdan, L. "The Structure of Parallel Cousin Marriage." *American Anthropologist* 61 (1959) : 17–29.

Nadvi, Abul Hasan Ali. *The Musalman. Social Life, Beliefs and Customs of the Indian Muslims.* Lucknow: Academy of Islamic Research and Publications, 1972.

Nanji, Azim. "Modernization and Change in the Nizari Ismaili Community in East Africa." *Journal of Religion in Africa* 6, no. 2 (1974): 123–39.

————. *The Nizari Ismaili Tradition in the Indo-Pakistani Subcontinent.* Delmar, N.Y.: Caravan Books, 1978.

Nasr, S.H., ed. *Ismaili Contributions to Islamic Culture.* Tehran, Iran: Weidenfeld and Nicolson, 1977.

Norris, H.S. *Indians in Uganda.* London: 1968.

Papanek, H. "Leadership and Social Change in the Khoja Community in Pakistan." Ph.D. diss., Harvard University, 1962.

Perry, Glenn. "The Arabs in American High School Textbooks" in *Journal of Palestine Studies* 4, no. 3 (Spring 1975) : 46–58.

Porter, John. *The Vertical Mosaic.* Toronto: University of Toronto Press, 1965.

Qureshi, Anwar I. *Islam and the Theory of Interest.* 2d ed. Lahore: S.H. Mohammad Ashraf, 1974.

Qureshi, Ishtiaq Husain. *The Pakistani Way of Life.* London: Heinemann, 1956.

Rotherhmund, Dietmar, ed. *Islam in Southern Asia.* Wiesbaden: Franz Steiner Verlag, 1975.

Said, Edward W. *Orientalism.* New York: Pantheon, 1978.

————. "Assessing U.S. Coverage of the Crisis in Iran." *Columbia Journalism Review* (March-April 1980).

————. "Inside Islam" in *Harper's* (January 1981) : 25–32.

Savory, R.M. ed. *Introduction to Islamic Civilization.* Cambridge: Cambridge University Press, 1976.

Scott, Stanley H. "Oral Methodology for Ethnic Studies" in *Ethnic Canadians: Culture and Education.* Regina: University of Regina, 1978.

Shaheen, Jack G. "The Arab Stereotype on Television" in *The Link*, vol. 13, no. 2 (April/May 1980) : 1–13.

Shalaby, Ibrahim M. "The Role of the School in Cultural Renewal and Identity Development in the Nation of Islam. Ph.D. diss., University of Arizona, 1967.

Siddiqui, Nejatullah. *Banking Without Interest.* 2d ed. Lahore: Islamic Publications, 1976.

Siddiqui, S.A. *Public Finance in Islam.* Lahore: S.H. Mohammad Ashraf, 1962.

Simmel, Georg. *The Sociology of Georg Simmel.* Kurt Wolff, ed. Glencoe, Ill.: Free Press, 1964.

Simpson, George E., and Yinger, J.M. *Racial and Cultural Minorities: An Analysis of Prejudice and Discrimination.* New York: Harper & Row, 1965.

Sitaram, K.S., and Cogdell, R.T. *Foundations of Intercultural Communication.* Columbus, Ohio: Charles & Merrill, 1976.

Smith, W.C. *Modern Islam in India.* London: Gollancz, 1946.

Smith, W. Robertson. *Kinship and Marriage in Early Arabia.* Cambridge: Cambridge University Press, 1885.

Stewart, D. *Early Islam.* New York: Time Inc., 1967.

Sweet, Louise E. "Reconstituting a Lebanese Village Society in a Canadian City" in *Arabic Speaking Communities in American Cities,* Barbara Aswad ed. Staten Island, N.Y.: Center for Migration Studies and Association of Arab-American University Graduates, 1974, pp. 39–52.

Tapiero; Norbert. *Les Idées réformistes d'al-Kawâkibi.* Paris: Les editions arabes, 1956.

Thompson, Gardner. "The Ismailis in Uganda" in *Expulsion of a Minority: Essays on Ugandan Asians,* M. Twaddle, ed. London: Athlone Press, 1974.

Van Nieuwenhuijze, C.A.O. *Sociology of the Middle East.* Leiden: J.E. Brill, 1971.

Vatuk, Sylvia. *Kinship and Urbanization.* Berkeley: University of California Press, 1972.

Wakf, B.A.B. *Islam, An Introduction.* Karachi: n.d.

Walji, S. "History of the Ismaili Community in Tanzania." Ph.D. diss., , University of Wisconsin, 1974.

Waugh, Earle H. "The Imam in the New World: Models and Modifications" in *Transitions and Transformations in the History of Religions,* Frank E. Reynolds and Theodore M. Ludwig, eds. Leiden, Holland: E.J. Brill, 1980, pp. 124–49.

Weber, Max. *The Sociology of Religion.* E. Fischoff, trans. Boston: Beacon Press, 1964.

Weeks, Richard V., ed. *Muslim Peoples: A World Ethnographic Survey.* Westport: Greenwood Press, 1978.

Werner, W., and Roth, Peter. *Doing School Ethnography* (Curriculum Praxis Monograph Series #2). Edmonton: University of Alberta, Department of Secondary Education, 1979.

Wilber, Donald. *Pakistan, Its People, Its Society, Its Culture.* New Haven, Conn.: H.R.A.F. Press, 1964.

Wolf, Umhau C. "Muslims in the Midwest" in *Muslim World,* vol. L, no. 1 (January 1960) : 39–48.

Wriggins, W.H. *Pakistan in Transition.* Islamabad: University of Islamabad Press, 1975.